# Trust the Text

John Sinclair is one of the most influential figures in world linguistics, an innovator who has revolutionized the study of spoken discourse and pioneered corpus-based research.

In this definitive collection, papers reflecting his most important work in the last decade have been collated and organized into meaningful sections, providing a clear statement of Sinclair's thinking and research.

- **Foundations** outlines the major theoretical principles on which subsequent chapters are constructed.

- **The organization of text** traces the development of Sinclair's insights into the relationship between text structure and dialogue.

- **Lexis and grammar** presents core papers on the description of vocabulary, its relationship with grammar and the role of corpus analysis in describing lexical patterns.

Featuring introductions and summaries of key arguments, *Trust the Text* is an essential addition to any linguist's bookshelf.

**John Sinclair** is President of the Tuscan Word Centre in Italy, which has an international reputation for corpus-based language research and teaching.

Edited with Ronald Carter, Professor of Modern English Language at the University of Nottingham.

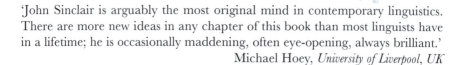

'John Sinclair is arguably the most original mind in contemporary linguistics. There are more new ideas in any chapter of this book than most linguists have in a lifetime; he is occasionally maddening, often eye-opening, always brilliant.'

Michael Hoey, *University of Liverpool, UK*

'Long before most linguists even knew that computerized corpora existed, John Sinclair was showing us how the study of large corpora revolutionizes our understanding of lexis in relation to grammar and meaning. This collection of essays forces the reader to confront the importance of lexical units larger than the word for both lexical and grammatical theory.'

Douglas Biber, *Northern Arizona University, USA*

'John Sinclair is an original thinker who trusts the text more than received ideas or orthodox linguistic opinions, however fashionable they may be. Readers who come to this book with an open mind will learn new things about language and will perhaps even change fundamentally in the ways they approach the study of language.'

Stig Johansson, *University of Oslo, Norway*

# Trust the Text

Language, corpus and discourse

## John Sinclair

*Edited with Ronald Carter*

Routledge
Taylor & Francis Group

LONDON AND NEW YORK

First published 2004
by Routledge
2 Park Square, Milton Park, Abingdon, Oxon, OX14 4RN

Simultaneously published in the USA and Canada
by Routledge
270 Madison Ave, New York NY 10016

*Routledge is an imprint of the Taylor & Francis Group*

Transferred to Digital Printing 2006

Typeset in Baskerville by The Running Head Limited, Cambridge

*British Library Cataloguing in Publication Data*
A catalogue record for this book is available from the British Library

*Library of Congress Cataloging in Publication Data*
Sinclair, John McHardy, 1933–
    Trust the text : language, corpus and discourse / John McHardy
    Sinclair
        p.   cm.
1. Discourse analysis. 2. Lexicology. 2. Grammar, comparative and
general. 4. Computational linguistics. I. Title.
P302.S455 2004
401'.41—dc22
                                                          2003024889

ISBN 0–415–31767–3 (hbk)
ISBN 0–415–31768–1 (pbk)

**Printed and bound by CPI Antony Rowe, Eastbourne**

# Contents

## For M.A.K. Halliday

I dedicate this book to Michael Halliday, because it was he who taught me to trust the text, along with many other precepts that have guided me throughout my career. He has been the most profound influence on my academic development, an inspiring teacher who combines the gift of clear and positive thinking with a delight in argumentation. I worked closely under his leadership for five years, and for the following forty years have rejoiced in having him as a close friend, however distant we are geographically.

This collection, as all my work, shows deep debts to Michael's training. He supported the start of corpus research in Edinburgh, and he encouraged my early attempts to understand lexis. He spoke very strongly for a focus on the spoken language, which led to my interest in the structure of discourse. He gave me confidence in writing grammars and in thinking for myself – what more could a budding linguist ask for?

# Acknowledgements

Many kind colleagues have helped the final form of these papers, mainly with constructive criticism, and sometimes with some valuable data. Since this volume represents my work over many years, I have taken their names from the individual papers and printed them, in alphabetical order below. To have had the attention and support of such a distinguished group of scholars has helped my work immensely, and I owe them a great debt.

Robert de Beaugrande, Adriana Bolivar, Ron Carter, Malcolm Coulthard, Frantisek Cermak, Jeremy Clear, Michael Hoey, Susan Hunston, Simon Krek, Ann Lawson, Anna Maurane, Giuseppe Palumbo, Jennifer Pearson, Martin Phillips, Randolph Quirk, Louise Ravelli, Wolfgang Teubert, Elena Tognini-Bonelli.

This collection of papers was proposed by Ron Carter, who selected the papers, suggested Routledge as publisher and carried the proposal through to contract. Then he arranged for a preliminary electronic manuscript to be prepared from the papers in various formats, and has continued to discharge all the duties of an editor, shepherding the text through all the stages to publication. I am extremely grateful for his support and hard work in bringing this book out – especially since this is not the first time. He was also the prime mover in my collection called *Corpus, Concordance, Collocation* some fifteen years ago.

John Sinclair
Florence
March 2004

# Introduction

## Ronald Carter

Analysis of extended naturally occurring texts, spoken and written, and, in particular, computer processing of texts have revealed quite unsuspected patterns of language . . . The big difference has been the availability of data . . . [The] major novelty was the recording of completely new evidence about how language is used . . . [The] contrast exposed between the impressions of language detail noted by people, and the evidence compiled objectively from texts is huge and systematic . . . The language looks different when you look at a lot of it at once . . .

It is my belief that a new understanding of the nature and structure of language will shortly be available as a result of the examination of large collections of text.

(Sinclair 1991: pp. xvii, 1, 2, 4, 100, 489)

## Background: the author

John Sinclair is one of the major figures in world linguistics. His earliest career was spent at the Department of English and General Linguistics at the University of Edinburgh but his work is associated most clearly with the Department of English Language and Literature at the University of Birmingham, where he held the foundation chair in Modern English Language from 1965 until 2000. He is currently co-founder and director of the Tuscan Word Centre in Italy which is known internationally for corpus-based language research and teaching.

John Sinclair has published and edited over 30 books and over 100 articles in the fields of grammar, vocabulary, discourse analysis, lexicography, stylistics, language teaching and corpus linguistics. In the 1970s he revolutionized the study of spoken discourse and in the 1980s he developed one of the largest-scale English language research projects the world has seen which has produced the 400 million-word Bank of English corpus and resulted in a whole range of innovative dictionaries, grammars and teaching materials as part of the Cobuild project. Published in 1987 and dismissed at the time by most major publishers, the first Cobuild dictionary was so influential that all dictionaries and reference books, especially those for learners of English as an additional language, are now based on corpora and have been affected by the principles of description and research which John Sinclair developed. In the 1990s and to the present day he has continued to innovate and push back frontiers of description, most markedly in the computational analysis of patterns of vocabulary and grammar, and the analysis of patterns of discourse, and he has developed theoretical accounts of the central importance of lexis in the theory of language.

## Background: theories and ideas

This book brings together some of the most significant papers written by John Sinclair in the past decade. They are papers in which he addresses some of the key questions about the nature of language and proposes new methodologies for their investigation. The papers build on questions posed since the 1960s, which the construction of large computerized collections of text are only now allowing answers to.

John Sinclair is in a distinct tradition of British linguistics. This tradition owes much to the foundations built by Professor J.R. Firth in the 1950s and extended by Professor Michael Halliday from the 1960s. It is a tradition that in theory and practice runs counter to the dominant worldwide traditions for the study of language instigated by Noam Chomsky in the 1950s and 1960s. For Chomsky, language is a cognitive, biological phenomenon and has to be studied by means of methodologies that trust the intuitions of the researcher. In this tradition there is distrust of real data and of extended naturally occurring texts and a reliance instead on invented, decontextualized sentences designed by and attested by the researcher only to substantiate the identification of structures, mainly grammatical structures, which are then claimed to be of universal significance. In this Chomskyan tradition there is no interest in language beyond the level of the sentence, there is no recognition that authentic data is of any significance and there is no acceptance that studies of large corpora of real language in use play any part in descriptions or theories of language. Most significantly, too, there is a clear sense that the analysis of meaning is not a primary purpose. Indeed, Chomsky has asserted on several occasions that 'grammar is autonomous and independent of meaning'.

The position of John Sinclair is determinedly against such an orientation to language description and theory. Sinclair is firmly in the Firthian tradition and has consistently argued that language should be studied in naturally occurring contexts of use, should work with extended examples – where possible complete texts – and should have at its centre the analysis of meaning. (See Stubbs 1996, for a fuller account of this Firthian tradition.)

In the 1960s Sinclair posed central questions about the centrality of lexis to language and pointed to its relative neglect within paradigms dominated by the analysis of grammar and phonology, often viewed as autonomous systems. Many of the questions posed, such as those concerning the significance of collocational patterns of language (see Sinclair 1966; Sinclair, Jones and Daley 1970) demanded the analysis of large quantities of text but at that time computational power and methods did not allow such investigation. Foley (ed.) (1996) is a collection of papers which exemplifies the continuity of John Sinclair's thinking between the 1960s and 1980s and its relevance for lexicography, as illustrated by the computational linguistic Cobuild project. The thinking is carried forward in the seminal *Corpus, Concordance and Collocation* (Sinclair 1991) which elaborated on these theories and synthesized them into important and influential new descriptive paradigms utilizing the evidence provided by extensive corpus analysis.

This book illustrates the extension of work in both theory and analytical practice based on John Sinclair's work in the 1990s. At the heart of this work is a recognition of the central importance of lexical units larger than the word. Engaged in writing the pioneering *Cobuild Learners' Dictionary* in the early 1980s, he became increasingly aware that certain long-held principles of linguistics (the primacy of syntax, the 'irregularity' of lexis) could no longer be sustained in the face of corpus evidence. Lexis seemed to be far from irregular; collocational patterns appeared everywhere in the lexical concordances generated from the corpus. Idiomaticity, far from being a marginal aspect of language, seemed to be ubiquitous and at least as significant as syntax in the construction of meaning (Sinclair 1991: 112). Fixed, repeated strings were ubiquitous in Sinclair's data, and, most markedly, in collocations that involve the most frequent everyday words. This led Sinclair to assert the existence of a tight bond between form and meaning, between sense and structure, and to the conclusion that collocations and idiomatic but very frequently occurring combinations were the real glue that held texts together.

John Sinclair illustrates time and again how lexical patterns and syntactic patterns cannot be divorced, in the process proposing, developing and refining theories of language which are in distinct contrast to those which characterized linguistic enquiry for much of the twentieth century. Sinclair underlines how theories of language cannot focus only on form and structure as if such features were autonomous and independent of meaning. In his theory of 'units of meaning', choices of lexical patterns entail patterns of meaning and even more precisely every distinct sense of a word is associated with a distinction in form. The inseparability of form and meaning is frequently returned to:

> in all cases so far examined, each meaning can be associated with a distinct formal patterning . . . There is ultimately no distinction between form and meaning . . . [The] meaning affects the structure and this is . . . the principal observation of corpus linguistics in the last decade.
>
> (Sinclair 1991: 496)

This descriptive and analytical position has exerted a major influence on research into and analysis of language within the past decade. It has affected the design of pedagogical materials such as course books, dictionaries and grammars, the place of linguistics in education, the analysis of literature and the fields, in particular, of discourse analysis and lexicology.

It is a deeply and uncompromisingly empirical position. The key word for Sinclair is 'evidence' and it appears in numerous places in the material collected together in this volume. By 'evidence' he means the data provided by extensive multi-million word collections of texts together with the extensive statistical support provided by the techniques of corpus linguistics. The theories proposed concerning units of meaning are thus supported by the evidence of larger amounts of data than has been seen before in the study of human language. As John Sinclair (1991: 4) himself puts it: 'The ability to examine large text corpora in a systematic manner allows access to a quality of evidence that has not been available before.' In this process the text itself cannot be neglected or be seen simply as some kind of illustration of a general point. The title chapter in this volume is 'Trust the text'. Every detail of the text has to be examined if a true picture is to emerge and that text too has to be seen not autonomously but as part of a network of other texts in the corpus so that the statements made about texts have to be verified with reference to other texts of the same or similar or of different types, each with their own disposition of linguistic features and each with their own provenance in the corpus. Descriptions of language are corpus-driven in that the corpus tells us what the facts are. And the larger and more representative the corpus the greater the attestation that is possible. It is in this way an innovative extension and enrichment of the Firthian tradition and one which stands in marked contrast to the Chomskyan view of the necessity for reliance on intuition and introspection and the evidence provided by a single linguist's knowledge of the language often in turn based on examples which he or she has invented for the purposes of theoretical exemplification.

However, in the midst of powerful theoretical development and the fascination of detailed empirical description of lexis, the wider contours of Sinclair's contributions to the study of language in text and context must not be neglected. Throughout his foundational work in the 1960s and at that time operating even more distinctly against the grain of current fashions, Sinclair asserted the importance of studying naturally occurring texts, spoken and written, and indeed argued that spoken language and written language are, interactively, organized in essentially similar ways. Like Michael Halliday, he also saw no obvious distinction between Saussure's *parole* and *langue* and certainly believed that descriptions of competence in a language could not be divorced from descriptions of performance in the use of that language. In the 1970s he created a corpus of spoken English discourse based on language use by teachers and pupils and utilized that data to propose models of analysis for the dynamic interaction and exchanges characteristic of spoken language (Sinclair and Coulthard 1975). The theories and models of language developed at that time have continued to be developed and refined and are characterized in this volume by chapters exploring the essentially dialogic nature of written discourse structure.

## Contents of this book

The papers collected in this book chart some of the main contours of John Sinclair's thinking, descriptive techniques and analytical practices over the past

20 years. Two papers were first published in the 1980s and provide points of backwards and forwards reference. The remaining papers date from 1990 through to 2001. Several of these papers have been published previously but often in Festschriften, specialized journals or edited collections. This publication brings key papers together and offers them as a coherent statement. All the papers have been edited and updated for this publication.

The volume consists of an introduction and three main sections structured as follows: Part I, 'Foundations', consists of two core chapters which outline major theoretical principles on which subsequent chapters are constructed. In the opening chapter the major principle of respecting and trusting the integrity of the complete text as a basis for linguistic description analysis and theory-building is articulated; in the second chapter a major theory of lexical organization and patterning is established as an organizing principle for subsequent chapters.

This is followed by a section of five chapters devoted mainly to work on written discourse structure. This part is entitled 'The organization of text', and develops important further insights into the relationship between text-structure and dialogic interaction by examining a range of text-types. 'Planes of discourse' and `On the integration of linguistic description', first published in the 1980s, outline a framework for the analysis of all situated language. The framework derives from the work described above on interactive spoken discourse in the 1970s but it is subtly extended here to embrace the organization of written text. In these chapters the importance of prospective and encapsulating structures is underlined as a plane of language which interacts with an autonomous plane concerned with discourse management. Throughout the section the importance of integrating the analysis of spoken and written language is underlined.

Part III is devoted to 'Lexis and grammar' and contains core chapters devoted to the description of vocabulary, its relationship with grammar and the role of corpus analysis in describing lexical patterns. The chapters work from the core chapters in the 'Foundations' section devoted to 'The search for units of meaning'. The section is rich in data and in examples of the varied range of insights into lexical patterning which corpus analysis reveals while at the same time proposing, extending and refining new theories of the organization of language rooted in the centrality of the lexical item.

## Conclusions and prospects

> The categories and methods we use to describe English are not appropriate to the new material. We shall need to overhaul our descriptive systems.
>
> (Sinclair 1985)

There is little doubt that the thinking exemplified in this book provides further foundations from which the existing limits of linguistic theory will continue to be questioned and challenged, and from which new frontiers of description can be crossed. The landscapes of language study are changing before our eyes as a result of the radically extended possibilities afforded by corpus and computational linguistics. And with every new advance it will be ever more likely that the text can and will be trusted.

Nottingham
July 2003

# Part I

# Foundations

# 1 Trust the text

This chapter was edited from a transcript of a keynote lecture given at the Seventeenth International Systemic Conference in Stirling, Scotland, in July 1990. Although not the earliest paper chronologically in this collection, it brings up to date previous work in discourse analysis and maps out the approach to corpora which is now known as 'corpus-driven linguistics'. In discourse analysis the chapter sets up a model of structural cohesion that applies equally to spoken and written discourse, and concentrates on written discourse. The background to this project is set out in Chapters 3 and 4, and the written analysis is pursued in Chapter 5. In the second half of the chapter it is argued that the received theories of language are not adequate to account for the mass of new evidence coming from early corpus study. This line of research is followed up in Part III — chapters 8–12 inclusive.

By way of a sub-title to this chapter, I should like to quote a short sentence from an article in *The European* (1–3 June 1990), by Randolph Quirk.

> The implications are daunting.

I shall refer to the discourse function of this sentence from time to time, but at present I would like to draw attention to its ominous tone. The implications of trusting the text are for me extremely daunting, but also very exciting and thought-provoking.

The argument that I would like to put forward is that linguistics has been formed and shaped on inadequate evidence and in a famous phrase 'degenerate data'. There has been a distinct shortage of information and evidence available to linguists, and this gives rise to a particular balance between speculation and fact in the way in which we talk about our subject. In linguistics up till now we have been relying very heavily on speculation.

This is not a criticism; it is a fact of life. The physical facts of language are notoriously difficult to remember. Some of you will remember the days before tape recorders and will agree that it is extremely difficult to remember details of speech that has just been uttered. Now that there is so much language available on record, particularly written language in electronic form, but also substantial quantities of spoken language, our theory and descriptions should be re-examined to make sure they are appropriate. We have experienced not only a quantitative change in the amount of language data available for study, but also a consequent qualitative change in the relation between data and hypothesis. In the first part of this chapter I hope to raise a point about description based on the appreciation of this fairly fundamental appraisal.

Apart from the strong tradition of instrumental phonetics, we have only recently devised even the most rudimentary techniques for making and managing the recording of language, and even less for the analysis of it. In particular we should be suspicious of projecting techniques that are suitable for some areas of language patterning on to others.

This is my first point. Until recently linguistics has been able to develop fairly steadily. Each new position in the major schools has arisen fairly naturally out of the previous one. However, the change in the availability of information which we now enjoy makes it prudent for us to be less confident about reusing accepted techniques.

My second main point is that we should strive to be open to the patterns observable in language in quantity as we now have it. The growing evidence that we have suggests that there is to be found a wealth of meaningful patterns that, with current perspectives, we are not led to expect. We must gratefully adjust to this new situation and rebuild a picture of language and meaning which is not only consistent with the evidence but also exploits it to the full. This will take some time, and the first stage should be an attempt to inspect the data with as little attention as possible to theory.

It is impossible to study patterned data without some theory, however primitive. The advantage of a robust and popular theory is that it is well tried against previous evidence and offers a quick route to sophisticated observation and insight. The main disadvantage is that, by prioritizing some patterns, it obscures others. I believe that linguists should consciously strive to reduce this effect until the situation stabilizes.

The first of my points takes us into the present state of the analysis of discourse, which is now some 20 years old and worth an overhaul; the second plunges us into corpus linguistics, which, although even more venerable, has been rather furtively studied until becoming suddenly popular quite recently. They might seem to have very little in common, but for me they are the twin pillars of language research.

What unites them is:

a  They both encourage the formulation of radically new hypotheses. Although they can be got to fit existing models, that is only because of our limited vision at present.

b  The dimensions of pattern that they deal with are, on the whole, larger than linguistics is accustomed to. Both to manage the evidence required, and even to find some of it in the first place, there is a need to harness the power of modern computers.

The most important development in linguistic description in my generation has been the attempt from many different quarters to describe structures above the sentence and to incorporate the descriptions in linguistic models. The study of text, of discourse, including speech acts and pragmatics, is now central in linguistics. Since the early 1950s a number of approaches have been devised that attempt to account for larger patterns of language. Although large-scale patterns are clearly affected by, for example, sociological variables, they still lie firmly within the orbit of linguistic behaviour for as long as linguistic techniques can be used as the basis of their description.

No doubt we quite often begin a new study by projecting upwards the proven techniques of well described areas of language. To give an example, consider distributional techniques of description which began in phonology. These led in the early 1950s to attempts by, for example, Zellig Harris, to describe written text using essentially the same methods, by looking for repeated words and phrases which would form a basis for classifying the words and phrases that occur next to them. This is just the way in which phonemes were identified and distinguished from allophones, the basis of the famous 'complementary distribution'. Now there are only a relatively small number of phonemes in any language, numbered in tens, and there are a relatively large number of words, numbered in tens of thousands. The circumstances are quite different, and in the pre-computer era this kind of research faced very serious problems. The unlikelihood of finding exactly repeated phrases led Harris to the idea that stretches of language which, though physically different, were systematically related, could be regarded as essentially the same. This was articulated as grammatical transformation. It is an object lesson in what can go wrong if you project your techniques upwards into other areas without careful monitoring and adaptation. In the event, transformations provided the key feature with which Chomsky (1957) launched a wave of cognitive, non-textual linguistics.

Discourse study took off when speech acts (Austin 1962) were identified in philosophy. It took a development in a discipline outside linguistics to offer a reconceptualization of the function of the larger units of language. However, much of the description of discourse since then has been the upward projection of models, worked out originally for areas like grammar and phonology. I cheerfully admit *mea culpa* here, in having projected upwards a scale and category model in an attempt to show the structure of spoken interaction (Sinclair et al. 1972a). It has been a serviceable model, and it is still developing, along lines which are now suitable for capturing the general structure of interactive discourse. Recent work on conversation by Amy Tsui (1986), on topic by Hazadiah Mohd Dahan (1991) and by others incorporating the relations between spoken and written language are continuing within the broad umbrella of that model while making it more convenient as a vehicle for explaining the nature of interaction in language.

Louise Ravelli's study of dynamic grammar (1991) is an interesting exercise in turning the new insights of a theoretical development back on to familiar ground. It is in effect a projection downwards from the insights of discourse into some aspects of language form.

While using familiar tools is a reasonable tactic for getting started, we should also work towards a model of discourse which is special to discourse and which is not based upon the upward projection of descriptive techniques, no matter how similar we perceive the patterns to be. In this case, for the description of discourse, we should build a model which emphasizes the distinctive features of discourse. A special model for discourse will offer an explanation of those features of discourse that are unique to it, or characteristic of it, or prominent in discourse but not elsewhere.

Many of the structural features of discourse are large scale and highly variable. As the units of language description get larger, the identification of meaningful units becomes more problematic. The computer is now available to help in this work.

However, we should not use the computer merely to demonstrate patterns which we predict from other areas of language study. It will labour mightily and apparently with success, but it may also labour in vain. Mechanizations of existing descriptive systems are present in abundance. Many teams of scholars have made excellent, but limited, use of the computer to model a pre-mechanized description of part of language form, and tested the model against data. The computer will expose errors and suggest corrections; it will apply rules indefatigably, and it will continue to tell us largely what we already know.

Instead I would like to suggest that we might devise new hypotheses about the nature of text and discourse and use the computer to test whether they actually work. Computers have not been much used in this way so far in language work; their main role has been checking on detail. Gradually computers are becoming capable of quite complex analysis of language. They are able to apply sophisticated models to indefinitely large stretches of text and they are getting better and better at it. As always in computer studies, the pace is accelerating, and this will soon be commonplace.

I would like to put forward one hypothesis, or perhaps a small related set of hypotheses, which should simplify and strengthen the description of discourse. It is a stronger hypothesis than one normally encounters in discourse, and it is one where the computer can be used in a testing role. It is explicit enough to identify a large number of cases automatically. Where it fails the cases will be interesting to the analyst, because in such cases the hypothesis is either wrong or not properly stated, or the evidence is too vague or idiosyncratic to be covered by general statement.

This hypothesis draws on something by which I set very great store – the prospective features of spoken discourse. For me the study of discourse began in earnest when I classified initiations in exchanges according to how they pre-classify what follows (Sinclair 1966; quoted in Sinclair and Coulthard 1975: 151, see also 133). This approach broadened into the view that a major central function of language is that it constantly prospects ahead. It cannot determine in most cases what actually will happen, especially not in spoken interaction, but it does mean that whatever does happen has a value that is already established by the discourse at that point. So the scene is set for each next utterance by the utterance that is going on at the moment. Over the years, the more that attention has been focused on the prospective qualities of discourse the more accurate and powerful the description has become.

In contrast much of the analysis of written language as text has concerned retrospective pattern. Patterns of cohesion, of repetition, reference, replacement and so on. Complex patterns emerge, linking parts of a text to each other. Some become very complex indeed, and sample texts have many lines drawn from one part of the text to another to indicate ties, links, chains, etc. I accept, as I am sure most scholars do, that written and spoken language are different in many particulars, but are they as different as the styles of analysis suggest? Is it really true that we mainly find prospection in the spoken language and retrospection in the written language? That would suggest that they are very different indeed.

Of course there are backward references in conversation. But why are they not apparently as important to the analyst as they are in the written language? Vice versa there are prospections that can be identified in the written language, as Winter (1977) and Tadros (1985) have shown.

People do not remember the spoken language exactly and so they cannot refer back to it in quite the simple way that they can with the written language. Because we have written text in front of us to check on, it is apparently easy to rely on retrospective reference. But do we really in the normal course of reading actually check back pronominal reference and so on? I doubt it. The point could no doubt be checked by doing studies of eye movements but I doubt if many researchers would consider it viable enough to require checking.

Informal experiments which colleagues and I did many years ago supported the commonsense view which is that, in general, people forget the actual language but remember the message. And so the question that I would like to ask is: 'Do we actually need all the linguistic detail of backward reference that we find in text description?' Text is often described as a long string of sentences, and this encourages the practice of drawing links from one bit of the text to another. I would like to suggest, as an alternative, that the most important thing is what is happening in the current sentence. The meaning of any word is got from the state of the discourse and not from where it came from. A word of reference like a pronoun should be interpreted exactly like a proper name or a noun phrase. The reader should find a value for it in the immediate state of the text, and not have to retrieve it from previous text unless the text is problematic at that point.

The state of the discourse is identified with the sentence which is currently being processed. No other sentence is presumed to be available. The previous text is part of the immediately previous experience of the reader or listener, and is no different from any other, non-linguistic experience. It will normally have lost the features which were used to organize the meaning to shape the text into a unique communicative instrument.

From this perspective, there is no advantage to be gained in tracing the references back in the text. The information thus gleaned will not be relevant to the current state of the discourse because previous states of the text are of no interest to the present state of the text; nor is it important how the present state of the text was arrived at.

I reiterate this point because, although it is straightforward, it is not an orthodox position and yet it is central to my argument. There are minor qualifications to be made, but nothing should disturb the main point. The conceptual difficulty arises, I believe, from the fact that the previous text is always present and available to the analyst, and the temptation to make use of it is too strong.

The notion of *primed frames* in Emmott (1997) is promising. Some form of mental representation of the text so far, the state of the text, must be building up in the mind of a competent reader, and must be available for interpreting the text at any particular point. It would be a digression in this argument to discuss positions concerning mental representations, because my concern is to explain how the text operates *discoursally* – while someone is experiencing its meaning. Very roughly we can understand it as the previous sentence minus its interactive elements – whatever enabled it to be an interaction at a previous stage in the text – plus the inferences that have been used in order to interpret the text at this particular point.

Let us take as a starting position the view that 'the text' is the sentence that is being processed at any time and only that. The text *is* the sentence that is in front of us when an act of reading is in progress. Each sentence then is a new beginning to the text. Each sentence organizes language and the world for that particular location in the text, not dependent on anything else. (No wonder, by the way, that we have had such problems in the past about the definition of a sentence, if it is indeed synonymous with the definition of a text. The paradox of the structure which represents a 'complete thought', but which is often verbalized in a form that is clearly part of a larger organization, is resolved.)

The relation between a sentence and the previous text is as follows: each sentence contains one connection with other states of the text preceding it. That is to say it contains a single act of reference which encapsulates the whole of the previous text and simultaneously removes its interactive potential. The occurrence of the next sentence pensions off the previous one, replaces it and becomes the text. The whole text is present in each sentence. The meaning of each previous sentence is represented simply as part of the shared knowledge that one is bringing to bear in the interpretation of a text at any point.

My position, then, is that the previous states of the text up to the one that is being processed are present in the current sentence in so far as they are needed. Previous sentences are not available in their textual form, but in a coherent text there is no need to have them. The same interpretive mechanism that we use to identify proper names, or other references from the text into our experience of the world, is suitable for processing that part of our experience which has been produced by previous text.

If this view is accepted, the way is clear to concentrate in description on the communicative function of each sentence and not to worry about what its textual antecedents might have been.

I now return to my original text, *The implications are daunting*. This text is obviously an act of reference to the whole of the preceding sentence, because the phrase *the implications* does not carry within itself a clear indication of what it refers to. The word *the* says that the reference of the noun group is knowable, and *implications* need to be implications of something. We may assume that the whole of the preceding sentence is whatever has implications. The preceding sentence reads like this:

> The Japanese use Western languages not merely to market their goods but to improve their products by studying those of their rivals.

The act of reference works if readers are satisfied that the two sentences can be interpreted in this way.

This sentence also prospects forward to the sentences that we have not yet read. This is one of the *advanced labelling* structures that Tadros (1985) has described in detail. If you mention *implications* in this way, you have to go on to list them; so we may assume that the next sentence or sentences will be understandable as implications. The quoted sentence tells us in advance that what follow are implications. Here is what follows:

> Not merely must the business have personnel with skills in different languages but the particular languages and the degree of skill may vary from person to person according to his or her job within the business. They may also vary from decade to decade as new markets open up in different countries.

These are the implications. So the hypothesis that I am putting forward is that the text at any particular time carries with it everything that a competent reader needs in order to understand the current state of the text. It encapsulates what has gone before in a single act of reference, so that the previous text has exactly the same status as any other piece of shared knowledge. In many cases it also prospects forward and sets the scene for what follows.

The sentence that follows *The implications are daunting*, quoted above, does not contain an act of reference, and so it constitutes a counter-example straight away. The reason is that this sentence is fully prospected by its predecessor. If you think for a moment of spoken discourse, you find that an answer, which is prospected by a question, does not contain an act of reference that encapsulates the question. It would be bizarre if this were the case: the occurrence of the answer is made understandable by the prospection of the question, and yet the answer would encapsulate the question and so cancel its discourse function.

A question can indeed be followed by an utterance that encapsulates it; for example, *That's an interesting question*. Such utterances are called *challenges* (Burton

1980) just because they encapsulate the previous utterance and cancel its inter-active force.

We therefore conclude that the prospection of a sentence remains pertinent until fulfilled or challenged, although the sentence itself is no longer available in the normal business of talking or writing. Prospected sentences do not contain an act of reference, though they may, of course, themselves prospect. Prospection thus provides a simple variation in text structure. If a sentence is not prospected by its predecessor, it encapsulates it, and by so doing becomes the text.

In this chapter it is possible to give only the very broadest outline of this set of hypotheses. There is a lot of detail and a number of qualifications, and it will become much more elaborate as ways are developed of coping with dubious examples. But the basic idea is simple, and probably testable by present tech-niques. Most acts of reference can be identified by currently available software. The proposal is much simpler than many other models of text, because it selects the features of sentence reference and prospection as being particularly impor-tant in structure. If it turns out to be adequate for a starting description of text then it should commend itself because of its simplicity. It also simplifies the busi-ness of understanding text structure, in that it points out that each successive sentence is, for a moment, the whole text. This could lead eventually to a really operational definition of a sentence.

So my first main point is a double-edged one. I put forward some proposals for text structure as illustrations of strong and testable hypotheses. I suggest we should use the ability that we now have to perceive the higher structures of lan-guage and also the powerful computing tools that we now have and that we should find out how reliable and how useful our hypotheses are.

Much of the description of the higher organization of language has remained at the stage of patterns and labels. Little has been done to describe restrictions or to explain the reasons for the patterns, i.e. to make a proper structural description. Similarly, many investigations in language, particularly in areas like stylistics, have remained at a relatively modest level of achievement for a very long time, simply because of the technical problems involved in validating state-ments. Very detailed and careful analysis is required in stylistics, and it is still usually done by hand (though see the *Journal of Literary and Linguistic Computing, passim*). We are now in a position to be bold, to look for testable hypotheses which may simplify and clarify the nature of text and discourse. It is not enough that a particular description of language can actually provide a set of boxes into which text can be apportioned. We must look for models which help the text to reveal itself to us.

If we are going to take advantage of the computer's ability to test hypotheses over large stretches of text, there is a price to pay, but the opportunity is worth paying for. The price is the requirement of precision of statement, which will add pressure to move linguistics towards scientific rigour; the opportunity is the freedom to speculate and get fairly quick feedback from the computers about the accuracy and potential of the speculations. Far from restricting the theorist, the computers will actually encourage hunch-playing and speculation at the creative stage. The wealth of data and the ease of access will however encourage the compilation of statements which are firmly compatible with the data.

The relationship between the student of language and the data is thus changing. My other point is that we as linguists should train ourselves specifically to be open to the evidence of long text. This is quite different from using the computer to be our servant in trying out our ideas; it is making good use of some essential differences between computers and people. A computer has a relatively crude and simple ability to search and retrieve exhaustively from text any patterns which can be precisely stated in its terms. Now of course we cannot look with totally unbiased eyes at these patterns, but I believe that we have to cultivate a new relationship between the ideas we have and the evidence that is in front of us. We are so used to interpreting very scant evidence that we are not in a good mental state to appreciate the opposite situation. With the new evidence the main difficulty is controlling and organizing it rather than getting it. There is likely to be too much rather than too little and there is a danger that we find only what we are looking for.

I would like to summarize the kinds of observations which are already emerging from such studies, the kinds of studies that have been done in Cobuild and elsewhere. Sometimes they cast doubt on some fairly well established areas of conventional language description.

I shall begin at the lowest level of abstraction, the first step up from the string of characters, where word forms are distinguished by spaces. It has been known for some time that the different forms of a lemma may have very different frequencies. (The forms of a lemma differ from each other only by inflections.) We generally assume that all the forms of a lemma share the same meanings, but we are now beginning to discover that in some cases, if they did not share similar spelling, we might not wish to regard them as being instances of the same lemma. For example, take the lemma *move*. The forms *moving* and *moved* share some meanings with *move*, but each form has a very distinctive pattern of meaning. Some of the meanings found elsewhere in the lemma will be realized, and some will not. In the word *moving* for example there is the meaning of emotional affection, which is quite prominent.

This kind of observation makes us realize that lemmatization is not a simple operation; it is in fact a procedure which a computer has great difficulty with. Of course, with evidence like this it is quite difficult to persuade the computer that lemmatization is a sensible activity. The difference between *move* and *movement* is not noticeably more extreme, yet *movement*, being a derived form, would be expected to constitute a diffferent lemma from *move*.

Such complexities have also been found in several other European languages in a project sponsored by the Council of Europe. When you think of a language like Italian, blessed with a multiplicity of verb forms, and of the prospect that in principle each of those could be a different semantic unit, and also of the fact that there is evidence in many cases that this is so, then you can see the kind of problem that lies ahead. Bilingual dictionaries may soon grow in size substantially as the blithe assumption of a stable lemma is challenged.

Second, a word which can be used in more than one word class is likely to have meanings associated specifically with each word class. Just to give one example, the word *combat* as a noun is concerned with the physical side of combat, and as a verb is concerned with the social side. There is an exception: in the phrase 'locked in combat', *combat* is used in the social meaning although it is a noun. The exception draws attention to another useful point – that the correlations of meaning and word class break down when the words form part of some idiomatic phrase or technical term.

We have not yet made estimates of the proportion of the vocabulary which is subject to this phenomenon, but in the compiling of the Cobuild dictionary (Sinclair, Hanks et al. 1987) we tried to identify the predominant word class of each meaning of each word. We were pretty flexible in judgement and kept the detail to a minimum. Even so if you look at a few pages of the dictionary you will get the strong impression that meaning correlates with word class.

Third, a word may have special privileges of occurrence or restrictions in group structures. For example there is a class of nouns whose members occur characteristically as prepositional objects, and not as subjects or objects of clauses; *lap* as a part of the body is one such. There is a large class of nouns whose members do not occur alone as a group or with only an article; they have to be modified or qualified in some way. I shall not develop this point here because Gillian Francis (1985) gives an excellent account of the phenomenon as applied to nouns. This work is a close relation of valency grammar, which is likely to see an upsurge of interest in the next few years.

Fourth, traditional categories, even major parts of speech, are not as solidly founded as they might appear to be. A recent computational study (Sinclair 1991) of the word *of* revealed that it is misleading to consider it as a preposition. Only occasionally, and in specific collocations with, for example, *remind*, does it perform a prepositional role. Normally it enables a noun group to extend its pre-head structure, or provides a second head word. In due course the grammatical words of the language will be thoroughly studied, and a new organizational picture is likely to emerge. We must not take for granted the lexical word classes either.

A fifth type of pattern occurs when a word or a phrase carries with it an aura of meaning that is subliminal, in that we only become aware of it when we see a large number of typical instances all together, as when we make a selective concordance. An innocent verb like *happen*, for example: if we select the most characteristic examples of it we find that it is nearly always something nasty that has happened or is going to happen. Similarly with the phrasal verb *set in* – it is nasty things like bad weather that set in. This feature associates the item and the environment in a subtle and serious way that is not explained by the mechanism of established models.

As a corollary to this, I must emphasize that a grammar is a grammar of meanings and not of words. Grammars which make statements about undifferentiated words and phrases leave the user with the problem of deciding which of the meanings of the words or phrases are appropriate to the grammatical statement. Most dictionaries give us very little help, and since distinctions in meaning are arrived at without any systematic consideration of grammar (apart from the Cobuild dictionaries) they cannot be used as evidence in this case. Each grammatical feature will probably correlate with just one meaning, unless it is a very common word, or a word of very multifarious meaning, in which case the same grammar may apply to two or three meanings. But the coincidence of distinct environmental patterns with the shades of meaning of a word is remarkable, and is confirmed all the more as we examine the detail in more and more instances.

Sixth and last, and for me the most interesting result of this research concerns the area of shared meaning between words and between phrases; the results of collocation. Put fairly bluntly it seems that words in English do not normally constitute independent selections. I cannot speak with much confidence yet about other languages, with different principles of word construction, except to say that the underlying principle, that of collocation, is certainly to be found operating in languages like German and Italian, and on that basis one can predict with fair confidence that shared meaning will be a feature.

One way of describing collocation is to say that the choice of one word conditions the choice of the next, and of the next again. The item and the environment are ultimately not separable, or certainly not separable by present techniques. Although at this point I risk my own censure about the upward projection of methodology, I find myself more and more drawn to Firth's notion of prosody in phonology to apply to the kind of distribution of meaning that is observed in text when there is a large quantity of organized evidence. Successive meanings can be discerned in the text, and you can associate a meaning or a component of meaning or a shade of meaning with this or that word or phrase that is present in the text. But it is often impossible in the present state of our knowledge to say precisely where the realization of that meaning starts and stops, or exactly which pattern of morphemes is responsible for it. This may be simply an unfortunate stage in the development of the description, but I do not think so. I think that there probably is in language an interesting indeterminacy. Once you accept that in many or most cases of meaningful choice in English the words are not independent selections, but the meanings are shared, then you are in an area of indeterminacy from which I cannot at the moment see any exit. It is no longer possible to imagine a sharp division between one type of patterning which behaves itself and conforms to broadly statable rules, and another which is a long list of individual variations, and then to insist that they both create meaning at the same time.

Now a model which does not take into account this point is going to represent the language as carrying more information (in the technical sense of information theory) than it actually does. The patterns which are marginalized by our current attitudes include everything from collocation of all kinds, through Firth's colligations, to the conditioned probability of grammatical choices. This is a huge area of syntagmatic prospection. If a model claims to include all such features, but does not explain their effect on conventional grammar and semantics, it will exaggerate the meaning that is given by the choices. That is a fairly serious misrepresentation if the grammar creates more meaning in a set of choices than is mathematically possible.

In the way in which we currently see language text it is not obvious how each small unit of form prospects the next one. We identify structures like compounds, where the assumption is of a single choice, or idioms, although the precise identification of these is by no means clear-cut. The likelihood is of there being a continuum between occasional, quite independent choices and choices which are so heavily dependent on each other that they cannot be separated, and so constitute in practice a single choice.

At present what we detect is a common purpose in the overlapping selection of word on word as if these are the results of choices predetermined at a higher level of abstraction. The choices of conventional grammar and semantics are therefore the realizations of higher level choices. Phrasal verbs are quite an interesting case in point, recently documented in a dictionary that Cobuild has published. Phrasal verbs are difficult to enumerate or identify because there are so many grades and types of co-selection that the relevant criteria are difficult to state and even more difficult to apply. But contrary to what is often claimed, each word of a phrasal verb does contribute something semantically recognizable to the meaning of the whole. In some cases, it is mainly the verb, and in other cases it is mainly the particle.

For instance the particles index in the *Collins Cobuild Dictionary of Phrasal Verbs* (Cobuild 1989) shows that the particle can often guide you to the meaning through a semantic analysis of the phrasal verb. A particle like *along* for example combines with common verbs such as *get* or *come* to make a range of linked meanings. From a basic sense of 'travel' there is the related meaning *progress* in literal or figurative terms. In parallel to this is the meaning of 'accompany', as found in *tag along*, among others. This develops into the notion of 'accept', and collocation with *with* is strong. We can draw a diagram (Figure 1.1). The phrasal verbs are semantically ordered in this analysis

The meaning of words chosen together is different from their independent meanings. They are at least partly delexicalized. This is the necessary correlate of co-selection. If you know that selections are not independent, and that one selection depends on another, then there must be a result and effect on the meaning which in each individual choice is a delexicalization of one kind or another. It will not have its independent meaning in the full if it is only part of a choice involving one or more words. A good deal of the above evidence leads us to conclude that there is a strong tendency to delexicalization in the normal phraseology of modern English.

Let me try to demonstrate this by looking at the selection of adjectives with nouns. We are given to understand in grammar that adjectives add something to the noun, or restrict the noun, or add some features to it. That is no doubt true in some cases, but in the everyday use of adjectives there is often evidence rather of co-selection and shared meaning with the noun. Here are some examples, using recent data from *The Times*, with grateful acknowledgement to the

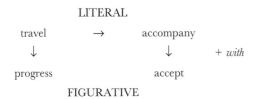

LITERAL

travel     →     accompany

↓                       ↓        + *with*

progress               accept

FIGURATIVE

*Figure 1.1* Semantic analysis of phrasal verbs with *along*.

editor and publishers. Classifying adjectives are more prone to show this, but it is common also in qualitative adjectives.

Here are some nouns that are modified by *physical:*

    physical assault
    physical confrontation
    physical attack
    physical damage
    physical attribute
    physical proximity
    physical bodies

In these cases the meaning associated with *physical* is duplicated in one facet of the way we would normally understand the noun. The adjective may focus the meaning by mentioning it, but the first meaning of *assault* is surely physical assault. It is not suggested that of all the different kinds of assault this is identified as one particular kind, namely physical assault. This co-selection of noun and adjective does not make a fixed phrase, nor necessarily a significant collocation; it is just one of the ordinary ways in which adjectives and nouns are selected. The selections are not independent; they overlap.

Here are some nouns that occur with *scientific*:

    scientific assessment
    scientific analysis
    scientific advances
    scientific study
    scientific experiment

Here *scientific* is fairly seriously delexicalized; all it is doing is dignifying the following word slightly.

Here are some nouns that occur with *full*:

    full enquiry
    full range
    full account
    full consultation

full capacity
full circle

These are mainly types of reassurance more than anything else. We would be unlikely to have an announcement of a partial enquiry.

Here are some nouns that occur with *general*:

general trend
general perception
general drift
general opinion
general consent

In all these cases if the adjective is removed there is no difficulty whatsoever in interpreting the meaning of the noun in exactly the way it was intended. The adjective is not adding any distinct and clear unit of meaning, but is simply underlining part of the meaning of the noun.

In such ways we can see that many of the word-by-word choices in language are connected mainly syntagmatically; the paradigmatic element of their meaning is reduced to the superficial. The same phenomenon occurs with qualitative adjectives such as *dry* in *dry land*, *dry bones*, *dry weight* (which is perhaps slightly technical), or *loud* in such combinations as *loud applause*, *loud bangs*, *loud cheers*.

The co-selection of adjective and noun is a simple and obvious example. There are many others. For example, there are in English many phrases which behave somewhat like idioms; they are built round a slightly specialized meaning of a word that goes with a specific grammatical environment. Take, for example, the framework AN . . . OF, one of the commonest collocations in the language. Consider the words that go in between those two words, in collocation with the word that immediately follows. There may be quite a small range: for example, with *an accident of* there is an *accident of birth*, *an accident of nature*, *an accident of society*. The whole phrase *an accident of* seems to have an idiomatic quality (Renouf and Sinclair 1991).

These are subliminal idioms which were heralded many years ago (Sinclair et al. 1972b). They do not appear in most accounts of the language and yet they are clearly found in texts. We understand them as centring on a slightly specialized meaning of a word in a common grammatical environment and in a regular collocation. This alignment of grammar and lexis is typical of co-selection.

The sub-title of this chapter is *The implications are daunting*. Relating this sentence to the points I have made, clearly *daunting* is a member of an odd lemma. There are no finite forms 'daunt', 'you daunt', etc. Further, *daunting* is obviously co-selected with *implications*. I do not know what other things can be daunting, but the collocation of *implications* and *daunting*, with those inflections, and in either an attributive or a predicative syntax, illustrates the shared meaning in that phrase. So the sentence also does duty as an example of co-selection.

In summary I am advocating that we should trust the text. We should be open to what it may tell us. We should not impose our ideas on it, except perhaps just to get started. Until we see what the preliminary results are, we should apply only frameworks that are loose and flexible, in order to accommodate the new information that will come from the text. We should expect to encounter unusual phenomena; we should accept that a large part of our linguistic behaviour is subliminal, and that therefore we may find a lot of surprises. We should search for models that are especially appropriate to the study of texts and discourse.

The study of language is moving into a new era in which the exploitation of modern computers will be at the centre of progress. The machines can be harnessed in order to test our hypotheses, they can show us things that we may not already know and even things which shake our faith quite a bit in established models, and which may cause us to revise our ideas very substantially. In all of this my plea is to trust the text.

# 2 The search for units of meaning

In the mid-1990s I was invited to co-edit an issue of *Textus*, the journal of the Italian society of English academics, just at the time that the first findings of corpus research were beginning to suggest an alternative model of the lexicon. This chapter was published in *Textus* IX, 1996, and is the place where it is proposed that a unit called the lexical item is established as a higher rank of lexical structure, above the word. An outline structure of this new unit is suggested, based on exhaustive descriptions of the corpus evidence for several candidates. Chapter 8 is a direct follow-on from this.

## The case for extended units of meaning

The starting point of the description of meaning in language is the word. This is one of two primitives in language form, the other being the sentence. The sentence is the unit that aligns grammar and discourse, and the word is the unit that aligns grammar and vocabulary.

The alignment of grammar and vocabulary is very clear in inflected languages, where in the typical case one morpheme, the lexical one, is invariable and the other, the inflection, varies with the local grammar. This kind of model is absorbed by users of such languages in basic education, and is very strong.

I would like to draw attention to another, more generalized, feature of the independence of the word as we perceive it. In the majority of writing and printing conventions, words are separated by spaces, and thus have the physical appearance of discrete units. One of the early stages in learning to read is the recognition of words as units, and this is built firmly into our general model of language. A text is therefore seen as a succession of discrete items, those items being words.

The word, however, does not reign unchallenged as the basic unit of language. American linguistics of the first half of this century put forward the morpheme, the smallest unit of grammar, as a more suitable foundation, and the surge of interest at that time in unwritten languages, and non-European ones, gave strong arguments. Some scholars preferred the Item and Arrangement model (IA), where the initial steps in describing the structure of a language are the identification of the morphemes and their patterns of arrangement.

Words are made up of single morphemes or their combinations, and so on to sentences and discourse. The other model, Item and Process (IP), again began with the morpheme, but instead of arrangement this model envisaged the morphemes going through processes, such as pluralization, in order to produce the variety of words that are seen, particularly in inflected languages. So, in Hockett's famous paper (1954), the argument raged over whether *baked* consisted of two morphemes, *bake* and *ed* placed one after the other, or *bake* which had gone through the process of having its time reference changed to the past, which was signified by the change in its shape.

Hockett acknowledged at the beginning of his paper that he had accidentally overlooked a couple of millennia of European scholarship in this field, but carried on regardless. This provoked Robins (1959) to advocate a third model, WP (Word and Paradigm), where the word was recognized as the foundation unit, and the equivalent of Process in IP was the *inflection* of the word. This model had developed in the study of the European classical languages, and Robins argued for its wider relevance.

All three of these models concentrated on the smaller units of language, and in dealing with larger units dwelt almost exclusively on grammar. IC, or Immediate Constituent Grammar showed the IA model in action, and was very popular in the 1950s. Harris (1954) found that multi-word stretches of language did not recur, and proposed the transformation as a device for considering as equivalent stretches which differed systematically.

None of these models takes lexis seriously into account, though Harris gets much closer than anyone else. The starting point of this chapter is the observation that words enter into meaningful relations with other words around them, and yet all our current descriptions marginalize this massive contribution to meaning. The main reason for the marginalization is that grammars are always given priority, and grammars barricade themselves against the individual patterns of words.

A glance at any dictionary will confirm the status of the word as the primary unit of lexical meaning. A dictionary lists the words of a language and alongside each one provides an account of the meaning or meanings. Since the common words of a language typically can have several meanings, these are usually listed in separate paragraphs – Table 2.1 gives an example. The model is clear – *words* are the units of language but are prone to multiple ambiguity.

The phenomenon attracts a great deal of academic activity, because it has to be accounted for. Most of the explanations are historical, and show the way word forms can coalesce in time, and meanings can specialize and diverge. Theories of meaning arise, with concepts such as 'core meaning' (Carter 1987), and scientific experiments are conducted with the aim of providing evidence to support the theories.

Dictionaries, however, also show that the equation 'word = unit of meaning', while reliable in general, has to be qualified in a few cases. Compounds, for example, typically consist of two words, each of which has an independent existence, but together they make a meaning that is different from the normal

*Table 2.1* Extract from *Cobuild Dictionary* (1995), p. 1,538

---

**'shot / ʃɒt/  shots**

1 **Shot** is the past tense and past participle of shoot.

| | |
|---|---|
| 2 A **shot** is an act of firing a gun. *He had murdered Perceval at point blank range with a single shot . . . a man fired a volley of shots at them.* | N-COUNT |
| 3 Someone who is a good **shot** can shoot well. Someone who is a bad shot cannot shoot well. *He was not a particularly good shot because of his eyesight.* | N-COUNT<br>adj. N |
| 4 In sports such as football, golf, or tennis, a **shot** is an act of kicking, hitting, or throwing the ball, especially in an attempt to score a point. *He had only one shot at goal.* | N-COUNT |
| 5 A **shot** is a photograph or a particular sequence of pictures in a film. *I decided to try for a more natural shot of a fox peering from the bushes . . . He received praise for the atmospheric monochrome shots in David Lynch's* The Elephant Man. | N-COUNT |
| 6 If you have a **shot** at something, you attempt to do it; an informal use. *The heavyweight champion will be given a shot at Holyfield's world title.* | N-COUNT<br>usu. sing.,<br>usu. N *at* n |
| 7 A **shot** of a drug is an injection of it. *He administered a shot of Nembutal.* | N-COUNT<br>usu. N *of* n |
| 8 A **shot** of a strong alcoholic drink is a small glass of it; used especially in American English . . . *a shot of vodka . . . spirits and liqueurs, served in a shot glass.* | N-COUNT |

---

putting together of their individual meanings. *Blackbird* is the usual example; a blackbird is a black bird, but not all black birds are blackbirds. In addition, the bigger dictionaries often include a few paragraphs at the end of the entry where a number of idiomatic phrases are listed, with explanations to show that these also claim a meaning in combination that they do not have in simple concatenation – Table 2.2 gives one from Cobuild (1995). The low prominence of these features, and the almost total absence of provision for them in the grammar, makes it clear that they are considered as marginal phenomena, almost aberrations, exceptions that prove the rules.

I say 'almost total absence' because although the traditional parsing and analysis was quite pure in this respect, the business of language teaching has brought into prominence one type of combination in English that is so common it cannot really be ignored. This is the phrasal verb, the verb plus particle that conjures up an unpredictable meaning; the scourge of the learner. The structure does not fit the model, neither semantically nor grammatically, because a single meaning-selection straddles a major structural boundary. As a result, dictionar-

*Table 2.2* Extract from *Cobuild Dictionary* (1995), pp. 694–5

| | |
|---|---|
| 12 If someone or something **gives the game away**, they reveal a secret or reveal their feelings, and this puts them at a disadvantage. *She'd never been to a posh mansion, and was afraid she might give the game away . . . The faces of the two conspirators gave the game away.* | PHRASES<br>V inflects |
| 13 If you are **new to** a particular game, you have not done a particular activity or been in a particular situation before. *Don't forget that she's new to this game and will take a while to complete the task.* | v-link<br>PHR |
| 14 If a man or woman is **on the** game, he or she is working as a prostitute; an informal British expression. | v-link<br>PHR |
| 15 If you beat someone **at** their own **game**, you use the same methods that they have used, but more successfully, so that you gain an advantage over them. *He must anticipate the manoeuvres of the other lawyers and beat them at their own game . . . The police knew that to trap the killer they had to play him at his own game.* | PHR after v |
| 16 If you say that something is **all part of the game**, you are telling someone not to be surprised or upset by something because it is a normal part of the situation that they are in. *For investors, risks are part of the game.* | v-link<br>PHR |
| 17 If you say that someone is **playing games** or **playing silly games**, you are emphasizing your disapproval of the fact that they are not treating a situation seriously and that you are annoyed with them. *This seemed to annoy Professor Steiner. 'Don't play games with me' he thundered. . . . From what I know of him he doesn't play silly games.* | V inflects<br>PRAGMATICS |
| 18 If you say **the game is up**, you mean that someone's secret plans or activities have been revealed and therefore must stop because they cannot succeed. *Some thought they would hold out until Sunday. The realists knew that the game was already up.* | V inflects |

ies for the learner usually make special provision for phrasal verbs, and grammars for learners make apologies for their very existence.

Besides compounds and phrasal verbs we can mention idioms, fixed phrases, variable phrases, clichés, proverbs, and many technical terms and much jargon, as examples of recognized patterns where the independence of the word is compromised in some way. In conventional descriptions of a language, whether lexical or grammatical, they are tucked away, well off-centre. They seem to be anarchic, individual, unstable, one-off items that just do not fit into a tidy description. Unlike phrases and clauses which fit together in Chinese boxes with labelled bracketing, these spill out all over the place, fit no hierarchical place, and relate in mysterious ways to word meaning. Sometimes the criterion given for identifying phrasal verbs, idioms, etc., is that the meaning is not the same as the sum of the meaning of the constituent words. Unfortunately that is not a formal criterion – see the discussion in the Introduction to Sinclair, Moon et al. (1989) – and the individual words in an expression can be in all sorts of relationships to the meaning:

a  none of the words may appear to contribute directly to the meaning of the expression (*bear on* = be relevant to)
b  some may, while others may not (*to beat someone up*)
c  each still seems to mean what it normally means (*the rain beats down*).

This last type is usually called a *collocation*, a frequent co-occurrence of words; it does not have a profound effect on the individual meanings of the words, but there is usually at least a slight effect on the meaning, if only to select or confirm the meaning appropriate to the collocation, which may not be the most common meaning. So in 'the rain beats down', the meaning of 'beat' is '[to hit] hard, usually several times or continuously for a period' (Cobuild 1995).

It is thus clear that there are many cases in texts where the independence of the choice of words is compromised, because other patterns cut across them and constrain them. In grammar we are familiar with concord rules, and the predictions of grammatical choices (e.g. that the choice of a transitive verb predicts an object); in this chapter the constraints are simply extended to include lexical constraints as well.

Because lexical constraints operate often at the level of word choice, it is possible to use numerical methods to gather and evaluate the evidence without the labour of preprocessing the text. This is very helpful now that electronically held text corpora are increasingly available to researchers and access to large corpora – over 200 million words *in The Bank of English* – makes the results much clearer because the large range of variation of expression can be penetrated to reveal the underlying regularities.

### Statistics

It should be stressed here that the use of numerical methods is normally only the first stage of a linguistic investigation, and this kind of work should be distinguished sharply from the heavy reliance on statistical methods in some styles of linguistic-analytical operations such as parsing or translation.

In gathering and organizing corpus evidence, the first focus is on repeated events rather than single occurrences. This initial state does not mean that unique, one-off events are necessarily ignored, but rather that they cannot be evaluated in the absence of an interpretative framework provided by the repeated events.

So a language pattern – however defined – has to occur a minimum of twice. This is a primitive test of significance in itself, in that the exact recurrence of an event is rather unlikely to be an accident, but it is of course not normally a sufficient condition. Ultimately the inherent likelihood of an event has to be related to the frequency of its occurrence in order to determine its linguistic role. In practice, for language, unlike many other areas of research, only events that recur are worth assessing the significance of; no matter how unusual, a single occurrence is unremarkable in the first instance.

This position is consistent with the collection of corpora for their representative quality, rather than the investigation of the meaning and function of any particular text. When a reliable description of the regularities has been assembled, then individual texts can be read against it, and at that time the individual instance will make a balanced impact by comparison with the norms.

At present the only available measure of significance is to compare the frequency of a linguistic event against the likelihood that it has come about by chance (Clear 1993). Since language is well known to be highly organized, and each new corpus study reveals new patterns of organization, a relationship to chance is not likely to be very revealing.

## Open choice and idiom

Complete freedom of choice, then, of a single word is rare. So is complete determination. As in ethics, freedom and determinism are two conflicting principles of organization which between them produce a rich continuum. I have called their linguistic correlates (Sinclair 1987) the *open-choice principle* and the *idiom principle*. The preponderance of usage lies between the two. Some features of language patterning tend to favour one, some the other.

Tending towards open choice is what we can dub the *terminological tendency*, which is the tendency for a word to have a fixed meaning in reference to the world, so that anyone wanting to name its referent would have little option but to use it, especially if the relationship works in both directions. Another tendency – almost the opposite – is the natural variation of language, so that very little indeed can be regarded as fixed.

Tending towards idiomaticity is the *phraseological tendency*, where words tend to go together and make meanings by their combinations. Here is collocation, and other features of idiomaticity. Many of these patterns seem almost purely linguistic (like Halliday's (1966) famous *strong tea* and *powerful engine*, where on semantic grounds the adjectives should be interchangeable, but on collocational grounds they are not). The linguistic patterns are of course supported strongly by tendencies in the world at large for objects and events to associate with each other. So, for example, both *door* and *window* have *room* as a significant collocate – here language does little more than correlate with the world, and adds little distinctive pattern, unlike *slammed* with *door* or *seat* with *window*, where collocational selectivity is evident.

Where then is the boundary between a relatively independent item and one with such a strongly determining environment that we are tempted to extend the item boundary and recognize a phrase? One hypothesis, to be explored in this chapter, is that the notion of a linguistic item can be extended, at least for English, so that units of meaning are expected to be largely phrasal. Some words would still be chosen according to the open-choice principle, but probably not very many, depending on the kind of discourse. The idea of a word carrying meaning on its own would be relegated to the margins of linguistic interest, in the enumeration of flora and fauna for example.

Part of the supporting argument for this hypothesis is that words cannot remain perpetually independent in their patterning unless they are either very rare or specially protected (for example by being technical terms, if indeed that status offers the protection that is often claimed for it). Otherwise, they begin to retain traces of repeated events in their usage, and expectations of events such as collocations arise. This leads to greater regularity of collocation and this in turn offers a platform for specialization of meaning, for example in compounds. Beyond compounds we can see lexical phrases form, phrases which have to be taken as wholes in their contexts for their distinctive meaning to emerge, but which are prone to variation.

It is often pointed out that so-called 'fixed phrases' are not in fact fixed; there are very few invariable phrases in English. Nevertheless, in discussions, descriptions and the teaching of languages, the myth of fixedness is perpetuated – as if *variation* was a minor detail that could safely be ignored. However, the argument of the present paper is that this variation gives the phrase its essential flexibility, so that it can fit into the surrounding cotext.

The variation is often systematic, and widespread – i.e. other lexical phrases vary along the same lines. We also look for structure, perhaps of a lexical kind as well as grammatical, so that we can claim that different components of the phrase carry out distinct functions; this 'division of labour' is a strong hint of a larger unit of meaning. If the evidence of a very large corpus tends to support this position, then phraseology is due to become central in the description of English.

In considering the corpus data, we shall begin in an area of patterning that on intuitional grounds should be relevant – the area of very frequent collocations, idioms, fixed phrases and the like. If we are to find evidence of extended units of meaning, it is surely there that we should look. A typical idiom in English is built around *naked eye*. Then we will consider a frequent collocation that would not normally be thought of as idiomatic – *true feelings* – to see if the analysis reveals additional constraints. Then we will choose an uncommon word – *brook* as a verb – to study how a single word can be closely integrated into its cotext without setting up anything that might be called an idiom; finally we will sketch out one aspect of the use of the very common word *place* to confirm that the interdependence of meaning and cotext is not confined to the marginalia of language.

### *Naked eye: outline description*

In life, some things come in pairs – arms, legs, ears, eyes, etc., to think only of the human body. This pairing cuts across the regular relationship of singular and plural in nouns. Normally we can expect the plural of a noun to refer to more than one of whatever the singular refers to, but with pairs the singular is not as often required as the plural. It is therefore available for other functions.

For example, most uses of the form *eye* are not in a singular/plural relationship with *eyes*. The point is made in the Introduction to Sinclair, Clear et al. (1995), where there is shown to be very little overlap between the 'top twenty' collocates of these two word forms; *blue* and *brown* collocate only with *eyes*, while *caught* and *mind* collocate only with *eye*, as part of multi-word expressions to do with monitoring, visualizing, evaluating.

We shall examine in detail the expression *naked eye*. There is no useful interpretation for this phrase based on the 'core' meanings of the two words, e.g. 'unclothed organ of sight', although we can work back from the phrasal meaning, roughly 'without (the) aid (of a telescope or microscope)' and make a metaphorical extension to *naked* which fits the meaning. Notice that, once established, it is dangerously easy to reverse the procedure and assume that the metaphorical extension is obvious. It is not; *naked* in the collocation *naked eye* could equally well mean 'unprotected', 'without eyelids', 'without spectacles, contact lenses, etc.', and the collocation *naked eye* could easily mean 'shocked' (?they stripped in front of the naked eyes of the watchers) or 'provocative espionage device' (?American use of their naked eye spy satellites has caused Iraq to retaliate), or a dozen other metaphorical extensions of the semantic features of the two words involved.

The data analysed for this study comes from *The Bank of English*, which contained in mid-1995 a total of 211 million words of current English from a wide range of sources. There are 154 instances of *naked eye*, reproduced without editing in Appendix 2.1 (see pp. 45–7). Three pairs of lines are identical, and would normally be removed by the retrieval software on the grounds that they are probably repeats of the same example, leaving 151 different concordance lines. These 151 lines constitute our data.

By inspection of the concordances, it is clear that there is greater consistency of patterning to the left of the collocation than to the right, so we move in our study step by step to the left. There is so much detail to be dealt with in even 151 lines that the main argument may get hopelessly obscured; hence this study is in two parts. The main argument is set out here with a few illustrative examples, and the discussion of the atypical, odd and wayward instances is returned to in the section 'Naked eye: detail', pp. 40–4 below.

The first position to the left of *naked eye* (designated N-1) is occupied by the word *the*, in 95 per cent of the examples. The deviant examples are explained as the influence of regular features of English – the concord of personal pronouns and the nominalization of noun phrases. Therefore it is established that *the* is an inherent component of the phrase *the naked eye*.

We now turn to position, N-2, immediately to the left of *the*. Two words dominate the pattern – *with* and *to*:

*Table 2.3* Position N-3

| see 11 | seen 14 | total 25 |
|---|---|---|
| visible 48 | invisible 16 | total 64 |
| | N-3 position | grand total 89 |

> . . . you can see with the naked eye . . .
> . . . just visible to the naked eye . . .

The other prepositions are *by, from, as, upon* and *than* (though some grammars do not recognize *as* and *than* as prepositions). The total number of prepositions in this position is 136, which is over 90 per cent. The word class 'preposition' is thus an inherent component of the phrase, accounting for over 90 per cent of the cases.

What we have done, in terms of our analysis, is to change our criterion from collocation to *colligation*, the co-occurrence of grammatical choices (Firth 1957b) to account for the greater variation. The pattern observed here is not full colligation, because it is the co-occurrence of a grammatical class (preposition) with a collocating pair, but it is an extremely useful concept at this stage of our investigations.

Roughly 10 per cent of the instances do not have a preposition at N-2. These show what we might consider to be a short form of the phrase, primarily used as the subject or object of a clause, where a preposition would be inappropriate:

> . . . the two form a naked-eye pair . . .

The short form is found both in general use and in a semitechnical use – see Part 2 for details.

We now consider N-3, and leave on one side the short and technical instances (reducing the total number to 134). It is immediately clear that variations on two words – *see* and *visible* – dominate the picture.

All of these are prominent collocations, restricted to the two word classes 'verb' and 'adjective'. On this occasion colligation, being divided between the two, is not as important as another criterion, that of *semantic preference*. Whatever the word class, whatever the collocation, almost all of the instances with a preposition at N-2 have a word or phrase to do with visibility either at N-3 or nearby. This new criterion is another stage removed from the actual words in the text, just as colligation is one step more abstract than collocation. But it captures more of the patterning than the others.

Having established a criterion of this kind, we seek to maximise it. Even single occurrences of words can be included so long as they have the selected semantic feature, which is what we are counting. So, among the verbs we find *detect, spot, spotted, appear, perceived, viewed, recognized, read, studied, judged* – and the verb *tell*, which is used in a meaning similar to *detect*.

> . . . you cannot tell if . . .

Other adjectives at N-3 are *apparent, evident, obvious* and *undetectable*, each having a semantic feature of, roughly, 'visibility'. The criterion of semantic preference implies a loosening of syntactic regimentation, and in turn this means that the strict word-counting on which we have based positional statements is not as appropriate as it was earlier. While the majority of 'visibility' indications are to be found at N-3, quite a few are at N-4, and a scattering are even farther away or on the right hand side of the expression. The details are given in the section 'Naked eye: detail', below, pp. 40–4.

At this point we draw attention to a concord rule that has been obscured by the step-by-step presentation, which presents the prepositional choice before the semantic one. This rule is a correlation between the 'visibility' choice and the preposition choice, depending on the word class of the semantic preference. Adjectives take *to*, and verbs take *with* in all but a very small number of cases.

We should revise the statement about colligation to say 'collocation with the preposition that collocates normally with the chosen verb or adjective in the chosen construction'.

We have one more step to take – to look at the selections to the left of N-3 and see if there is any further regularity that might be incorporated into the phrase that we are studying. We must expect that in many cases the concordance line is not long enough, and in a thorough study we would have to look at extended contexts; if

> 'visibility + preposition + *the* + *naked* + *eye*'

is all one basic lexical choice, then a reasonable context of four or five words on either side would in most cases take us beyond the limit of the printed line. To avoid adducing a great deal of extra evidence, we shall concede at the outset that there are likely to be some indeterminate cases.

It is clear from a superficial glance that there is little or no surface regularity, but closer examination, set out on pp. 40–8, justifies one further element in the structure of a lexical item. We postulate a *semantic prosody* of 'difficulty', which is evident in over 85 per cent of the instances. It may be shown by a word such as *small, faint, weak, difficult* with *see*:

> . . . too faint to be seen with the naked eye . . .

and barely, rarely, just with *visible*:

> . . . it is not really visible to the naked eye . . .

or by a negative with 'visibility' or *invisible* itself, or it may just be hinted at by a modal verb such as *can* or *could*:

> . . . these could be seen with the naked eye from a helicopter . . .

A semantic prosody (Louw 1993) is attitudinal, and on the pragmatic side of the semantics/pragmatics continuum. It is thus capable of a wide range of realization, because in pragmatic expressions the normal semantic values of the words are not necessarily relevant. But once noticed among the variety of expression, it is immediately clear that the semantic prosody has a leading role to play in the integration of an item with its surroundings. It expresses something close to the 'function' of the item – it shows how the rest of the item is to be interpreted functionally. Without it, the string of words just 'means' – it is not put to use in a viable communication. So in the example here, the attention to visibility and the strange phrase *the naked eye* are interpreted as expressions of some kind of difficulty (I am told – Tognini-Bonelli, personal communication – that the literal translation of the phrase in Italian – *a occhio nudo* – has the same semantic trace but does not correlate with a prosody of difficulty).

Having arrived at the semantic prosody, we have probably come close to the boundary of the lexical item. In any case, with only the short lines of data that are made available for this study, we lack the evidence with which to continue the search. However, we have enough already on which to base the description of a compound lexical item. We shall describe its elements in the unreversed sequence, the textual sequence.

The speaker/writer selects a prosody of difficulty applied to a semantic preference of visibility. The semantic preference controls the collocational and colligational patterns, and is divided into verbs, typically *see*, and adjectives, typically *visible*. With *see*, etc., there is a strong colligation with modals – particularly *can*, *could* in the expression of difficulty – and with the preposition *with* to link with the final segment. With *visible*, etc., the pattern of collocation is principally with degree adverbs, and the negative morpheme *in-*; the following preposition is *to*. The final component of the item is the *core*, the almost invariable phrase *the naked eye*.

Note that this analysis makes two important observations, which tend to confirm the existence of this compound lexical item:

a   The beginning of the item is very difficult to detect normally, because it is so variable; on the other hand the end is fixed and obvious. But if the analysis is correct, the whole phrase must be seen as the result of a single choice, with no doubt a number of subsidiary internal choices.
b   The initial choice of semantic prosody is the functional choice which links meaning to purpose; all subsequent choices within the lexical item relate back to the prosody.

Here, then, is one model of a lexical item consisting of several words, and with a great deal of internal variation. The variation, however, disappears when the description invokes an appropriate category of abstraction, and despite the variation there is always a clearly preferred selection right down to the actual words. The variations are negligible around the core, and can be explained by the tension between different constructional pressures; further away from the core they become more varied, allowing the phrase to fit in with the previous context, and allowing some more detailed choices to be made.

## *True feelings*

Seeking confirmation of this model, we turn to a less likely example, a common collocation that would not normally be considered idiomatic – *true feelings*. A dictionary might gloss it as 'genuine emotions', and that would be fairly accurate as far as the semantic side was concerned. But if we study the occurrence of this phrase in the same way as *the naked eye*, we find similar restrictions on the choices. For the sake of space, we will not offer a step-by-step analysis, but summarize the position as follows:

At N-1, immediately before the collocation, there is a strong colligation with a possessive adjective:

> . . . we try to communicate *our* true feelings to those around us . . .

If not, then another possessive construction will be found, in particular *the true feelings of* . . . In 84 cases retrieved from a large corpus, there were seven of these and one noun in the *'s* form. Only three examples had no possessive at all.

At N-2 there is a clear semantic preference for 'expression' – usually a verb. *Express* itself occurs in one or other of its forms nine times, and *communicate, show, reveal, share, pour out, give vent to, indicate, make public*. Occasionally the 'expression' element is to be found after the phrase, or on either side, as in *make . . . perfectly clear*.

At N-3 and beyond there is a semantic prosody that we may label 'reluctance', as in *will never reveal, prevents me from expressing, careful about expressing, less open about showing, guilty about expressing*, etc. The prosody is sometimes close to 'inability', as in *try to communicate, incapable of experiencing, unable to share*.

The patterning so far is very similar to *naked eye*. However, in a number of cases we find that the semantic preference and the semantic prosody are fused – like *invisible* above. For *true feelings* the verbs are such as *conceal, hide, mask, disguise, giving an inkling of, deny, not be keenly aware of*. Closely related are *acknowledge, betray, admit*.

Our conclusion is that the collocation *true feelings* is the core of a compound lexical item which has the following inherent components:

> a semantic prosody of reluctance/inability
> a semantic preference of expression (and a strong colligation of a verb with the semantic preference)

a colligating possessive adjective
the core

So, not only are our true feelings our genuine emotions, but we use this particular collocation when talking about our reluctance to express them, even to ourselves. The collocation is almost never used except as part of this compound lexical item.

This result is remarkably similar to *naked eye*, although the collocations were chosen to be as different as possible.

### Brook

Let us seek our next example in an area of the vocabulary where the word is commonly thought to be rather independent of context – the area of infrequent words. We select the word *brook*, and confine ourselves to its use as a verb meaning approximately 'tolerate', ignoring the more common noun *brook* meaning a small stream.

All the evidence from c. 200 million words is presented in Appendix 2.2 (see p. 48). Here there is no initial collocation, but a quick examination of the immediate environment of *brook* shows negatives at either N+1 (*no*) or N-1 (*not, n't, cannot*), N-2 (*not, inability*) or N3 (*not*). This covers all the examples, and so is inherent in the expression. *Brook*, verb, is thus part of a compound lexical item.

At N+2 we find a semantic preference of 'intrusion' realized by a strong collocation of interference and prominence given to delay and opposition, and a 100 per cent colligation with nouns. Where N-1 is negative, the emphatic *any* often comes at N+1.

Moving to the left-hand side, we come across colligation with modal verbs, mainly expressed by *will* and *would*, supported by *'ll* and *'d*. Sometimes the modality is lexicalized, and we find *determination, (in)ability, in no mood to, vowing to*. Only three instances have no modal; one is a general statement:

. . . Artemis-type women brook no nonsense from their menfolk . . .

one is contemporary:

. . . Eritrea's rulers brook no interference from . . .

and one is just odd:

. . . they brook no brickbats . . .

The case is made for modal colligation as an inherent component of the compound item.

Moving further to the left, we find a semantic prosody that is difficult to express. It partly concerns the absence of something (in this case first and second person subjects), and partly includes words like *said, make/made clear, shows, indica-tion*. In all the instances except one, the 'brooking' is one stage removed as something reported of someone else, and the phrase includes a threat of retalia-tion or even punishment. The person who refuses to brook intrusion is an authority figure – a president, a country, mother and father, teachers, the army, the Tigers (a Tamil separatist group in Sri Lanka). The prosody can be crudely expressed by 'reported threat by authority', and it is pretty clear in most of the cases even in the line as printed. The one instance of a first person subject makes the threat element clear, and the assumption of authority:

> . . . Warn them that, on this one, we'll brook no interference . . .

The usual semantic gloss on *brook* as a verb is 'tolerate', and, as far as it goes, this is true. 'Tolerate' can replace *brook* in all the examples without disturbing their message. But *brook* is always negative; it expresses intolerance, not toler-ance; the intolerance is of intrusive behaviour by another.

There is an inherent component of future modality in the expression, which shows that the possible intrusions are into plans or policies, and that the expres-sion is a threat or warning. The displacement by report of the threat, and the frequent naming of authority figures as subject of *brook*, complete the expression of a semantic prosody.

There is another, rather elusive element of the prosody that we have not so far reconciled with the data. This phrase is emotionally charged with the com-mitment of the threatener to carry out the threat. Some of it may be in the words chosen as objects, especially where the negative comes in front of *brook* – *petulant isolation, challenge, protests, criticisms, defeat, contradiction* and *treachery*. In the other cases – the majority – the emotional charge is in the position of the nega-tive, governing the noun rather than the verb. Compare:

> I will not make any promises
> I will make no promises

> (constructed examples)

Both rhythmically and structurally, the second seems to carry a great deal of emotional commitment, while the first is almost tentative.

This example illustrates the reason for the choice of the term *prosody*. The precise extent of the prosody, and the nature of its realization, cannot be deter-mined in advance; and once it is identified with a phrasing it will be part of the meaning even if it has no clear expression. For example Artemis-type women must be interpreted as dominating in order to fit the prosody; the appointment which would brook no delay must be a very important one for the person con-cerned, etc.

Here, then, in the case of a single infrequent verb, is to be found a very similar pattern to those we have seen of collocations.

### *Place*

For one final brief example we will turn to the frequent end of the vocabulary. *Place* is one of the commonest words in English, and has 50 paragraphs in the Cobuild dictionary (1995), some of which present several senses. Sense 13 is – in informal English – where someone is living or staying, and the phrasing of the definition 'Your *place* is the house or flat where you live; an informal use' already signals two important points. One is the possessive *your* and the other is the informality of the expression.

To illustrate the structure of this item in a short space, I shall use only one of the most typical versions of it. In principle, any possessive could colligate with *place*, but *my* is very common at N-1 and I shall consider only this. At N-2 we find a preposition, with a strong collocation for *to*. At N-3 there is very often another colligation, with an adverb of place, *back, home, over, round, up, down*, and combinations such as *back home*. The directional meanings of these words is barely relevant, since they all mean the same thing, and they seem mainly to contribute to a prosody of '*informality*'. When there is no adverb, there is usually a verb of travel – a form of *come* is a strong collocation, and *go, walk, bring, make it, take*. Where there is an adverb, the verb is found in front of it. There is a clear semantic preference for the expression of travel.

The verb *invite*, which occurs occasionally, gives expression to an important semantic prosody – in this case not the only possible use of place with the meaning 'home', but a typical one. Clear invitations are common:

> . . . Would you like to come back to my place for a while . . . (NB the person invited might not have been there before, and so is not going back)

and so are references to invitations, e.g.

> . . . if she was coming to my place I would check . . .

or quasi-invitations:

> I decided to take him to my place to sleep it off . . .

or indications of easy social informality:

> . . . She came over to my place with a friend . . .

To conclude, then, we have strong evidence for a compound lexical item which has a semantic prosody 'informal invitation', a semantic preference for 'local travel' which is realized by colligation of a verb of movement and optionally a directional adverb, with *come* and *over* as typical collocations. A strong colligation with a preposition (collocate: *to*) and a possessive (collocate: *my*) precede the single word core, place.

## Conclusion

The case for compound lexical items will be made by piling up evidence of the kind illustrated in this chapter, and apparently pervading much of the vocabulary. So strong are the co-occurrence tendencies of words, word classes, meanings and attitudes that we must widen our horizons and expect the units of meaning to be much more extensive and varied than is seen in a single word.

In the early days of the study of lexis (e.g. Sinclair 1966) there was provision made for the likelihood that the word and the lexical item would not always coincide. However, the state of computing 30 years ago would not allow a more sophisticated measure than the word. Now the position is different – the early studies have established that there is a considerable amount of co-selection among words that co-occur, and the present state of corpus linguistics makes it feasible to investigate the phenomenon over large volumes of evidence.

A great deal of the patterning reported here is readily computable, and most of the rest will probably yield in time to heuristic procedure. A start can be made on an inventory of the units of meaning of English.

If the model of a lexical item offered in this chapter turns out to be the only one, and the computational search is successful, then a text will be analysed into a string of units, each statistically independent of those on either side. The major structural categories that have been proposed here – collocation, colligation, semantic preference and semantic prosody – and their inter-relationships, will be elaborated and will assume a central rather than a peripheral role in language description.

The impact that this perspective on language will have on conventional phrase, clause and sentence grammar may be considerable. There is clearly a shared set of descriptors with grammar in the internal structure of the item – negatives, medals, possessives, etc. It is to be expected from the evidence presented above that elements of the internal structure will recur many times, and this position is supported by much ongoing research. Both externally and internally, we might end up with a potentially very simple lexicogrammar.

It should be noted that this model does not exclude single words that are apparently chosen on open-choice principles and do not make collocational, etc., patterns, nor appear among semantic preferences – words that leave no trace of their use. Even such words do not need another model – they are examples of the limiting case of the lexical item proposed here.

It is of course likely that this lexical item is only one of several. One possibility is a type of item based on a grammatical core rather than a lexical one. 'Collocational frameworks' were proposed by Renouf and Sinclair (1991) and need further study. In these the core is one or more frequent grammatical words, usually discontinuous, like *the . . . of.*

Models that arise from corpus-driven studies, like the one proposed here, have a holistic quality that makes them attractive. The numerical analysis of language is aligned closely with the meaningful analysis; lexis and grammar are

hardly distinguished, surface and abstract categories are mixed without difficulty. As a result some of the problems of conventional description are much
reduced – for example there will be little word-based ambiguity left when this
model has been applied thoroughly. Although a great deal of research has to be
done to find the units and make the description coherent, the gain for students
and users of language should be well worth the effort.

## Naked eye: detail

Here is a more detailed account of the structure of the *naked eye* item, following
up most of the minor variations. It is a central part of the methodology at this
stage that every instance has the same weight as any other, and that selection is
on the basis of the number of instances of a certain kind. No instance is ignored
or overlooked; however, in exposition, the discussion of detail can obscure the
main force of an argument.

In this chapter the detailed analysis of *naked eye* is presented here; for reasons
of space the detailed analysis of the other studies is omitted.

### *Position N-1*

The first position to the left, as already mentioned, is nearly always occupied by
the word *the*. There are eight exceptions: *your* (2), *our*, *a*, *to* (3); in one example
the phrase is surrounded by typographical tags indicating that it is the title of an
article, and we omit this one because it gives no useful evidence.

The cases of possessive adjectives illustrate a latent tension in the phraseology:

> . . . anything you can see with your naked eye . . .
> . . . you could see it with your naked eye . . .
> . . . that we can't even see with our naked eye . . .

The subject pronouns *you* and *we* set up an expectation of concord, which cuts
across the strong requirement of *the* as a component of the phrase. In the above
cases, which are from informal spoken sources, the concord rule has won; in
other examples (the majority) the decision goes the other way.

The example with *a* instead of *the* has *naked eye* in a noun-modifying position
– *a naked-eye pair* – and this is supported by another example, not part of this
data but collected from a similar source:

> . . . A Naked-Eye Supernova . . .

This usage suggests a technical use of the phrase *naked eye*, where it refers to a
precise measure of luminosity. Used as a modifier in a nominalization, it has no
article. In the three instances of *to naked eye* the same structure occurs, and the
phrase modifies *visibility*, *brilliance* and *observation*. In some of these examples the
phrase is hyphenated.

### Position N-2

We now turn to the position immediately to the left of *the*. Apart from *with* (47) and *to* (77), there are 17 other prepositions, and 10 other words which we will deal with in turn. The variation is greater than that of N-1, but the two main collocations are strong, constituting the great majority of the instances. We can refine the figures as follows:

a    we remove from the total the examples already identified as nominalizations, since their structural environment cannot be expected to conform to the main patterning; note however that two of them:

> . . . flared to naked eye visibility . . .
> . . . flared up to naked eye brilliance . . .

already suggest another regularity within the technical use of the phrase. We thus remove four instances, leaving 146. In the other deviant examples at N-1 the choice is of possessive, and therefore the surrounding structure is not affected; so we retain these.

b    we introduce colligation, the co-occurrence of grammatical choices. As well as *with* and *to*, the other prepositions are *by, from, as, upon* and *than* (though some grammars do not recognize *as* and *than* as prepositions). The total number of prepositions in this position is 136, which is over 90 per cent.

The seven instances of *by* show tension between the general grammatical rule for the formation of the passive and the collocational 'pull' of the phrase. All the examples are passive, and the agent phrase of the English passive is normally introduced by *by*. This conflicts with the otherwise dominant use of *with* after verbs and in these seven cases the general rule holds, though in the majority of the instances it does not.

*From* is used twice, in both cases revealing another phraseological tension:

> . . . signs hidden from the naked eye . . .
> . . . it was clear, both from the naked eye and re-runs, that . . .

The verb *hide* takes *from* as its normal preposition, especially in the form *hidden* – *\*hidden to the eye* would sound very odd. The other example couples *the naked eye* with *re-runs*, using *both . . . and*, thus getting into difficulties, since *to* will not go with *re-runs* in this context, and *from* is not one of the collocating prepositions in our phrase.

The single instance of *as*, and one of the two with *than* are of a technical nature, because of the assumption of a previously known measure of luminosity. The other instance of *than*

> . . . using nothing more than the naked eye . . .

is a good example of the phrase in its minimal form. Here the impersonality of *the* gives it the general reference that is associated with it.

There are ten instances remaining, where the word at N-1 is not a preposition. Of these, nine are similar to the one just quoted, where *the naked eye* means approximately 'anyone using their unaided sight'. In one of these cases there is a blend of two idiomatic expressions with *eye*, similar to *hidden from*, discussed above:

> . . . far beyond what meets the naked eye . . .

*Meets the eye* has an independent existence.

The example with *that* at N-2 is strange, but shows the phrase as a noun modifier, similar to the technical use.

The one remaining instance is a title, shown by the initial capital letters.

### *Position N-3*

In Part 1 we identified 104 instances of the semantic preference of 'visibility'. To complete the picture we omit the short forms and technical uses, (though some of them show this semantic preference) and concentrate on the 28 lines unaccounted for.

When we move from physical evidence (collocation) to structural (colligation) to semantic criteria, we must expect less regimentation of position, and more variation generally. Also each step backwards in the concordances has itself introduced some variety of expression – hardly any at N-1, a little more at N-2 and quite a lot at N-3. Each variation has the potential of introducing further variation in its vicinity.

If we collect the instances with *it* at N-3 we usually find a verb of visibility at N-4. *See* occurs three times in this position, also *view*. *See* also has *ourselves* at N-3. Sometimes N-4 is the preposition *at*, and the verb at N-5 is a form of *look*. Once we find the adjective *indistinguishable* at N-5. So the semantic *preference* is present, but slightly displaced from its commonest position.

In another 18 instances the word at N-3 is not closely related to the phrase we are studying, and the structure has displaced the 'visibility' expression even farther to the left (13 cases), and sometimes even to the right of the rest of the phrase (5). Typical examples are:

> . . . they look like stars to the naked eye . . .
> . . . appear like a thin line to the naked eye . . .
> . . . To the naked eye there was no trace of any . . .

In three cases the visibility expression is beyond the end of the concordance line as printed, but they have been included in this category for the sake of simplicity.

Thus in 133 lines out of 134 we can claim that a semantic preference for an expression of visibility is an inherent component of the phrase; usually a verb or adjective, usually at N-3, and frequently a form of *see* or *visible*.

One instance remains:

. . . To the naked eye he is easily one of the fittest . . .

There is no realization here of the visibility expression and it has to be inferred. The construction *To the . . . eye* is commonly used, and many other adjectives could occur in it. This instance is probably closest to the short form of the phrase, and we can now identify an element of the relation between the short form and the full form. The short form implies visibility but does not express it; it is therefore semantically dependent on the full form.

## Position N-4

We can build up the notion of difficulty by studying the first few lines of the concordance line by line. The first instance is:

. . . too small to see with the naked eye . . .

Are there any more, suggesting difficulty of visibility? The second instance is:

. . . that can be seen with the naked eye (very few of these) . . .

The word *can* weakly indicates overcoming a difficulty. The third instance is similar. The fourth is indeterminate, but one can reasonably infer that viewing the moon without a telescope is not very rewarding. Number 5 has *could*, number 6 *not really*, and number 7 *cannot always be perceived*. These are all instances of a *semantic prosody* of 'difficulty'. This may just be hinted at by a modal verb such as *can* or *could* or more directly by a negative with 'visibility' (of which we already have recorded 16 examples of *invisible*), or by some other means.

Clear lexical expressions of difficulty are given in 22 cases of words like *small* with *see*. Then there are 15 negatives. Another 14 express the opposite of difficulty in this context – *so big, entirely obvious, bright, clearly visible*, etc., and these are included because they state or imply that this case of visibility is unusual. For example:

. . . It's so big you can see it with the naked eye . . .

This makes a total of 51. Then there are 15 instances of *can* or *could* without a negative and with *see* or a similar verb. Sometimes the implication of difficulty is clear even in this brief context:

. . . 5 mm wide, but you can see it with the naked eye . . .

It is normal in English to use a modal verb, usually *can*, with a verb of physical perception instead of the simple present tense. The incidence of *can see*, etc., is thus unremarkable. But in turn it may be argued that people are only likely to report on what they can see or hear when there is some doubt or difficulty, in which case the normal usage supports our interpretation here. So, while the high incidence of modals suggests a small secondary organization around the verb *see*, the instances can be counted as at least consistent with the 'difficulty' prosody.

The remaining examples require interpretation, because there is no clear expression of difficulty on the surface. Nevertheless, in all but a dozen cases, it is fairly obvious that observation with the naked eye is considered inadequate or problematic, especially when contrasted with some other means of observation. A few examples:

> . . . A man's face may look smooth to the naked eye. But magnified, it . . .
> . . . We see, with the naked eye now it is so close . . .
> . . . the first to be seen with the naked eye for 400 years . . .
> . . . a star cluster that, to the naked eye, looks like a faint frosting . . .
> . . . us to see thousands of stars with the naked eye, and millions with an optical . . .

In my reading, there are 35 of these, which added to the rest gives a total of 103 instances that either express the prosody of difficulty or are likely to be understood as invoking it, as against 12 which could be interpreted without it, for example:

> . . . Jupiter and Saturn are visible to the naked eye . . .

Although there is an implied contrast with other objects that are not visible to the naked eye, this example is close to the technical use and records the visibility without raising questions of difficulty.

Of course, we have artificially restricted ourselves to a very small context, and several of these cases may give evidence of the prosody nearby; but we have no reason to believe that the prosody cannot be neutralized or reduced substantially in impact by other choices in the vicinity.

# Appendix 2.1

| | | |
|---|---|---|
| agents too small to see with the | the naked eye | and so they much preferred |
| binaries that can be seen with | the naked eye | (very few of these) or through |
| our galaxy that you can see with | the naked eye | Now to expand our horizons: The |
| is like viewing the moon with | the naked eye | . You see a disk with some |
| of thing you could look at with | the naked eye | 'Would you like to |
| it is not really visible to | the naked eye | . About five years ago, a |
| cannot always be perceived by | the naked eye | and said, 'As I've gotten |
| even though nothing is visible to | the naked eye | . We should trust our patients |
| the opening is not visible to | the naked eye | . Typically, the closed |
| photoaging changes are visible to | the naked eye | . And even more disturbing |
| little rooftop house. Viewed with | the naked eye | , she was nothing more than a |
| is visible with | the naked eye | . While stroke path can be with |
| outlets. These could be seen with | the naked eye | from a helicopter, and the water |
| human ovum is barely visible to | the naked eye | . The corpus luteum forms in the |
| small. It can easily be seen by | the naked eye | . The time of ovulation in |
| is large enough to be seen by | the naked eye | . The ovary still contains the |
| the surveyor's map. Invisible to | the naked eye | beneath a shroud of poison ivy, |
| to iris borer. Invisible to | the naked eye | , the young borers work their |
| plants that you can see with | the naked eye | just as much as those for which |
| is almost invisible to | the naked eye | . For as his newly curvaceous |
| by many besides those visible to | the naked eye | . People from varied stations |
| which Parsons could not see with | the naked eye | ; with Parson's only |
| a strip of water so wide | the naked eye | can barely see the far shore |
| passage among them, visible to | the naked eye | . Time to settle down for a |
| muted one could look at it with | the naked eye | . The air smelled of summer's |
| like a wiggling speck of dust to | the naked eye | , like nothing more than dining |
| from the deck of his ship with | the naked eye | , these are very faint aren't |
| becomes immediately apparent to | the naked eye | . The opening of each envelope is |
| is the first supernova seen with | the naked eye | for nearly 400 years. The last |
| was the first to be seen with | the naked eye | for 400 years and is relatively |
| was the first to be seen with | the naked eye | for 400 years and is relatively |
| and sewage clearly visible to | the naked eye | . And the sewage is not only bad |
| to earth to be visible with | the naked eye | . That was almost four years |
| bright comet which was visible to | the naked eye | and passed extremely close to |
| than the faintest star visible to | the naked eye | on a dark night. The fourth |
| bright comet which was visible to | the naked eye | and passed extremely close to |
| anything you can see with | your naked eye | , probably has adequate amino |
| distant objects invisible to | the naked eye | . These were picked up by the |
| at it directly, not even with | the naked eye | . Never ever put your eye to a |
| at it directly, not even with | the naked eye | . Never ever put your eye to a |
| in 1963, they look like stars to | the naked eye | , but closer examination of the |
| blood and matter were visible to | the naked eye | 'Dabs?' Thorne queried. |
| to view or carry out repairs. To | the naked eye | there was no trace of any |
| rubber and quite invisible to | the naked eye | unless you were crouching down |
| going on that you can't see with | the naked eye | . Nature is secretive, Matt. |
| the two was nearly visible to | the naked eye | . Finally, they stood face-to- |
| was a transformation invisible to | the naked eye | , and certainly unbeknown to |
| record what we see ourselves with | the naked eye | . If identical objects are at |
| of making themselves visible to | the naked eye | eventually. But it' |
| they are rarely visible with | the naked eye | , which is why many experts |
| ceques now visible to | the naked eye | only as the alignment of Inca |
| if the lights were invisible to | the naked eye | . Other regions |
| scarlet of Zanzibar. We see, with | the naked eye | now it is so close, European |
| carcinoma can be recognized with | the naked eye | . It comes away in fragments |

flat warts are often invisible to the naked eye , but are detected with a

cannot tell by looking at it with the naked eye whether you are clear or not

Yes, and to the naked eye the liquid produced will appear

on a level that is invisible to the naked eye . SHIELDS Your circle might want

it. The worms cannot be seen by the naked eye . Horses grazing the paddock

dust particles (those visible to the naked eye ), but are sufficiently loose to

Double Cluster. Easily visible to the naked eye , these two clusters lie more

of Desert Rats, invisible to the naked eye , could be seen clearly and in

13 years and will be visible to the naked eye all week (it'll be by far the

a machine,' McGhee remarked. 'To the naked eye he is easily one of the fittest

so small they cannot be seen with the naked eye I asked the curator which was

that we can't even see with the naked eye . But I'm just saying that the

look weak and sun-bleached to the naked eye . Backlighting sometimes

too small to see with the naked eye , known as Quorn. A relation

its effects cannot be seen by the naked eye . For a better

than red, are just visible to the naked eye and feed mainly under the

and can be almost invisible to the naked eye . On an ideal scalp, the

lines and are fairly visible to the naked eye . Especially common in pregnant

deterioration is invisible to the naked eye , the condom no longer offers

most closely equates with what the naked eye naturally sees, I find this

variation on Damon Blur to the naked eye , giggles disbelievingly at this

mites are too small to see with the naked eye . The answer is to spray

that inspection of the film with the naked eye failed to spot any visual

former is easier to detect with the naked eye than in the latter. The

manifesto ART Naked eye Limp cocks and sagging

of mould spores undetectable to the naked eye a time bomb or respiratory

in lettering barely visible to the naked eye . He witters on about how rising

individual pixels visible to the naked eye . I want to record my

currently producing a program – The Naked Eye – looking at the human life

difficult to spot a fault with the naked eye But a look at Jose Maria's

inch, appears like a thin line to the naked eye . Kasell: Changes will be

the mines using nothing more than the naked eye . When asked about the year

go up. You could see it with your naked eye Chadwic; Yeah. Wells:

the tires that aren't visible to the naked eye You have to take this to the

small and difficult to spot with the naked eye , but others should be clearly

with the neighborhood and using the naked eye to compare them with existing

So it's a kind of a fight because the naked eye and the viewer see things

itself far beyond what meets the naked eye . Now, remember, now, this

bacterium ever—it's visible to the naked eye . ADAMS: And the ups and

it's so big you can see it with the naked eye . Richard Harris has more.

a hot dog, so it's visible to the naked eye . Now, according to conventional

something that you don't see with the naked eye . Unless you're involved, you

I E it is only just visible to the naked eye . It exists in a petri dish full

with a curved front which to the naked eye looked flat. And that was

summer, and still not visible to the naked eye . No wonder the chorus of

times too faint to be seen with the naked eye , and would be difficult to

and all have to be judged by the naked eye on a crucial split second of

late tackle from Ablett. To the naked eye it looked a questionable

distant object readily visible to the naked eye . On a dark, moonless night it

1992 INVISIBLE to the naked eye and floating 12 miles above the

when it was clear, both from the naked eye and re-runs, that he never made

A man's face may look smooth to the naked eye . But magnified, it resembles

of the ecosystem. But using the naked eye to count the devilism-looking

But this molecule is invisible to the naked eye because it is only 20 angstroms

hat of all. You cannot tell with the naked eye if the crown is on back-to

Regulus on the 22nd as the two form a naked-eye pair low in the W evening sky,

marks supposed to be invisible to the naked eye which have been put into the

| | | |
|---|---|---|
| stars we dub Orion's sword. | The naked eye | often perceives the Sword as |
| to be seen since SN 1987a flared to | naked eye | visibility in the large |
| has not been entirely obvious to | the naked eye | . The best clues he has given to |
| hemisphere was visible to | the naked eye | the first such since the |
| Jupiter and Saturn are visible to | the naked eye | , and have been known since pre- |
| than the faintest star visible to | the naked eye | . Observations began again in |
| arc, 30,000 times as accurate as | the naked eye | . The less accurate Tycho |
| which is frequently visible to | the naked eye | and can form up to 30 percent |
| was, could have been visible to | the naked eye | . The striking appearance of the |
| still 15 to 20 times fainter than | the naked eye | can see. During August, |
| red light than can be seen with | the naked eye | . In August, Richard Ellis |
| the faintest stars visible with | the naked eye | . Even with their CCD detectors |
| fainter than anything visible to | the naked eye | . Smette recorded 10 |
| for the particular oil, but to | the naked eye | the graphs appear to be |
| us to see thousands of stars with | the naked eye | and millions with an optical |
| Nova Cygni, could be seen with | the naked eye | . Today it is barely visible |
| The last supernova visible to | the naked eye | . But its radiations could be |
| In 1600, an obscure star flared up | to naked-eye | brilliance, then faded: we now |
| 4.2, making it visible to | the naked eye | in dark areas. Novas are |
| star that can be seen with | the naked eye | . But, they say, it could reach |
| of anatomy as studied with | the naked eye | had progressed as far as it |
| was the first to be visible to | the naked eye | since 1604. Then on 28 March |
| star that can just be seen by | the naked eye | . It looked brighter than all |
| is just large enough to be read with | the naked eye | , and positioned near the hole |
| constellation as we view it with | the naked eye | . Loop III contains no brilliant |
| much too small to be visible to | the naked eye | . They are created by suspending |
| indistinguishable from it with | the naked-eye | observations available at the |
| dimmer than any object visible to | the naked eye | . In 1987, another group of |
| in the night sky visible to | the naked eye | in his book Sky Phenomena: A |
| in his book Sky Phenoman: A Guide | to Naked Eye | Observation of the Stars |
| saw stars that were invisible to | the naked eye | . By watching sunspots there |
| their dimness none is visible to | the naked eye | , even though most of the stars |
| first supernova to be visible to | the naked eye | since the German astronomer |
| seen In a Star cluster that, to | the naked eye | , looks like a faint frosting on |
| sticks to can be spotted with | the naked eye | , and fished out with tiny |
| flakes of settled snow appear to | the naked eye | . If it is not homogeneous, and |
| reality' by improving upon | the naked eye | ; and unlike virtual reality, it |
| Australians than is evident to | the naked eye | are refusing to be coerced |
| light to detect signs hidden from | the naked eye | , different chemicals and fuming |
| 5 mm wide, but you can see it with | the naked eye | ', said Dr Hoggett, 'That is |

## Appendix 2.2

| | | |
|---|---|---|
| again shown its determination not to | brook | any challenge to its authority. It |
| about the ANC, about its inability to | brook | any criticism or opposition. Like |
| another indication that SLORC cannot | brook | any objections or protests against |
| authenticity? Anthea: It doesn't | brook | any messing around. There is no |
| President Assad will be in no mood to | brook | any more. Treachery, however |
| s absolutely useless. We will not | brook | any decision by any court from |
| the Government honest and we will not | brook | any attack on his independence |
| unenthusiastic for Delorism, will not | brook | Britain's petulant isolation from |
| become a state of mind that does not | brook | contradiction. Yet a few modest |
| armed with an attitude that will not | brook | defeat. The opening scene of the |
| country's crisis was too urgent to | brook | delay. But this is a symptom of |
| of mediocre academics who don't | brook | disagreement with their world view |
| pounds 15 billion a year and do not | brook | dissent even from governments. |
| put upon', but did not readily | brook | interference. His Ere, who |
| the proud Cleopatra would not | brook | . Learning of his plans, she |
| judicial inconsistencies which would | brook | no more of Malcolm's /or Rose's |
| enemies within Germany that he would | brook | no opposition. Calling upon his |
| minded determination of the Tigers to | brook | no opposition in the Tamil areas of |
| Yitzhak Shamir bas said Israel will | brook | no interference concerning the |
| do it at once She would | brook | no argument or oppositions and on |
| a leap. But Fisher's determination to | brook | no opposition meant that defective |
| and those influenced by its rays will | brook | no denial in seizing their |
| needs or wants. Artemis-style women | brook | no nonsense from their menfolk, as |
| and intolerant teachers, as they will | brook | no mispronunciation or mis-accent |
| anger in her companion's veins would | brook | no control, and Sarah Ellis has |
| thin enough to make it clear they'd | brook | no interference, and his jaw was |
| Warn them that, on this one, we'll | brook | no interference. And if, by some |
| had an urgent appointment which would | brook | no delay. HMS I1Ka |
| of action for herself. one that would | brook | no interference. Pallas and Hart |
| of the country. And the army will | brook | no weakening of its power. In 1988, |
| fantastic. They fear no mocking, they | brook | no brickbats and from the moment |
| insistent about the tasks that will | brook | no delay but there is a need for |
| it was a sovereign state, and would | brook | no interference it its internal |
| ummer, and made it clear that he would | brook | no dissent from the ERM line. |
| a pistol. and Epstein himself would | brook | no opposition. He once ordered |
| most whiskers, and he will definitely | brook | no lip from anyone. Moscow |
| avoid the terrifying Hackman who will | brook | no vigilantes in his town and |
| rove inadequate, the minister would | brook | no criticism of the Government's |
| Tibet was in its isolation. He would | brook | no delay, calling for informal free |
| f the motherland. 'The peoples will | brook | no interference,' warned another |
| aughter. Meanwhile, Eritrea's rulers | brook | no interference from their de jure |
| François Mitterrand, vowing to | brook | no interference from France's |
| eft in the care of those who would | brook | no contradiction, feminism became |
| or what have you) and they will | brook | no delay. This feat has never |
| has made it plain that he will not | brook | obstruction of his reconstruction |
| again, it was in a voice that didn't | brook | resistance. You just told me that |
| Department. The Constitution does not | brook | riddles, solved or unsolved. |
| most likely, that she did not | brook | self-indulgence, laziness, or |
| that society would not always | brook | such nonsense. They had only to |
| out – that Mrs. Thatcher would not | brook | the thought of a husband and wife |

# Part II
# The organization of text

# 3 Planes of discourse

This chapter was a contribution to a Festschrift for Ramesh Mohan, then Director of the Central Institute of English and Foreign Languages (CIEFL), Hyderabad, India. Professor Mohan was a literary scholar who worked his way through stylistics to an interest in language and language teaching. The paper was published in 1982 in S.N.A. Rizvi (ed.) *The Two-fold Voice: Essays in Honour of Ramesh Mohan*, Pitambar Publishing Co., India.

It seems appropriate for this volume to offer a piece on the relation between a language and its literature. The main deficiency of the present descriptive apparatus is an overall theoretical framework within which approaches which are essentially linguistic and those which are essentially literary can both be accommodated and indeed integrated, so that they relate to each other not as alternatives but as complementary studies, meeting in the acceptance of major categories.

Literature is a prime example of language in use; no systematic apparatus can claim to describe a language if it does not embrace the literature also; and not as a freakish development, but as a natural specialization of categories which are required in other parts of the descriptive system. Further, the literature must be describable in terms which accord with the priorities of literary critics. In this effort a first step is the incorporation of *evaluation* within linguistic theory and language description.

Linguistics is a subject which has advanced on the theoretical front quite dramatically in recent years, but which has not been able to reach over to the essentially evaluative quality of literature. Indeed it has even emphasized the objectivity of its descriptions of literary texts, particularly in defending its stance; stylistics, the 'bridge' area between linguistics and literature, has neither established a sound theoretical position of its own, nor grafted itself securely onto either of its parent disciplines.

The study of English literature has never been a strongly theoretical activity, and it pays little attention even to its own analytical traditions, retaining fiercely the central independence of the critical intellect. Although recently a French-based structuralist movement has found some supporters, there are at least as many opponents.

I would like to offer a tentative outline of a framework for locating not only literary but all instances of language in use. The origin of this work is in discourse analysis, where advances were originally made in the study of spoken interaction. Written language seemed to lack the features that were evident in speech, but lately attention has turned to the desirability of incorporating both modes of language within the one framework. Seeing written language as essentially interactive, and attempting to describe it as such, is a difficult process, but early results are encouraging. The set of categories that arises from this work can be applied to literary texts also, with some modifications which feed back into a more illuminating picture of the whole.

I do not propose to define evaluation here, because it will be exemplified in various forms in what follows, and its features are not yet clear enough for a restrictive definition to be reliably formulated. I would claim, though, that it is a consequence of interaction, of the difference between people which must be expressed or implied verbally, so that they can share their experiences and not just their information.

Language in use has two aspects: at one and the same time it is both a continuous negotiation between participants, and a developing record of experience. The negotiation aspect highlights interaction and will be called the *interactive plane* of discourse. In conversation interactive activity is clearly seen operating in real time; securing and yielding the right to talk, constraining the interpretation of what follows, and attempting to steer the discourse towards the goals of the individual participant. In writing it is not so prominent, because normally only one participant composes each document, and the relevant interaction is an imagined construct of the writer, leaving each of his readers with an adjustment problem. Long stretches of written text may be devoid of the traces of moment-by-moment interaction because there is no structural need for it; as in expository prose. It is simple and instructive to compare written and spoken versions of a common communicative event – instructions on how to do something or get somewhere, for example. Where a misguided writer, searching for an informal style, concocts a pseudo-conversation with his imagined reader, an actual reader is likely to have increased problems of adjustment, stretching to impotent fury. As an example, here is the opening of Weaver 1964:

> This book is, in one sense, about thinking. About a certain way of thinking, that is. You may have the idea that it is dull to think about thinking, and perhaps you even have the idea that it is unprofitable or too difficult to improve the way you think. But, you see, you had to think to come to those conclusions. And how certain are you that your conclusions are sound?'

The other aspect of language in use is the developing record of experience. On a small scale, in a conversation, say, or reading a letter, it can be seen as a gradual sharing of relevant experience by recalling previous words and phrases and reworking them in the new contexts provided by a movement on the interactive plane. That is a simple model of sentence construction, but adequate for the moment. On a larger scale this process can be seen as a continuous internalization of experience, from the world outside to the inner space of language. The process is both individual and collective, and, where written down, forms the most explicit record we have of human evolution.

In principle, nothing exists or happens which cannot be represented verbally (though in practice the strict and complex organization of language leads to difficulties). Language models experience and is assumed to be adaptable enough for the job, but the price to be paid is representation through a largely pre-existing organization. Poets complain of the shackles.

The stage-by-stage tally of the record of experience will be called the *autonomous plane* of discourse, because it is concerned with language only and not with the means by which language is related to the world outside. If we can use the word *text* to designate both spoken and written language-in-use, then the organization and maintenance of text structure is the focus of the autonomous plane.

This is a dynamic view of language. As we put language to use, we make text by negotiating our affairs with each other. At any one point, the decisions about what effect utterances should aim at, what acts they should perform or what features of the world they should incorporate, are decisions on the interactive plane. Each segment of activity thus has an existential quality. But at the same time it is building up from text which has gone before, readjusting, working in the new material with the old, and maintaining records, moment by moment. Decisions in this intra-textual area are made on the autonomous plane.

Different aims in human affairs will lead to text that emphasizes one of these planes more than the other. A job which involves communal control of a carefully timed process will show a lot of interactive decisions – like David Abercrombie's (1956) example of experts moving a grand piano up a spiral staircase. No need to keep much record of experience here, no time to articulate complex sentences. On the other hand, the success of the activity depends on a vast amount of shared experience. If we remove access to the autonomous plane altogether the result, difficult to imagine, would be interaction which made no assumptions of shared experience and led nowhere, lacking the ability to internalize the world. There would be no syntax, no vocabulary, no textual reference.

The point about vocabulary is important because words are often held to refer to or signify directly events or items in the world. But this is only possible if two conditions hold:

a  if there is a prior shared experience of, roughly, definition of the word in the speech community,
b  if the text structure at the point of using the word allows access to that meaning.

Since both the record of shared experience (a) and the organization of text structure (b) are the responsibility of the autonomous plane, it is clear that the relation between a vocabulary item within the language and a class of objects or events is complex and necessarily involves the autonomous plane. So stretches of conversation which seem to exist almost entirely in the immediate interaction are likely to be heavily dependent on previous activity on the autonomous plane.

Similarly, long stretches of expository prose direct immediate emphasis on to the organization of the propositional content, and the reader seems to be given very few interactive clues. There is no place for real-time management, because both the time factor in composition and the time factor in any single reading are independently in the control of the respective participants. The whole written work is also assumed to be continuously at the disposal of the participants, in contrast with an average spoken encounter, which is heavily affected by the speed of decay of the sound wave, and the restricted verbal memory of participants. Aspects of turn-taking, directing address, interruption, etc., are not relevant in most writing. We might conclude that there is no reason arising from the situational constraints why written prose should not be a string of verbalized content propositions, with appropriate logical connections. If so, then all other features of written text organization are candidates for a place on the interactive plane. Work in identifying and describing these features is not far advanced, but they include:

a    predictions, which in Tadros's terms (1981) are commitments made by the writer at one point in the text, to perform another act of discourse subsequently (e.g. *enumeration*, in which a numeral placed before a noun that has no direct referent in the real world commits the writer to present a corresponding list. *There are five types of . . .*).

b    anticipations, which are similar to predictions but are not commitments. The writer inserts signals which allow him, but do not commit him, to perform a subsequent act. If he takes up the option, it is interpreted retrospectively as arising from the anticipation. For example, *Fruit drinks usually contain high quantities of sugar*, where *usually* anticipates, but does not predict, a subsequent contrast with fruit drinks which do not contain high quantities of sugar.

c    self-reference, when the propositions concern the text itself (*This book is . . .*).

d    discourse labelling, when the acts are named as they occur (*Heat is defined as . . .*).

e    participant intervention, when the author adopts directly his participant status on the interactive plane (*We allow wide margins for error*). This feature is usually coupled with one of the others, particularly (d), where the passive voice in the example above conceals a deep structure first person subject. *It is interesting to note that . . .* is another typical example.

f    cross-references, and much of the standard textbook apparatus, which offer alternatives to the linear sequence of text (see Roe 1977).

The only apparent motivation for these and other features of written text is to present the text interactively. Despite the structural complexity that is introduced, this kind of text is largely preferred to the minimal expression of necessary content.

An exception was made above to the 'logical connectors', as if they formed a separate or separable system of links between syntactic units, and could therefore be restricted to the autonomous plane because their concern was with intra-textual management and not interactive control. But language is not normally as neatly organized as this, and the words and phrases which realize such connections have clear interactive roles of which logical connectors are a subset. Careful research is needed in this area to describe the function of the logical connectors without the prior assumption that logical structures have a separate existence, mapped rather confusedly onto text.

If research continues to confirm that two distinct planes of discourse are necessary in an adequate model, the next question that arises is the relationship between them. Every utterance, it is asserted, is to be described on both planes, no matter how intractable the surface representation may appear. For the purposes of this chapter, *utterance* can be taken as equivalent to *sentence* in the written language and *move* in the spoken language (see Sinclair and Coulthard 1975: 120).

We must search for an explicit representation of the two planes in a single utterance, and we find it in the *performatives* of J.L. Austin 1962. The linguistic conditions are set out in Lecture V and the characteristic sentence structure is a main clause (first person subject, simple present tense performative verb; object, if present, second person; optional adverbial *hereby*), followed by a subordinate reported clause (optional conjunction *that* or equivalent nonfinite verb structure, or, in the case of performative verbs that question, conjunctions *if* or *whether*). If all utterances could be transformationally derived from such structures, then the syntactic category of *report* would be the relationship between the two planes, with the interactive plane performing an action explicitly, and the autonomous plane reporting the content. Examples of explicit performatives are:

> I bet that you can't do that.
> I promise you that I'll be good from now on.
> I implore you to help me.
> I claim that I'm innocent.
> I wonder if that's true.

Work in pragmatics has shown that it is extremely difficult to detail the derivations in a generative-transformational model; however, that it is more or less to be expected, since the model restricts itself to the autonomous plane, and allows for no differentiation between participants (Chomsky 1965: 3). It has no dynamic, and offers no explanation of why people should talk to each other. The view of language presented here gives equal prominence to interaction and text-maintenance, and seeks to locate *report* on neither plane, but as that category which relates the two planes to each other, however it is realized in any given instance. It is not necessary that every utterance has an explicit paraphrase in forms of performative and report, because the vagaries of any particular language would soon turn up plenty of counter examples. Report is, in general, the mechanism by which linguistically expressed content is related to speech acts performed (Searle 1969: 29).

Report transfers attention from the interactive to the autonomous plane within an utterance. Between utterances there is found an operation called *plane-change* which transfers attention in a different way. By referring to a preceding utterance with discourse labels like *question* or *reply*, a speaker or writer encapsulates the old interaction in his new one, and the discourse proceeds, in a sense, talking about itself. There are many signals of this operation as well as discourse self-reference items; words like *exercise* in the classroom, *formalities* at customs, *agenda item* in committee meetings can be used; or the reference pronouns *this* and *that*. They all share the ability to refer to a preceding utterance as merely a stretch of language, recognizing in some way its interactive force but not necessarily attending to it. Plane-change is the principal technique of evasion in discourse, but has in general a major organizing role. Consider the following constructed example:

a   What's your name?
b   Why do you ask?
c   Don't talk to me like that.
d   Are you trying to be rude?

Each successive utterance ignores the interactive potential of the previous one, and replaces it with a new one, thus appearing to move onto a higher plane of discourse relative to its predecessor. Since there are only two planes of discourse, the effect is to push the preceding utterance down to the autonomous plane, from which its contribution can be later retrieved if need be.

Returning to *report* for a moment, it is clearly a recursive operation. Reports can be made within reports ad infinitum. *He said that she felt that he knew that she wondered* . . . But there are only two planes of discourse, and all subsequent reports after the first are on the autonomous plane, following the rules of syntax. The reason is that once the transfer is made from interactive to autonomous, the particular sensitivity to interaction is replaced by attention to the syntactic and lexical decoding.

To distinguish the first report from subsequent ones, I shall use the term *subreport* for the latter. The first actually effects a plane-change; any successors merely simulate one. No further plane-changes occur, and further marks of interaction such as *you see, I mean*, are seen as parentheses, and not as the surprise appearance of main clauses to which the surrounding discourse is subordinate.

There is one other major category of text structure to be introduced, and then the framework is complete. This is called *quote*, and is the introduction of one text within another. The quoted text is assumed to maintain its integrity –

the reasons for its linguistic patterning are not sought with reference to the other outer text within which it occurs. Its own language is thus highlighted, because it is protected from the exigencies of the surrounding syntactic and lexical patterns, and it is not responsive directly to considerations of the socio-linguistic situation within which it occurs. This is roughly what Jakobson (1960) means in his famous definition of the poetic function as that which projects 'the principle of equivalence from the axis of selection into the axis of combination'.

Quote may well be seen as a parallel, alternative operation to report, but there is one important difference, namely that quote cannot effect a transfer from the interactive to the autonomous plane. It is fairly obvious in that quoted text is borrowed from some other situation where it would have had an interactive role, and it is supported, in English anyway, by the fact that performative utterances cannot introduce quotations without first going through a report stage. So quotes occur only on the autonomous plane.

We have assumed so far an undefined unit of sentence size, and insisted that each successive one is responsive to both planes. The interactive plane identifies two participants, of which at any moment one is the 'I' of the discourse, and the other one 'you'. There is an important condition on language events of this type, which is implied in felicity conditions in speech acts and Grice's (1975) Maxim of Quality. Briefly, the 'I' of the discourse − P1 we shall call him or her − is interpreted as *averring* the reported propositions, the averring being modified by any expressed or implied performative relationship. It is thus nonsense to say *the moon is round, and that is not the case*. This is a paradox not noted in Hofstadter's (1981) interesting collection. Given the complexities of authorial identification and stance, it is important to note that the study of language defines one relation between author and text, and considers all others to be dependent on it. We shall call this unique relation of interactive and autonomous planes the *outer* situation, in which the language is actually communicative.

If an author wishes not to aver a proposition, he signals this by attributing it to someone else, including the nameless subject of a passive or the ubiquitous *one*. Thus it is a report from the start and the attributed proposition will be couched in a sub-report or quote. Initially in a sequence of such structures, there will be an explicit reporting syntax. The consequences of this curious but common event are discussed in Tadros (1981) dealing with the expository prose of economics.

> Examples would be: Some writers claim that market forces will always control profits. It is frequently maintained that . . .

I now want to characterize *fact* in a slightly curious way, because *factive* is an accepted category in linguistics. First of all, I am not concerned with whether anything actually happened or not, because the interest in that lies in the world outside discourse. If a participant avers that the moon is round, that is the nearest we get in language to the moon being round. Nor am I concerned with whether anyone *believes* that something happened or not, because that also is in the real world.

The contrasting state, that of fiction, is brought about by an author detaching himself from the responsibility of averring each successive utterance, but not attributing them to any author in the real world – either no one at all, or a fictitious narrator. The utterances therefore lose their status as being identified with a participant in any real situation.

What, then, is their status? It is noted by Tadros (1981) that instances of authorial detachment in her material predict evaluates to follow – that is to say, the author expounds someone else's point of view in order to give a critical opinion of it. The evaluation is the point of the stratagem, and is the method by which the author signals a return to averring.

We can extend this notion to fiction. In a work of any length, participants contract to suppress their natural expectations of continuous averral, and assimilate utterances into a single artefact which will lead to a final evaluation – a laugh if it is a joke; an appreciation of the moral if it is a parable; a more complex response if it is a poem or a play. Coleridge's famous phrase 'that willing suspension of disbelief for the moment, which constitutes poetic faith' (*Biographia Literaria*, Chapter 14) applies exactly to the state of fiction in this description. The author signals 'I do not aver the following utterances, but I assure you that there will be an opportunity for positive evaluation when I have finished'. The audience allows him this posture, and therefore considers the factual relationship as suspended during the performance of the artefact.

Literary critics talk of readers identifying with fictional characters, and the same narrative leads to a different experience when presented as fact or fiction. If factual status entails authorial averral, this seems a similar notion to the readers identifying with the author. In fiction they have no such given viewpoint, no predetermined link through from each utterance to the real world. It becomes possible for them to be offered a viewpoint within the fiction, and identify with that.

To review the discussion so far, I should like to build up a simple diagram. First of all, the two planes of discourse and their relationship of report:

*Figure 3.1*

The lines are curved to suggest a portion of a circle, where everything inside has to do with language, and outside is the real world. In this dynamic view of discourse the interactive plane is the interface between the real world and the inner world of language, whether viewed individually or collectively.

Two dimensions are not enough for this diagram, so we must imagine it as a cross-section of a cylinder, the length of which is the time base, and consider a longitudinal section.

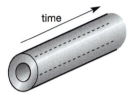

time

*Figure 3.2*

A section through the rim of the cylinder would be represented as

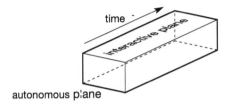

time

interactive plane

autonomous plane

*Figure 3.3*

Simplifying this, and segmenting it for utterances, we get

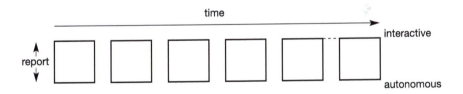

time

interactive

report

autonomous

*Figure 3.4*

Plane-change can be represented as follows:

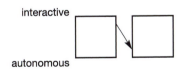

interactive

autonomous

*Figure 3.5*

On the autonomous plane, the first choice of further layering is between (sub-report) and quote, e.g.

> I aver that X said that . . . (sub-report)
> I aver that X said ' . . .' (quote)

according to whether the new material is subject to the continuing syntactic and other restraints, or whether it is an interpolated text.

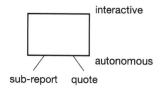

*Figure 3.6*

The same choice is recursive thereafter. A cross-cutting set of choices affects the distribution of utterances on the autonomous plane, whether the original P1 continues to aver the embedded utterances or makes an attribution to another.

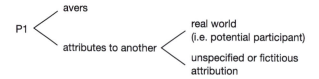

*Figure 3.7*

Putting these together, we can locate a particular combination called the *inner situation* which will be described in a moment.

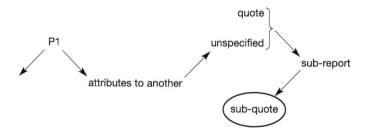

*Figure 3.8*

Characterized in language, this sounds like

> I report that an unspecified author said that one of his characters said ' . . .'

The idea of a state of fiction has recursive potential, but, as with a report within a report or quotes within quotes, only the first in the series creates the state of fiction. There can be facts within fiction, but only if *fact* is understood in the sense of 'expressions of true propositions' rather than as used here for discourse facts. There cannot be discourse facts within fictions. So novels can and do mix historical events with fictitious ones, without affecting the overall state of fiction.

Dialogue occurs in quotes, as a further recursive layer, but slightly different because there are likely to be features of moment-by-moment interaction which are indications of a remote speech situation. We then have to postulate an *inner* situation in order to interpret the utterances, by an act of imagination, whether or not the quotes are the special case of fiction. But as well as their direct imaginary value, the same utterances have a value in the outer, real situation. Since quoted they draw attention to all the details of the language chosen; this reverses the normal language–situation relationship. Normally we expect the language chosen in an utterance to be appropriate to the occasion on which the participants are speaking, or the circumstances of presentation of a written document. In quotes, however, we may not have much evidence of the imaginary inner situation. Some hints may be given in the surrounding report, or in stage directions, or in the internal content. But part of the imaginary situation is likely to be constructed by considering the features of the quoted language, and the kind of situation that might be appropriate to them.

Let us consider briefly the framework within which we can discuss the language of a recent novel – I shall take David Lodge's *How Far Can You Go?* (1980) as representative, although it contains some unusual interactive features.

First of all, it is clear from the dust-jacket, endpapers, format, and title that it is a work of fiction. It begins:

> It is just after eight o'clock in the morning of a dark February day, in this year of grace nineteen hundred and fifty two.

The present tense might indicate a diary, which is an interactive text; but this opening is prefaced by a chapter title:

> I    How it was

The title indicates report. The first sentence of text, then, is a quote which is a fiction, within a report.

David Lodge enters into an interaction with an unknown set of readers, and all that he writes is describable on the two planes of discourse. He makes no utterances of explicit interaction, no 'I–you–hereby–present tense' performatives . He makes three implicit statements of interaction, namely the title *How*

*Far Can You Go?*, the dedication 'To Ian Gregor', and the act of copyrighting 'copyright © David Lodge 1980'. The publisher alternates with him as the main participant, and makes a number of technical statements announcing publication and dating it, reporting the ISBN number, acknowledging quotations, etc.

Because the novel genre is well-established, we can take several steps in interpretation. The bulk of the text is first reported on the autonomous plane. It is quoted, because the linguistic choices (e.g. the timing of the first sentence 'It *is* . . . 1952') are not constrained by the circumstances of any act of reading. Therefore the interpretive procedures are reversed, and the linguistic choices are used to create a remote situation – there is no outside information beyond the material on the detachable dust-jacket.

It is a fiction, in that the quotes are not attributed to anyone other than David Lodge, and yet he is not averring his text, utterance by utterance (nor is he in the absurd position of quoting himself). Therefore the status of the text as a whole, relating back to the interactive plane, is a reported fictional quote offered for evaluation.

The narrative text begins to incorporate explanations in the first paragraph: *for economy's sake; (it is a dialogue mass . . .)*. This feature is merely a matter of narrative chronology, but it does assert the presence of the imaginary author early on. At the top of page 3 there is the unusual paragraph,

Why?

This leads on to a string of questions in the next paragraph, and the beginning of the next:

To begin with the simplest case: . . .

There is now established an imaginary interaction between the imaginary author (not David Lodge, since he has indicated detachment from the outset) and the reader. On page 6 a new section begins *Before we go any further . . .* clearly indicating the imaginary author, and on page 7 the parenthetical *you understand* involves the reader and is distinct from the *you* that soon follows:

Most of your deceased relatives were probably there, which was why you prayed for them.

The verb tense indicates that this pronoun *you* refers impersonally to the characters in the novel. The same features continue; the reader is directly invoked on page 10:

( . . . would you, gentle reader? Did you, gentle Catholic reader?)

There are statements about the structure of the novel itself on page 14; and on page 15 the first 'I' of the imaginary author occurs. He is deciding what name to call a character.

> Let her be called Violet, no, Veronica, no Violet . . . for I like the connotations of Violet . . .

The imaginary author has both an *I* and a *we* function – a personal and an authorial.

David Lodge attempts to enter his own novel through the *I* persona by writing utterances for the *I* persona which are consistent with David Lodge in the outer situation. Pages 73–4 show the unusual effects of manipulating a complex discourse structure

> I have written about this before, a novel about . . .

The statement is true about David Lodge too – but we must stress the *too*, since the imaginary author is licensed to make any number of false statements, and this one has already made several thousand. Here the coincidence of historic truth between the real and imaginary authors tempts us to forget the original stance of detachment and assume that Lodge occasionally penetrates his own fiction and personally avers an utterance. It is an exploitation of formal ambiguity at the level of text, analogous to sentence-level figures of speech, but not a regular feature of the tradition of the English novel.

The imaginary author goes on to quote correspondence which he claims was received about this earlier book, and the section finishes

> Thank you again, Mr Jerhot, for your lovely letter.
> This book is not a comic novel, exactly, but I have tried to make it smile as much as possible.

Plausible it is, and there may well be a real Mr Jerhot, and a real letter. We readers do not know, although we are definitely invited to make a decision of a kind which is unusual in a novel. It is crucial to establish that David Lodge cannot return to the real planes of interaction within his own novel. He could try harder – he could say 'I, David Lodge, do solemnly swear before witnesses . . .' and print facsimiles of legal documents to attempt to get inside. But only the originals exist in the outer, real world.

In considering the aptness of his title *How Far Can You Go?* one strand of its meaning may be taken as an exploration of the limits of the discourse structure of the novel form, plausible again in the real world where Professor Lodge is a noted critic of narrative form.

Returning to more conventional aspects of the text of his novel, we find that the first evidence of an imaginary inner situation occurs early, on page 2, where some liturgical responses occur in quotes. Ordinary novel dialogues occur from page 20 onwards. They require us to construct a series of situations which are presented as entirely fictional, and relate the quoted utterances to those situations, in the first instance. Since the whole novel is a quote, I shall use the term *sub-quote* for those utterances which require the reader to create an imaginary pair of discourse planes in the inner situation.

There is a lot of circumstantial information offered in the surrounding text, reported to us through the fictional route that has been described. A further excursion into quotes represents a decision to move to another level of narrative, instead of reporting what was said under the normal syntactic conventions.

The quote on page 21, then, as an example:

> 'Did you get my valentine?' Dennis murmurs to Angela

is a sub-quote within a quote (the novel) within a report that has signalled fiction, all on the autonomous plane. Many further complexities arise as creative writers exploit the possible ambiguities of this array. For example, 'free indirect speech' as discussed in Pascal's *The Dual Voice*, is a report which shows in its language evidence of appropriateness to the speech style of one of the characters, so that it tempts the reader to interpret it as an unacknowledged quotation.

It is possible to locate literary language within an overall framework that relates it systematically to the other principal categories of verbal communication, using arguments derived from recognizing as central the dual planes of discourse. The range of configurations is endless but the framework is rather rigid, and the special effects of some literary texts arise from a characteristic playing upon the forms which is also evident at phrase and sentence level. The remoteness of the inner situations which the reader creates in reading literature is quite striking (see the diagrams above, pp. 58–60) and argues some sophistication of interpretation despite the familiar signals of the path to the inner situations.

The tradition of English literature has long allowed our imaginary author a fairly free hand in his simulations of discourse on the autonomous plane. It is only recently that apostrophes, direct addresses to the reader, and the like have become unfashionable; and the novel has had its extravagant moments before the recent experiments in form like Lodge's.

For further illustration I choose Burns's *Tam O'Shanter* for no better reason than that I am writing on Burns Night. This narrative poem contains many discourse diversions of a familiar kind. The imaginary author addresses his main character:

> O Tam! hadst thou but been sae wise
> As taen thy ain wife Kate's advice!

He addresses a section of his readership:

> Ah gentle dames! it gars me greet
> To think how monie counsels sweet,

How monie lengthen'd, sage advices
The husband frae that wife despises!

He continues:

But to our tale:–

But returns to direct address to Tam, John Barleycorn, and the witch Nannie. He apologises for his inadequate language:

But here my Muse her wing maun cour,
Sic flights are far beyond her pow'r;

and concludes the poem with direct advice to the reader:

Now, wha this tale o'truth shall read
Ilk man and mother's son, take heed:

Notice the attempt in the phrase *tale o'truth* to cross the fictional boundary – unlikely to convince in the case of Tam O'Shanter's experience.

To conclude this account of discourse planes, I would like to take as a further example an area of language use which is very distant from literature, but which yields parallels if described at a sufficiently abstract level. My objective is to demonstrate that the same set of categories is still appropriate, and can claim general applicability.

The discourse of language teaching is complex, particularly when the target language is also the medium of instruction. The same language is being used to control the business of teaching, and also instancing itself, practising itself, as it goes along. Small wonder that the students sometimes get confused, and for example, take as a model for repetition a question which was intended to elicit an answer!

As with literature, the category of evaluation is again needed, and again has a structural role.

In classroom discourse as a whole the characteristic teacher–pupil exchange, as reported in Sinclair and Coulthard (1975) consists of three moves:

Teacher Initiation
Pupil Response
Teacher Follow-up

The Follow-up move has several functions, but all of them are associated with evaluating the Response. If the Initiation is an elicitation, perhaps a question, and the Response is an attempt at an answer, the Follow-up will evaluate the answer according to the teacher's moment-by-moment appreciation of the lesson. This triad seems to be a microcosm of the most general pattern in discourse – two successive units in some recognizable relationship with each other, followed by a third which expresses and/or evaluates the relationship. In conversation it is fairly clear because of the regular turn-taking which guides us towards the unit boundaries; in expository prose it fits well with the structure of argument.

The simple structure of exchanges becomes specialized in language teaching, where students are often expected to practise using the language virtually regardless of the situational circumstances. The complexities of discourse thus introduced are described in detail in Willis (1981). When students produce such language-within-language they are *quoting*, and as noted in the discussion of literature above, attention is on the constructional detail. The utterances do not have any function or purpose beyond the particulars of their construction: they are not *averred*, in the sense in which I am using that word. They are followed by an evaluation by the teacher.

The state of fiction is achieved in the language classroom in at least two ways – by a practice based on stimulus materials which introduce fictional events and characters, and by the technique of role-play. Here, as Willis shows, the teacher directs the pupils to produce utterances or strings of utterances which are sub-quotes in an inner situation.

Not all instances of discourse make extensive use of the descriptive apparatus as these two. The apparatus itself is very simple – two only planes of discourse, linked by report, with the possibilities of plane-change and quote, the last three having recursive potential, except that the recursion only simulates further planes, because the original two planes are absolute. Fiction is seen as an extension of the device of P1 detachment, and quotes within quotes set up an inner situation. P1 detachment predicts evaluation because it stimulates interaction, and evaluation is a necessary consequence of interaction.

Although simple, the apparatus is powerful, because it should be able to analyse all instances of spoken or written language, and to analyse them relevantly from the point of view of experts in the specialized areas of language use.

# 4   On the integration of linguistic description

This chapter was commissioned by Teun van Dijk for a multi-volume *Handbook of Discourse Analysis* he was editing, published in 1985, London: Academic Press. This extract is from volume 2, pages 13–28. It follows up a number of points made in the previous paper, and makes a start on a suitable analytic method for written and spoken text, literary or non-literary.

## Introduction

This chapter outlines a descriptive system that is designed to bring out the underlying similarities of structure in all text and discourse. At present, despite theoretical frameworks that are general enough, descriptions are too dependent on the text or discourse type.

There is no attempt to trace the origins of the concepts and categories used, many of which will be familiar enough. To do so would overbalance the chapter and obscure the argument. For similar reasons, there is not a full bibliography; instead I have listed work that is not all easily accessed but that is relevant to the articulation of a fully integrated descriptive system.

The student of conversation is struck by the immediacy of speech events. Real time – the actual passing of seconds and minutes – is often the most influential feature of the context as participants play their parts in the complex fabric of verbal interaction. Timing is all important in turn taking and turn giving and turn holding; time is a major factor in the construction and delivery of a turn, and time is to be reckoned with in the business of keeping a check on how the conversation is going.

Each individual contribution to spoken discourse shows a curious tension between personal and social pressures. It is simultaneously co-operative and face threatening; it is a step toward the achievement of some personal goal, but it is put together in the knowledge that the goal can only be achieved through the construction of discourse, which by definition requires two participants. Because of this fundamental tension, it is easy to see discourse as essentially manipulative, and indeed it is often difficult to find morally reputable terminology for what seems to be going on.

The student of written language, in contrast to the student of conversation, is probably most impressed by the orderly nature of the events he is describing. Printed material is presented in accordance with thousands of conventions and is measured to thousandths of an inch. The text is read during preparation many times by different people, and in most cases time is not a structural influence. Where printed material has to be prepared against strict deadlines, as in newspaper production, every effort is made to neutralize the effect of time, and there is very little impromptu material in newspapers.

The responsibility for coherence lies with the utterer, which in the case of printed material is a composite entity including everyone who participated in the production of the text. The text appears to be quite static and non-negotiable; it is there, and it cannot be altered. It seems quite different from the ever-changing, hardly predictable movement of conversation. It can be described, and is normally described, as a complex contraption, and linguistic terms like 'structure' betray the underlying metaphor. Written language is not primarily seen as activity. Its relation to time is that of an unchanging record.

But in apparent contrast to the rigidity of written text, we are assured that each reading of it, even two readings by the same reader, is a unique communicative event. So the text has an interactive role that is related to time in a different way, since a reading of a text is an event in time. We can relate the fixed nature of a written text to the unique experience of any reading of it by making a reasonable assumption: since the main purpose of a text is to be read, its destined role in a series of interactions has a backwash effect upon its composition.

One further assumption is that a writer who is composing a text that is to be efficient interactively has an obvious model in conversation. From this a line of inquiry emerges that can lead to an integrated framework of description. If the same basic model is used in both documents and conversation, then, at least at an abstract level, the same categories of description are applicable. The influence of the particular medium, however, becomes stronger as we proceed toward realization, and we must guard against imposing categories appropriate to one medium on data from another.

## A dynamic model of discourse

An integrated description, deriving from a model of verbal interaction, describes language in use as written or spoken discourse. The model is dynamic rather than static, and we must consider this contrast in order to relate discourse description to traditional descriptions of language.

The main differences between a dynamic and a static model of discourse are (1) the dynamic model must show how the discourse proceeds from one point to another, and (2) the dynamic model must show how the components of the discourse play their part in the achievement of some purpose. In both cases, the differences take the form of additional requirements on the dynamic model. In the first case, the discourse is seen as a continuous movement from one state of affairs or *posture* to another. Our habits of studying language tend to obscure this movement, because we tend to study language with hindsight; when we are considering one stretch of language, we already know what happens next. In such circumstances, the importance of prospection, prediction, and the like is not as obvious as it should be.

In a dynamic model the elements of structure are described with reference to the state of the discourse at their point of occurrence, hence the unfolding or existential quality of discourse description. Only language that has already occurred can be taken as given; the description of subsequent items of language is conditioned by the state of the discourse at *their* point of occurrence.

Once the directionality of discourse has been fully appreciated, it follows that there is a marked difference in the way we describe previous and subsequent language. Each element of structure is considered both retrospectively and prospectively, but in different terms. Looking backward, the following issues are relevant to each element: (1) If the state of the discourse includes any firm predictions, does this element offer partial or total fulfilment of the predictions? (2) If the state of the discourse includes any prospections (less-than-firm predictions), does this element offer partial or total fulfilment of them? Looking ahead, the main issue can be stated as follows: (3) What framework of choice for the next element is created by the selection of this element?

Any utterance can follow any utterance – we are free agents. Although we tend to follow conventions in social behaviour, there are no absolute rules, because people make mistakes or make use of the conventions for more subtle tactics – irony, and so forth. However, each utterance sets the scene for the next. No matter what it is, the way it will be interpreted is determined by the previous utterances and in particular the immediately previous one. This is fairly obvious in question–answer pairs, but is a general feature of discourse. There are some complexities introduced by the hierarchic nature of discourse structure, because, for example, boundary utterances have a more far-reaching role than medial ones, but the main point is sound, and the prospective function of all utterances is of first importance.

The second requirement of a dynamic model balances the first by introducing purposefulness into the description. The dynamic view sees discourse as directional, a succession of changing postures; but it must be heading somewhere. We already have in the static models some notions of complete encounters and of finished artefacts in writing. Units of this kind link language and the physical world. With the addition of purposes that are recognized within the discourse, they are valuable units in a dynamic model. They provide a special kind of boundary.

The problem of purposes in language description is not that people believe human behaviour to be largely without purpose. Plans, goals and aims, for example, are readily admitted. The problem is mainly where to stop. Language activity is but one component of our general activity, which itself is largely purposeful. The separation of purposes that are recognized as being carried out through discourse from those that are not so circumscribed requires units that perform a linking role and relate complete patterns of linguistic activity to aspects of our general social behaviour. Hence the importance of identifying a unit at this interface.

Linguists are so accustomed to describing small-scale stretches of language that the contribution of each particular to the overall effect of an artefact may well be missed. In a dynamic model it is necessary to continue the directional description until a point is reached where the verbal activity performs in its totality some action that lies outside language. Each successive component has an effect that may be perceptible in passing but is certainly provisional until the artefact is completed and the overall action has been performed and is no longer negotiable except in terms of a subsequent artefact. An example from conversation is the polite refusal of an invitation that is eventually replaced by acceptance; often this kind of behaviour is within the normal social courtesies and recognized by participants. In writing it is commonplace for a writer to state a position that is contrary to the position he wishes the reader to adopt; the eventual effect can only be described when the artefact has unfolded in full.

The provisional interpretations of purpose are therefore subject to a back-wash effect from the artefact as a whole; the analyst can make final assignments in review. But in most cases the provisional interpretations are confirmed, and only in manipulative discourse of conversations between naive and sophisticated participants is there likely to be substantial reassignment.

It is normal, in fact, for speakers and writers to keep a running check on what they are doing, and much of this becomes part of the discourse. There is a whole vocabulary and syntax of language about language (point, question, object, etc.), so that the focus of the discourse can shift to the discourse itself. Less explicitly, many of the apparently meaningless words and phrases *(uhum, actually, well,* etc.) and devices (e.g., repeating a word or two of a previous speaker) in conversation are signals of how one speaker is interpreting the dis-course. Unless challenged, these are taken by the participant as signals of the provisional categorization of the discourse.

Despite the different circumstances of spoken and written language and the different realizations of linguistic categories, the view of a dynamic model is to see them as essentially similar. Both are interactive, both are directional, and both are purposeful. The description of formal written language is transformed by the application of a dynamic model, because much of its interactive quality is covert.

The fundamental categories of a description that integrates such disparate behaviour are more abstract than the normal categories of linguistics. But the job of integration must encompass further distinctions as well as those between speech and writing.

Literary discourse is treated as a special case even by linguists who claim that it is subject to the normal conventions of language description. The creation of the subject area of stylistics serves to insulate literature from the more mundane texts of everyday life. Patterns of language that are not remarked upon in non-literary text are invested with meaning in stylistics.

Despite these concessions, the literary critics have remained largely aloof, maintaining that there is a difference in kind between descriptive and evaluative study. However sensitive and painstaking a description may be, it does not engage with the central issues of criticism. There are other problems, too, about stylistics that can only be mentioned here, such as the lack of principle in selecting a focus of description, the uneasy status of interpretations from stylistic evidence, and the difficulty of description of long texts. There is little or no theory in stylistics; the value of its observations is related strictly to the results of individual studies.

If we view literary text as discourse, we must begin the description in the same way as with any other text, establishing first of all its location in the world around us. Who is addressing whom, on what occasion, and with what end in view? The analysis of the utterer shows that we must postulate at least two entities – an author in the real world and a narrator in a world of fiction. Such a distinction has been recognized in literary analysis for many years.

The relation between the author and the narrator is that the author reports the narrator but does not attest the truth of what the narrator says. Frequently this relationship is implicit, and the reader deduces from external evidence that sentences like 'I love you', or 'It is the year 2002' are not being averred by the author to the reader. In the absence of any such deduction, our normal assumption is that anything said to us or written to us is averred by the author or speaker to be true at the moment of utterance.

The purpose of a literary text is to secure from its readers a complex, evaluative interpretation; both globally (asking readers to answer questions like 'What does this mean to me?') and analytically (how the components of the artefact have their several effects). Such evaluations occur after an encounter with an artefact and do not need to be articulated.

So from a discourse point of view, literary text falls well within the categories that are already available for nonliterary text. The dynamic model requires an elaborate evaluation network for the description of any text; the oddity about literary text is that it has no function except to be evaluated. It is argued later in this chapter that stylistic evidence is no different from any other linguistic evidence.

An integrated approach to description should in fact be flexible enough to cover all distinctive varieties of a language, not just literary text. In the many studies of varieties that have accumulated over the years, the emphasis has been on distinctiveness and the descriptions fairly ad hoc. If an overall framework can be developed in detail, the varieties can be compared with each other on reliable criteria.

A dynamic model makes available the level of discourse necessary to mediate between form and purpose. Any particular pattern of syntax or lexis, or a combination of both, may have different functions in different types of text; thus allowing the small central organization of the language to be adapted to a wide variety of purposes.

Work is not yet very far advanced in this area; there are notes on characteristic features of a language variety, like the passive voice in formal prose; there are informal explanations of many of the features. But we do not have as yet any substantial research on, for example, the complementary distribution of features in different varieties. Research is needed on the levels of delicacy of classification of varieties that accords best with differentiating features. A serious deficiency is the lack of a framework of interpretation, through which the characteristics of a variety can be related to the generalized purposes of the variety.

For the present, we assume only a few major received categories such as narrative and expository writing and their spoken counterparts. Narratives are organized largely by time expressions and verb tenses, so if a reader or listener has prior knowledge that he will encounter a narrative, his expectations are attuned accordingly. He assumes that the time expressions are likely to be organizational rather than incidental. On the other hand, if he knows or quickly deduces that he is encountering expository language, he is alert to the sentence connectors, modal verbs, and the other realizations of textual organizations in expository writing. These tend to be in prominent positions.

There are probably not many texts that do not quickly indicate their primary classification, because the different organizations are frequently incompatible. It would be bizarre for example, for a narrative to report alternatives such as 'Mr Smith went out for lunch, or else he had sandwiches in the office'. Such a sentence can be worked into narrative under protective coverings such as:

1    Throughout his working life
2    I suppose that. . .

But without such an insulation, an author, whether as factual or fictional narrator, could hardly report alternative events.

A primary classification of discourse types is also valuable because no text is fully explicit about its organization as it goes along, and many are very covert. It is necessary to accept a default hypothesis, which states that in the absence of contra-indications, a linguistic item has the same function as its predecessor. When this is applied in description, the signals of maintenance or change of function must be accurately identifiable, and knowledge of the discourse type helps in the identification. Reference to chronology, for example, is prima facie taken as a signal of a change in posture in a narrative text; absence of such reference by default suggests a maintenance of posture. But in an expository text the presence or absence of chronological reference is unlikely to be structurally relevant.

We can now bring together the elements of an integrated descriptive system and apply them to some text examples. At the present stage of development, the descriptions are indicative only, and more varied application is necessary before they can be claimed to be comprehensive and reliable. But they illustrate the direction of current research.

## Applications of the model

### *Basic structure*

The minimum free element of structure in a discourse is the sentence or move (s/m), and these are considered equivalent. An integrating definition is attempted in due course, but in the meantime we can list what must be known about each s/m:

1  indications of interaction
2  the position of the author with reference to the text
3  attribution to narrator(s)
4  indications of argument
5  indications of self-reference
6  the dominant verb form.

These are not in any particular order, nor is it yet clear whether an order of priority will be established among them, particularly with reference to the primary classification of discourse.

### *Indications of interaction*

For each s/m, there has to be an identification of utterer and receiver, that is, those who would be referred to by the pronouns *I* and *you* if present. This requirement can be represented as:

I VB YOU

It must be understood that the above is a formula in the metalanguage of description. It does not imply that sentences can be paraphrased or generated in terms of the formula or that English happens to have a reliable class of performative verbs to realize the element VB. Although the conceptual origin of this kind of notation is speech act theory, it would be misleading to assume anything beyond the basic notion of illocutionary force.

*Table 4.1*

|  | Interactive |  | Autonomous |
|---|---|---|---|
| I VB | YOU |  |  |
| *I must compliment* | *you* |  | *on your hat* |
| *I promise* | YOU | THAT | *I'll come tomorrow at six* |
| *I AVER* | TO YOU | THAT | *it's getting late* |

In the analyses that follow, the descriptive apparatus is represented as very close to English, but only for clarity. Capital letters are used to identify the apparatus. To avoid ambiguity, the pronoun 'I' is rendered as *I* if it is part of the text or discourse and I if it is part of the metalanguage.[1]

### The position of the author with reference to the text

There is only one author of any s/m. He is the leftmost I in the analytic display. The minimum he can do is aver and that verb is used here as the signal of the default condition. The interactive segment of an s/m is placed first in the analytic display and is followed by a transition (usually expressible by THAT) to the remainder of the s/m, which is in the nature of a report in a broad meaning of the term. The analysis of s/ms by division into interactive and autonomous segments corresponds to the same distinction in planes of discourse and is a central feature of a dynamic model. Roughly speaking, the interactive segment depicts what is going on in the real world at the time of utterance, while the autonomous segment is a report about something that may include the current state of the real world but is certainly not restricted to it.

Any recurrence of *I* in the autonomous segment is thus in a report. An s/m does not normally return to the interactive plane after leaving it, and then only for running repairs like *obviously*, or *I understand*, which show in analysis as separate from the main structure of the s/m and are shown in parenthesis in the Interactive column.

*Table 4.2*

|   |   | *Interactive* | | *Autonomous* |
| --- | --- | --- | --- | --- |
| I | VB | YOU | | |
| *I* | *say* | TO YOU THAT | | *you do look happy* |
| I<br>[*I* | AVER<br>*understand*] | TO YOU THAT | | *the book is*<br>*being reprinted* |

### Attribution to narrator(s)

An author can attribute parts of his s/m to one or more narrators (a narrator is any subject that is not the leftmost I of the structure, nor the subject of the rightmost main clause). He can say, or write:

    3   Many people say that King Arthur actually lived.

We do not know if the author concurs with this belief or not; he merely avers that others believe it. Similarly,

4    It is generally supposed that glass is fragile.

An author can also report or quote by attribution to a named character in his discourse (including himself):

5    Peter said he was coming.
6    And then I said 'Look here!'

If, for whatever reason, a receiver decides that the autonomous segment is fictional, then the analysis introduces a fictional narrator F; a nonfictional but unidentified narrator is represented by N.

This possible layering of narrators is recursive and so has to be worked out separately for each text. It is entirely in the autonomous segment. In this analysis, at each transitional point there is a choice between report (THAT) and quotation (QUOTE). Note that the original author cannot quote himself.

*Table 4.3*

| Interactive | Autonomous | | |
|---|---|---|---|
| I AVER TO YOU THAT | *many people say* | *that* | *King Arthur actually lived* |
| I AVER TO YOU THAT | *it is generally supposed* BY N | *that* | *glass is fragile* |
| I AVER TO YOU THAT | *Peter said* | THAT | *he was coming* |
| I AVER TO YOU THAT | *I said* | QUOTE | *look here* |
| I AVER TO YOU THAT | F SAID | QUOTE | *Once upon a time* |

*Indications of argument*

The words and phrases of argument, logical connection, and so on, are important indicators of changes in posture. *But, however, or,* and sometimes *and,* are examples, as are the lexical paraphrases *in addition, as an alternative, on the other hand.*

Each time an author or narrator takes up a noticeably different attitude to his subject matter, there is a prima facie case for a change in posture. In the sentence,

7    I'd like to come but it's very expensive.

the second clause is interpreted as implying *I wouldn't like to come,* for the reason given.

Each prima facie change of posture is shown in the analysis by a new line.

*Table 4.4*

| Interactive | Autonomous |
| --- | --- |
| I AVER TO YOU THAT *I'd like to come* | |
| *But* | *it's very expensive* |
| I AVER TO YOU THAT | |
| *either* | *you've made a mistake* |
| *or* | *we've won a prize* |

A wide range of words and phrases contribute evidence of change of posture in addition to those that are associated with the construction of argument. *Actually, well, anyway, of course, in fact, for example* are common examples.

### Indications of self-reference

A change in posture is achieved whenever an s/m is explicitly referred to in the discourse. At any s/m boundary, there is an option open to speaker or writer.

a   He relates the next s/m to the preceding one by attending to its assumptions and prospections. For example, if asked a question he answers it.
b   He refers to the preceding s/m by a pronoun or a discourse vocabulary word, thus cancelling the requirement of dealing with its prospections. For example, if asked a question he says 'That's a very interesting question'.

### The dominant verb form

In most s/ms the verb of the main clause is taken as the dominant one. Sometimes there is more than one main clause and a change of verb form; in such cases it may be necessary to identify two s/ms.

Writers on narrative (e.g. Grimes 1975; Labov and Waletzky 1967) point out the importance of verb choices in the structure. Genette (1980) studies relative chronology in detail. Pearce (1977) uses verb choices as the cornerstone of his analysis of Joyce. In other types of writing and speaking, verb choices and related indications of timing are often signals of a change in posture. In practical analysis, usually the most revealing clue to structure is the disposition of the verb forms.

Any change between present and past, simple and continuous, modal and non-modal, perfect and non-perfect allows a change in posture.

This observation is just the tip of a grammatical iceberg which requires much further research into the relations between grammar and discourse. Theme, voice, and subject-referent, for example, are themselves interrelated and can create the kind of reorientation associated with a change in posture.

'Posture' is offered as the linking concept between internal and external patterning in s/ms. Certain configurations of syntax, compared with the previous s/m, provide evidence for an optional or obligatory change in posture. This evidence is then related to the current state of the discourse, and a decision is made about the place of the s/m in discourse structure.

In addition to the syntactic role of sentence elements, their lexical role and their physical disposition provide further evidence for discourse description. Patterns of lexical cohesion and stylistic devices such as parallelism cannot be easily integrated in a sentence-based description but are important features of discourse; the limitations of this chapter prevent full treatment of them.

## Examples

The examples that follow show prospective structuring only. That is only a half, or less, of the recoverable linguistic patterning. The retrospective links are not shown because a reliable description of them has not yet been achieved. But it is already reasonable to state how stylistic patterns, which are largely retrospective, can be integrated into a dynamic description of discourse. The principle is that any variation from the minimal, straightforward verbal expression of propositions can be interpreted as evidence for a change in posture or as evidence for maintenance of posture. From this very general position, the experience of analysis is gradually revealing the conventions of interpretations.

Three examples follow, one from written technical material, one transcribed from conversation, and one from literature. The analysis is in column layout, and changes in posture are shown horizontally. Since many of the structural features are recursive, each text prescribes for itself the number of columns and the classification of each. The examples are text fragments and so do not show the full hierarchy of patterning up to the artefact.

*Example 1: Written technical material*

> Cromenco's CDOS is claimed to be compatible with CP/M version 1.3. In other words, CP/M version 1.3 commands are embedded into CDOS. However, the reverse is not true: programs relying on CDOS's facilities might not run under CP/M. In addition, CDOS provides a number of additional facilities when compared to CP/M. CDOS uses a file system that is identical to CP/M so any diskette which may be read by CP/M may also be read by CDOS. There are minor differences: the system prompt used by CDOS is a period instead of a > sign. Also, the special CONPROC (Console Processor) program must be present on all system diskettes as a file. In CDOS another version of the PIP program is provided under the name XFER. It operates essentially like PIP with a few enhancements. However, PIP can also be executed under CDOS.
>
> (From ZAKS *The CP/M Handbook with MP/M*, Sybex, 1980)

*Table 4.5*

| Interactive | Autonomous | | |
|---|---|---|---|
| Interaction | Argument | Narrator | Self-reference |
| 1  I AVER TO YOU THAT | | N claims THAT | *Cromenco's CDOS is compatible with CP/M version 1.3* |
| 2 | *In other words* | | *CP/M version 1.3 commands are embedded into CDOS* |
| 3 | *However* | | *the reverse is not true* |
| 4 | | | *programs relying on CDOS's facilities might not run under CP/M* |
| 5 | *In addition* | | *CDOS provides a number of additional facilities when compared to CP/M* |
| 6 | | | *CDOS uses . . . read by CDOS* |
| 7 | | | *There are minor differences* |
| 8 | *Also* | | *The system prompt . . . a > sign* |
| 9 | | | *The special . . . as a file* |
| 10 | | | *In CDOS . . . the name XFER* |
| 11 | | | *It operates . . . with a few enhancements* |
| 12 | *However* | | *PIP can also be executed under CDOS* |

Notes

Most of the activities are indications of argument. There are a few interpretive problems: 4 – the verb *might* casts some doubt on whether this is the reverse of 2; 6 – from the previous line one anticipates a statement of additional facilities, while this seems to be about compatibility; 9 – is this a difference? In that case, it is a requirement of CDOS but not CP/M; 11 – although in fact a difference, this is not presented as one.

*Example 2: Conversation*

| | | |
|---|---|---|
| 1 | *A:* | Do you like Leicester George |
| 2 | *B:* | It's nice. . . yeah |
| 3 | *A:* | Do you find it grows on you |
| 4 | *B:* | Grows – like a limpet |
| 5 | *A:* | Well yes |
| 6 | *C:* | Yes or a wart |
| 7 | *A:* | mm |
| 8 | *B:* | No – it's OK. It's um like . . . any big town in the Midlands |

*Table 4.6*

| | Interactive | | Self-reference | Autonomous |
|---|---|---|---|---|
| 1A | I ASK YOU | IF | | *(DO) YOU LIKE LEICESTER* |
| | *George* | | | |
| 2B | *yeah* | | | |
| | I AVER TO YOU | THAT | | *It's nice* |
| 3A | I ASK YOU | IF | | *(do) you find THAT it grows on you* |
| 4B | I CHALLENGE YOU | ON | *grows* | |
| | I ASK YOU | IF | IT IS *like a limpet* | |
| 5A | *Well yes* | | | |
| 6C | *Yes* | | | |
| | I AVER TO YOU | THAT | IT IS *like a wart* | |
| 7A | *mm* | | | |
| 8B | *no* | | | |
| | I AVER TO YOU | THAT | | *It's OK* |
| | | | | *It's um like . . . any big town in the Midlands* |

Notes

Most of the activity is in the interactive segment, and utterance 4 shows a type of self-reference, where a word of the preceding utterance is picked out and talked about. The next three utterances maintain the concern with this word. *No* in utterance 8 indicates a shift of topic, and we understand the pronoun reference of *it* to be *Leicester* in utterance 1. Utterances 5 and 7 are entered only in the interactive segment because they do not express a proposition.

*Example 3: Literature*

> To be, or not to be – that is the question;
> Whether 'tis nobler in the mind to suffer
> The slings and arrows of outrageous fortune,
> Or to take arms against a sea of troubles
> And by opposing end them? To die, to sleep –
> No more; and by a sleep to say we end
> The heart-ache and the thousand natural shocks
> That flesh is heir to. 'Tis a consummation
> Devoutly to be wish'd. To die, to sleep;
> To sleep, perchance to dream.
>                                   (William Shakespeare, *Hamlet*, Act III, Scene 1, Collins' Text)

In this example, the elaborate recursion of attribution cannot be set out horizontally. The following is an alternative layout with notes.

*Table 4.7*

I AVER TO YOU THAT (Interactive)

    F SAYS QUOTE (Fictional Narrator)

        I AVER TO YOU THAT (see notes)

            *Hamlet* SAYS QUOTE (Narrator)

                I AVER TO YOU THAT (see notes)

|    | *Narrator* | *Self-reference* | *Argument* | |
|----|------------|------------------|------------|---|
| 1  | X SAYS QUOTE |                |            | *To be* |
|    |            |                  | *or*       |    |
| 2  | X SAYS QUOTE |                |            | *not to be* |
| 3  |            | *that is the question* |      |    |
| 4  | X SAYS QUOTE |                | *Whether* | *'tis nobler in the mind to suffer the slings and arrows of outrageous fortune* |
|    |            |                  | *or*       |    |
| 6  | X SAYS QUOTE |                |            | *to take arms against a sea of troubles and by opposing end them?* |
| 7  | X SAYS QUOTE |                |            | *To die, to sleep* |
| 8  | X SAYS QUOTE |                |            | *No more* |
| 9  | X SAYS QUOTE |                |            | *and by a sleep to say we end the heart-ache and the thousand natural shocks that flesh is heir to* |
| 10 | X SAYS QUOTE |                |            | *'Tis a consummation devoutly to be wish'd* |
| 11 | X SAYS QUOTE |                |            | *To die, to sleep* |
| 12 | X SAYS QUOTE |                |            | *perchance to dream* |

Notes

1  Only the first line (I AVER TO YOU THAT) is genuinely interactive; the other instances of this element, following the narrator F and the internal posture change X, are pseudo-interactive, since there is no real world situation in which they occur.

2  Each occurrence of X SAYS QUOTE is potentially a different X. A further stage in interpretation would be to decide if the X persona of 1 is the same as that of 4, and maybe 8 or even 12. Similarly, the X of 2 may be associated with 6, 7, 9, 10, 11, or only some of these. The framework of the analysis raises these questions.

3  The division into postures may well be challenged; also I have put ''tis nobler in the mind' as lying outside the following alternative, but a case could be made for 'in the mind' being a part of 5 only.

# 5 Written discourse structure

The stimulus for this chapter was a Festschrift for the fiftieth birthday of my closest colleague in Birmingham University, Malcolm Coulthard. During most of the 1970s we had worked together on the structure of spoken discourse, so for this chapter I turned to apply similar arguments to the written language, and present a usable analytic system. The paper follows Chapter 1, even to using the same text as example. It was published in 1993 in *Techniques of Description*, edited by Michael Hoey, Gwyneth Fox and myself, and published by Routledge.

## Introduction

This is a preliminary exploration of a new position on the structure of written text. It analyses a newspaper article by Randolph Quirk.

As a convenient starting point, let us assume that the text at any moment is seen as the sentence currently being interpreted. A reader is attending to one short stretch of the text at any time (and so, no doubt, is the writer when writing – at least the writer is responsible for making the text interpretable sentence by sentence).[1]

To Eugene Winter (personal communication)[2] structure is necessary because we cannot say everything at once. In any 'state of the text', then, we can expect guidance in the text to both what has gone before and what is yet to come. The sentence is regarded as the likeliest unit to carry the status of 'text of the moment'.

The relation between the state of the text and previous text is derived from an appreciation of the *interactive* quality of language. Language in use, whether written or spoken, is involved in the process of creating and sharing meaning between two participants. It therefore consists in part of features which organize the sharing of meaning, as well as features which create the meaning.

These features are usually inseparable. Each word, each intonation participates in both aspects of the organization of an utterance. As an example, here is a sentence from a recent letter to me:

We begin our fourth programme on 9 July.

As printed, out of context, it seems to be a simple piece of information. But on placing the sentence in context it can be seen as an integral component of a strategy of persuasion. The next sentence, the only other one in a brief paragraph, reads:

Can we have an official response from you regarding these suggestions?

The implication is that my response should be quick and definite, and since their commitments increase heavily on 9 July, I should, if possible, complete our business before that date.

The juxtaposition of these two sentences in a paragraph, without an overt connection, invites us to relate them by postulating a meaning of the same nature as 'so' though not identical to it. The absence of an explicit connection does not mean that the sentences are not connected in interpretation. We deduce, however, that provision for such a connection in the structure of each successive sentence is so important that, if it is not expressed, it is inferred.

The words and phrases which express connections between sentences are such as *so, therefore, on the contrary*. They are often called 'logical operators'. I would argue that they are part of the interactive apparatus of the language, progressively determining the status of a previous sentence in relation to the current one. In spoken English there are words and phrases which are clearly specialized towards expressing the interactive side of discourse meaning. These are the 'interactive signals' such as *well, ah, anyway, you see, after all, I mean*. The central tenet of the present argument – that a text is represented at any moment of interpretation by a single sentence – allows us to see that the logical operators and the interactive signals have essentially the same discourse function. One is associated with the speaker, but they both give coherence to the text and independence to the sentence. The similarity between them has been obscured by the strong physical presence of a written text, which is misleading since a text is actually interpreted bit by bit in a dynamic process.

### *Encapsulation*

There is support in the details of text organization for the view that each new sentence takes over the status of 'state of the text', and therefore that the previous sentence relinquishes that role. The support takes the form of a default hypothesis and the associated arguments.

The default hypothesis is that each new sentence encapsulates the previous one by an act of reference. By referring to the whole of the previous sentence, a new sentence uses it as part of the subject matter. This removes its discourse function, leaving only the meaning which it has created.

As a default hypothesis, this should be generally true and applicable and the analysis replicable. All cases where it is not true should be covered by explicit arguments. In a small proportion of cases we may accept that the encapsulation can be implied by the writer and reasonably inferred by the reader. If no such inference suggests itself, the text is interpreted as not coherent at this point. Texts are not expected to be totally explicitly coherent, and individual judgements on doubtful instances are expected to differ. The writing and reading of text is a human and not a mechanical activity.

Our hypothesis is that there is an underlying structure to discourse where each new sentence makes reference to the previous one, and encapsulates the previous sentence in an act of reference. It is a common discourse strategy for the discourse to refer to itself; where it is prominent and unexpected it is called *plane-change* (Sinclair 1981). This chapter argues that a less marked kind of self-reference is the basic coherence of text. If encapsulation were an absolute rule, and not just a default hypothesis, then the nature of text structure would be obvious. The current sentence would encapsulate the previous one, which in its turn had encapsulated its predecessor, and so on back to the beginning of the text. The current sentence would then be encapsulated in an act of reference in the next to come, and so on until the end of the text.

Any sentence, then, would be a precise manifestation of the whole text up to that point. Detail expressed in earlier states of the text would be recoverable through the encapsulations. The last sentence of a text would thus be a manifestation of the entire text, presented in an appropriate form for the discourse function which it was performing.

As a model of text structure, this is very attractive. It explains how texts can be organized and how their dynamism may be created and fuelled. It provides the basis for a powerful definition of coherence, and reduces cohesion to the identification of the act of reference only.

Other kinds of cohesion, referring to less than a sentence, are not regarded as textual in nature. We may clarify this point – for it is an important one – by suggesting that there are two quite different processes going under the name of cohesion. Failure to appreciate the distinction between them has hampered the development of models of text structure.

The first I would call 'point-to-point' cohesion, where, for example, a pronoun can be related back to a noun phrase earlier in the text, and can be said to 'refer' to it. This kind of pattern is clearly of frequent occurrence, and is the basis of most accounts of cohesion. It includes the rich field of lexical cohesion, where the recurrence of a word or phrase, or the occurrence of something reminiscent of a previous item, is noted. Each constituent of these patterns is less than one sentence long; normally a word or phrase, or at most a clause.

In contrast, the second process deals only with sentences or, occasionally, clause complexes, and it does much more than effect a tenuous connection between isolated constituents of sentences. It is the process of encapsulation, and it reclassifies a previous sentence by 'demoting' it into an element of the structure of the new sentence.

This kind of cohesion is clearly structural; the other is not so clearly structural. The model of text that I am putting forward has no place for retention of the actual words and phrases of a text so that such connections could be established (though see pp. 91–2 below on verbal echo).

The question remains as to where in a model 'point-to-point' cohesion should be located. An argument which I shall develop elsewhere is that when the discourse function of a sentence is superseded by the next one, its linguistic properties are discarded, and only what it expresses is retained. It is no longer a linguistic entity, but a part of shared knowledge. If it contains words and phrases of 'point-to-point' reference, these are interpreted with reference to shared knowledge, not to previous text.

If, by a process of progressive encapsulation of one sentence by the next, each sentence in turn encapsulates all previous sentences, then there is no need to search for actual stretches of text as referents, antecedents and the like. Nor is it necessary to identify precisely what stretches of text are referred to in cases of vague or general backward reference. It is sufficient that at least the immediately preceding sentence is encapsulated, thus transferring to shared knowledge all the meaning it has created, Cohesive devices will aid the work of inferencing so that the latest sentence will be understood in relation to the growing meaning of the whole communication.

This kind of model applies with little adaptation to both spoken and written language, and so offers the basis of an integrated description (Sinclair 1992a).

It is thus important to examine the relevance of this hypothesis and consider the instances which falsify it.

I should like to refer in detail to a feature article by Randolph Quirk in *The European* of 1–3 June 1990. The sentences are printed in numbered sequences in Appendix 5.1 (see pp. 98–100).

At this point I wish to say that I had no strong reasons for choosing this passage. It is always difficult to explain why a particular text is chosen, and one feels like a conjuror at a children's party, claiming innocence before pulling rabbits out of hats. Suffice it to say that of the various texts that I had easy access to, this one was of a suitable length, in a genre that is not regarded as specialized, and very competently written. It seems suitable as a first test of this hypothesis: if the hypothesis fails, it is unlikely to be worth trying on other texts; if it holds, success will encourage further study.

## Classification of sentences

There follows an analysis of the relationships between each sentence in the passage, the sentence before it and occasionally the sentence after it. First of all, the sentences which clearly and explicitly encapsulate their predecessors are listed in two groups according to the mechanism. 'Logical acts' show the use of the logical connectors and associated mechanisms such as ellipsis. The second group, 'deictic acts', is self-explanatory.

The next major category of coherence is prospection, and after that there is consideration given to verbal echoes and overlays of one sentence on another. Then I must turn to some problems, acts of selective reference, and doubtful or qualified assignments. A complete analysis is given in Appendix 5.2.

*Table 5.1* Logical acts

| | |
|---|---|
| 3.2b | *and* is a logical act which refers to and encapsulates the first half of the sentence and combines with a deictic act – see section on double acts of reference, p. 97. |
| 4.1 | *they should.* This is an example of ellipsis. The two words can be related to the whole of 3.2. In 3.2 *Those already . . . UK* firms names the referent of *they* and *must be prepared . . . self-study courses* names the referent of *should.* |
| | *however* means 'notwithstanding a previously stated position'. The previously stated position (PSP for short) is 5.1. |
| 5.3 | *And yet,* we interpret as 'despite some PSP' which is last expressed in 5.2. |
| 6.1 | *by contrast.* A contrast has to be *with* something, and we interpret the two contrasting positions to be those at 5.3 and 6.1. |
| 7.1 | *rather* is a logical act which encapsulates the first half of the sentence; it is thus an internal act of reference. There is another act of reference in this half sentence; see p. 87. |
| 8.2 | *And* is a logical act with a meaning here like 'as a confirmatory particular' to a PSP, which is 8.1. |
| 9.1 | *The implications.* The meaning of this noun indicates ellipsis, the implications must be of something, that is, of a PSP, which is 8.3. |
| 9.3 | *also.* We interpret *also* as 'in addition to some PSP' which is last expressed in 9.2. |
| 10 | *therefore.* We interpret *therefore* as a conclusion from a PSP, which we find is 9.3. |
| 10b | *and* is an internal logical act which encapsulates the first half of the sentence. There is a deictic act in this structure as well, see p. 87. |
| 11 | *None the less.* We interpret *none the less* as 'in spite of a PSP' which we find is 10. |
| 12.1 | *So.* We interpret *so* as 'because of a PSP', which we find is 11. |
| 12.1 | *too.* We interpret *too* as 'in addition to some PSP' which we find is 11. Each of so and too can encapsulate independently , see p. 83. |
| 12.2 | *also.* We interpret *also* as 'in addition to a PSP', which is 12.1. Note that there is another encapsulation in this sentence; see p. 83. |
| 12.4 | *in fact.* We interpret *in fact* as 'consistent with a PSP but reinforcing some aspect of it'. The PSP is 12.3. |
| 13.3 | *But.* We interpret *but* as 'notwithstanding a PSP', which is 13.2. |
| 13.4 | *And.* We interpret *and* as 'in addition to a PSP', which is 13.3. Note, however, that there is another encapsulation in this sentence. |
| 14.1 | *As a result,* we interpret this phrase as 'as the result of a PSP', which is 13.4. |
| 14.2 | *Yet.* We interpret this as 'in spite of a PSP', which is 14.2. |
| 16.3 | *too.* We interpret *too* as 'to add urgency to a PSP', which is 16.2. |

## *Internal acts of reference*

It was noted above and in note 1 that the sentence is only provisionally taken as the likeliest unit of test patterning; in some cases a substantial portion of a sentence, such as a clause complex, may be interpreted as acting fairly independently in the text. There are five instances of such internal patterns of reference, which are noted as they arise, in sentences 3.2, 7.1, 10, 15.2 and 16.2.

### *Logical acts*

These encapsulate the whole of the previous sentence, or the previous half of the same sentence. Numbering is by paragraph and sentence.

There is an interesting case in 15.2 'To *quote* . . .'. I did not immediately see this as a logical act of reference, but it is certainly initial, and depends for its interpretation on the previous text. The quotation it introduces would have to be germane to the previous text. It might be glossed as meaning 'In order to support a PSP, I quote ' . . . ', which shows that in this text it encapsulates 15.1. This usage is noted in Sinclair, Hanks et al. (1987), *to* para. 19.6.

### *Deictic acts*

These also encapsulate the whole of the previous sentence.

*Table 5.2* Deictic acts

| | |
|---|---|
| 3.1 | *things*. Deictic acts include lexical reference and repetition. Here the lexically weak word *things* is interpreted as referring to a PSP, namely the whole of 2.2. |
| 3.2b | *that* is an internal deictic acts which encapsulates the previous half of the sentence. There is also a logical act here – see above. |
| 7.1 | *This very obvious ethos*. This deictic act refers to the PSP which is the whole of 6.2. It is a complex act, which names the PSP as a 'very obvious ethos', and encapsulates it by reference. |
| 10b | *this* is a deictic act which encapsulates the first half of the sentence. It is internal, and is coupled with a logical act (see above). |
| 12.2 | *This* is a deictic act which refers to the PSP of 12.1. Note that there is a logical act also in this sentence (see above). |
| 13.4 | *this* is a deictic act which refers to the whole of 13.3. Note that it is combined with a logical act (see above). |
| 16.1 | *this subject* is a deictic act which refers to a PSP which is the whole of 15.2, or at least the quoted part of it. It will be discussed further in the section on acts of selective reference, p. 95. |

### First variation: prospection

So far we have shown that two-thirds (24 out of 36) of the non-initial sentences encapsulate the previous one wholly.

Of the remainder, a number show an alternative structure to that of retrospective encapsulation; this is *prospection*. Prospection occurs where the phrasing of a sentence leads the addressee to expect something specific in the next sentence.

Prospection is a major feature of text and discourse structure. Below the sentence it is found in a wide range of prefaces (see, for example, Tognini-Bonelli 1992). It is the central organizing principle of exchange structure in conversation (Sinclair 1992b) and it is already identified as a structural element in written texts (Tadros 1985).

Prospection takes precedence over retrospection quite naturally, because the precedence is built into the sequence of events. The prospective acts relevant to a sentence are made in the previous sentence, while its retrospective features are not apparent until the sentence itself has occurred.

The act of prospection means that the interactive force of a sentence extends to the end of the sentence following. Indeed, it has been pointed out for many years that in one of the most obvious prospections in the spoken language, the question, the next utterance is interpreted in advance. The question sets the parameters with which the next utterance is evaluated; its relevance is measured against the presumption of a perfectly fitting answer.

In these circumstances, a sentence cannot simultaneously fulfil a prospection and encapsulate the utterance that makes the prospection. The former requires maintenance of the discourse function of the previous utterance, and the latter requires the cancellation of that discourse function.

In the spoken language this is fairly obvious operationally. The interactive quality of the prospecting sentence is of necessity retained throughout the next sentence. Otherwise it is not easy to see how a participant can become aware that a prospection has been adequately dealt with.

One kind of prospection is the introduction of quoted speech, usually through an *attribution*.

4.2   *his message* is a prospective deictic act which is satisfied by 5.1.

If a quote is more than a sentence long, as in this case, the attribution is maintained as a basis of interpretation, but textually we return to the same rules as before after the first sentence, each new sentence relating to at least one of its neighbours.

Indeed, 4.2 is the only prospective attribution in this passage that involves more than one sentence. Towards the end there are two candidates for consideration as internal prospection:

15.2   *To quote the Prince of Wales again:* prospects the quotation that follows, within the sentence.

16.2 the statement; also the exhortation: each prospects a following quotation.

Another kind of prospection is approximately what Tadros (1985) calls *advance labelling*. It rests on the addressee interpreting a word or phrase as something to be elucidated in the following sentence.

9.1 gives a fairly clear example. The implications are about to be stated, and indeed they are, beginning with 9.2.

12.2 flexible response is elucidated in the whole of 12.3.

13.1 The notion of perceived disadvantage is elucidated in the whole of 13.2.

There must be a margin of variation in interpretation here, and for the analyst a risk of arguing from hindsight. In addition to the above, I assume that in a normal reading of a passage such prospections as the following would occur. With *monoglot* in 2.1, it seems to me that the writer is now committed to developing the notion 'monoglot' in the next sentence, as he does. The word appears prominently in 1, and 2.1 disentangles it from cuisine and myths, leaving nothing else to talk about.

Another is *competitive* in 7.2, which to me prospects 8.1 fairly clearly. 'Competitive' has been in the air since *cannot afford to* in 3.1, and now has final position in the sentence and paragraph.

In some cases a sentence introduces a new topic and is thus clearly a preliminary to the next. That is to say, if a reader stops at the prospecting sentence he/she can predict with fair confidence that the following sentence will pick up the new topic and develop it.

There are two places in the text where the subject matter abruptly changes, and the lack of preparation for the new subject indicates that there is a textual device at work. If we can distinguish between the overall topic and the immediate subject matter, then this device changes only the subject matter. The approach to the topic does not change.[3] For example, 4.1 introduces *the Prince of Wales* as the subject of the new sentence, and there has been no hint (beyond the editor's introduction) that Prince Charles might be referred to. The sentence stands out as a considerable reorientation of the text, and moves from a general group, *those who think . . .* , to an individual. The sentence is equative and performs the function of selecting the Prince of Wales as a new topic, and relating him to the preceding text. It is almost certain that the following sentence will feature the Prince of Wales. 4.1 is thus classified as prospective.

This pattern occurs again more clearly in paragraph 16. In 16.1, *a large advertisement . . .* is now a new topic, and so the pronoun *It* in 16.2 is prospected by 16.1.

There is a very difficult case in 7.1, in which *the precept* can be interpreted as a prospection of 7.2. However, this interpretation may not be generally agreed, and the case will be discussed in the section on qualified assignments on p. 95.

There is a point of some potential importance arising from the analysis of the two clear cases, those of 4.1, 4.2 and 16.1, 16.2. We identify the first sentence in each case as performing the function of introducing a new topic. This is done without reference to the second sentence or any subsequent one; it is done by interpreting the first sentence with reference to the state of the text. 4.1 and 16.1 thus each contain a prospective act.

The second sentence in each case is interpreted as developing the new topic, and so fulfils the prospection. This forward-facing analysis contrasts with the direction of pronominal reference, where traditionally it would be said that the pronouns *he* in 4.2 and *It* in 16.2 refer to *the Prince of Wales* (4.1) and *a large advertisement* (16.1) respectively – a backward-facing analysis.

The claim in this chapter is that the forward-facing, or prospective, analysis is more relevant to the explication of discourse. It is hierarchical, explaining the sentence connection with reference to a higher-order structure of topic introduction and development (see Hazadiah 1991). The retrospective analysis is less powerful because it concerns merely subsentences (and often subclause elements). It is also of doubtful relevance because of our assumption that in the normal reading process the actual language of earlier sentences is not available for acts of reference.

There are two points of clarification to be made about prospection, before we leave it.

1  It was stated above that a prospection refers forward to the next sentence. The possibility arises that one or more sentences may intervene, without any overt indication of their intervention.

   When a substantial amount of text from different sources has been described in the terms of this chapter, it will be possible to check how contiguous must be the sentences involved in a prospection. Certainly, in the spoken language, if a prospection is interrupted it must normally be reactivated by a specific signal, as we find in side sequences (Jefferson 1972) and insertion sequences (Schegloff 1972). Perhaps a similar mechanism is to be found in written discourse.

   It would be consistent with the overall description of discourse to expect that a prospection must be attended to in the very next sentence. Prospections are not retained indefinitely until attended to, and if their fulfilment is to be postponed, this will probably have an effect on the structure.

2  One difference between spoken and written language is that it is mandatory in coherent written discourse that prospections are fulfilled. In conversation it is fairly common for the discourse to move its focus in such a way that a prospection is just ignored, because neither participant ensures its fulfilment.

This major difference may well affect point 1 above, because if the fulfilment *must* occur in the written language, then no doubt it can be tactically delayed.

### First exception: verbal echo

In order to make the case against the textual relevance of 'point-to-point' cohesion, I may well have slightly overstated it. It is hardly likely that a reader specifically erases each successive sentence (unless it prospects) before beginning to read the next one. More likely, the process of reading is much more untidy. What is more, there is plenty of evidence in poetry, advertising, oratory and verbal humour to refute the idea of complete textual erasure. There are different kinds of memories, some of which seem to operate independently of the necessities of the reading process. All sorts of stylistic features like rhyme and antithesis depend on comparing the present state of the actual text with a previous one.

This point is not a total reversal of my original position. I believe that, when reviewed in the light of this chapter, a great deal more prospection will be acknowledged than hitherto. We have not been encouraged to stress the directional element in text, and so the prospective quality of, for example, poetic form, has not been emphasized. Also the dual nature of poetry reading, made clear by Fish (1970), suggests that not all genres conform to a standard set of reading conventions.

However, to accommodate any doubts about the availability of previous text, it is perhaps more accurate to suggest that the reader's attention shifts to the textual reality of the new sentence and relates that to the state of shared knowledge which has been created by the text so far. Awareness of previous words and phrases will die away sharply, though the traces, especially of something striking and memorable, may be retained with sufficient clarity to be reactivated.

There is some evidence in spoken language that speakers indicate co-operation and convergence by reusing each others's actual words. In the example below, each country named is repeated by the next speaker. No new information is provided but the participants indicate their co-operative intent.

    *M:* North America, that's right.
    *P:* North America, we were right. Holland, you were right about that.
    *M:* Holland, right. Thailand, oh good.
    *P:* Thailand, good. Oh we know something then. Greece, yes.
    *M:* Greece . . .

                                                       (data from Cobuild)

In the next example, the patient keeps using the word *heart*, which the doctor replaces by *chest*, to indicate that he does not share the patient's view of the topic, although he does not challenge the veracity of the patient's story.

    *D:* And what's been the matter recently.
    *P:* Well I've er pains around the heart.
    *D:* Pains in your chest then.
    *P:* Yeah round the heart.

    *D:* Whereabouts in your chest.
    *P:* On the heart side, yeah.

There is one candidate for verbal echo in our text: 13.1, where *perceived disadvantage* seems inescapably to recall *perceiving . . . disadvantage* in the previous two lines, ending 12.4. It cannot be considered an encapsulation because it only refers to one small part of the sentence, and indeed, it shifts the topic by picking up what appears to be unimportant in 12.4.

    The effect of this verbal echo on the coherence of the text is to change the topic while maintaining superficial cohesion. Paragraph 11 is about the differing status of languages, and paragraph 12 is about the problems this inequality may create.

### Second exception: overlay

Sometimes there is no obvious act of reference in a sentence with respect to the one before it, and yet the two appear to be closely connected – in fact, they are often almost paraphrases of each other. In such cases the new sentence takes the place of the old. In terms of the structure of the text, the new sentence can be seen as similar to encapsulation, in that it replaces its predecessor. To see two sentences as virtual paraphrases of each other is a complex act of interpretation, and not something that can always be reliably assessed. Perhaps there is an underlying default structure, so that we expect from experience that a simple juxtaposition of sentences is most likely to signal an overlay. The new sentence has a new orientation, which can be discovered by noting the way it varies from the old. For example, 2.1 closely follows the phrasing of paragraph 1. Anthony Burgess and his novel disappear, and also the complex of myths. The word *insular* is qualified by *less*, *cuisine* is demoted to parentheses, *monoglot* is heavily emphasized by *disastrously* and by its final position in the sentence.

    The new sentence performs the function of focussing on *monoglot* whereas the original sentence was more diffuse. (Hence the interpretation that *monoglot is* a prospection for 2.2.)

    6.2 is a rephrasing of 6.1. The meaning is couched as a generalization in 6.1, and as two generalized instances in 6.2. It should be noted that 6.2 is hardly less general than 6.1; the instances do not signal a movement from general to particular; it is just another way of expressing the generality.

    8.3 is an interesting case. It rephrases 8.2 quite carefully but focuses on the Japanese. Consider the parallels (Table 5.3).

    Here our interpretation of the new focus depends on understanding the significance of 'The Japanese', perhaps by associating *The Japanese* with *powerful rivals* in 8.1. This inference turns an otherwise innocuous piece of information into a menace, and strengthens the argument of 8.2.

    It is inaccurate and simplistic to see 8.3 as a particular case of 8.2 or 8.1. 'The Japanese' are not identified with *businesses* in 8.1 nor with *sales force, middle management, personnel . . .* in 8.2, but specifically with *powerful rivals*. The parallels

*Table 5.3*

| Sentence 8.3 | Sentence 8.2 |
| --- | --- |
| The Japanese use Western languages | language skills |
| not merely to | not just |
| market their goods | for the sales force |
| but | but |
| to improve their products | research and development |
| | new ideas and processess |
| by studying | so that they can learn |
| those of their rivals | to keep in touch with trends in other countries |

*Table 5.4*

| Sentence 15.1 | Sentences 14.1, 14.2 |
| --- | --- |
| although English is the language most widely used in international trade | it is precisely the native speakers . . . English |
| it should not be automatically | these are the very people . . . |
| assumed by native English speakers | complacent |
| to be the most satisfactory | who have to be . . . most |
| choice for negotiation with clients | sensitive about the choice of language in negotiation |

shown in comparing 8.3 and 8.2 above concern the similarity of the propositions, not the identity of referents.

There is one other case, of doubtful clarity: 15.1 and both 14.1 and 14.2. 14.2 is included because its expression of complacency is reflected in *At long last* (15.1). See Table 5.4.

The Germans drop out, and so does assiduity in foreign-language training, though the early phrases of 15.1 – *UK businesses are waking up to the realisation* – offer a dim comparison.

I think we may say that 15.1 covers largely the same ground as paragraph 14, and may be classified as overlay.

It should be noted that in suggesting a similarity of meaning between adjacent sentences, there is little or no role played by the actual words and phrases, or their position and ordering. This overlaying is thus not claimed to be textual.

The comparative layout above is intended to show only the correspondence of meaning. Instead, I suggest that the first of each pair has been 'detextualized', in that its meaning has been transferred to an area of shared knowledge of the participants, and as the new sentence is understood and interpreted, the repetition of meaning becomes obvious, though not textually dependent.

In this way overlaying can be distinguished from verbal echoing, which is specifically textual. No doubt we shall come across mixed and doubtful cases – and I have returned many times to consider the first two sentences in our text because of the extent of verbal repetition. But in the present state of the model I would like to keep them distinct.

## Coherence

At this point, we have assigned each sentence in the specimen text except 3.2 to a category which concerns its relation with the sentence that has occurred before it. It makes an act of reference, or it fulfils a prospection, or it echoes or overlays the previous sentence.

Most of the assignments have been fairly straightforward, involving the whole of the previous sentence. Contentious cases centre on the following:

1  acts of selective reference, where less than a sentence is encapsulated;
2  qualified links, which are not clear for one reason or another.

There are two other matters to be cleared up.

1  Some sentences participate in more than one act of reference. Some of these are closely linked, some apparently independent of each other.
2  In particular, we have identified a number of internal acts of reference, which may suggest that we revise the original assumption that the orthographic sentence is the best minimal unit for text structure. In the text–order analysis, the sentences we choose to divide are those whose two parts behave as two separate sentences in terms of this analysis. This is a circular argument, but a satisfying one nevertheless. That is, we do not make arbitrary or intuitive divisions of sentences.

Let us now explore the notion of *coherence*. A text can be said to be coherent when each successive sentence can be assigned wholly and without difficulty to one of the relationships that have been illustrated in this chapter so far. It may not be necessary, however, for a text to show coherence consistently, and a reader's impression of our specimen text might well be of perfectly acceptable coherence although there are doubtful points in the analysis. We assume that all addressees expect texts to be coherent, and actively search for coherence in difficult text. But if a given text were found to consist of a string of sentences which did not show these relationships, we may predict that the coherence would be difficult to appreciate.

This line of argument also suggests that there is little difference between cohesion and coherence. Our initial hypothesis picks out those cohesive patterns which concern a whole sentence, and rejects all the others (which will be dealt with on another occasion, but which are held to be nonsignificant in text structure). The sentence-size cohesive patterns turn out to be the elements of coherence.

It would be rash to claim that the sentence connections described in this chapter are all and only the matter of coherence, and that a text is guaranteed to be coherent if it follows the rules. But it is certainly claimed that an understanding of the nature of text as presented here, and operational skills developed from it, will be of advantage in comprehension and composition.

### Third exception: acts of selective reference

In the previous discussion, two sentences were noted as containing reference to only part of the preceding sentence; and there was no prospection in the preceding sentence to warrant such selection (as there is in 4.1 in relation to 4.2 and 16.1 in relation to 16.2). These are 13.1 and 16.1 (in relation to 15.2).

In 13.1, a nominalization clearly picks up the phrasing of 12.4. What seems to be almost an afterthought in 12.4 becomes the 'topic sentence' for the next four paragraphs (though note that *disadvantage* in 15.2 is another view of the matter). This is the clearest case in the passage of a change of topic brought about by a cohesive reference to a minor part of the preceding sentence.

In 16.1 the deictic phrase on *this subject* refers to 15.2, but only to the second part of it. However, it was suggested above that 15.1 is merely an introductory preface to 15.2, and in such a case the sentence (paragraph 15 in this case) may safely be divided into two linear units. With this reallocation the act of selective reference disappears.

There is one other case which deserves comment in this section. 8.2 repeats in inverted commas *'every aspect'*, which is a phrase from the preceding sentence. The encapsulation is already achieved, if weakly, with the first word in the sentence, *And*. The change of topic, then, has a similar effect to 13.1, in that it picks out what was a minor element of 8.1. The verbal echo here is at its most explicit, being an actual quotation in inverted commas.

### Qualified assignments

Many of the assignments that have been made depend on my personal interpretation of the text. I am more confident of some than of others, and in a few cases I feel it is necessary to express doubt about the clarity of the relationship I perceive.

This is not a critical comment on the author, his text or the analyst, but a recognition that creation and perception of text structure is not exact or fully determined, but is subject to the process of interpretation.

Clearly, there is a broad band of variation possible in texts between demonstrable incoherence and over-explicitness. There is also variation across a single text, where the quality of the coherence may not be even. Peaks and troughs may alternate in various patterns, still to be described.

Linguistic description at this point comes into contact with prescription and critical opinion. Standards of coherence may be expected in a society for various types of text, and the most seemingly objective description may have inescapable prescriptive implications.

All that is offered here is a review of those assignments about which there may be reservations. There are five of them, out of 36 non-initial sentences, which does not seem to be a proportion that is likely to disturb the overall coherence of the article.

The coherence is less than clear in structural terms at 3.2. The message of 3.2 is relevant at that point, and there are indications of an urgent call to change. But 3.2 is not clearly prospected, nor does it encapsulate its predecessor, nor is there a plausible case for stylistic rephrasing.

As a general rule in interpretation, in the absence of a clear indication we reverse the argument and ask 'what is the kind of relationship that, using all the powers of inference available, you would assume in this case?' My answer to this question is that 3.2 poses the contrary to 3.1 – a logical act like 'on the contrary' or 'instead' would fit with my interpretation.

Hence I propose to reassign 3.1 to logical acts, but with a caution that the act is inferred and not expressed.

We turn to 7.2, which is involved in two qualified assignments. The problem lies in identifying what is meant by *the precept* in 7.1. If it means, approximately, the message of 7.2 then this sentence is a fulfilment of the advance labelling of 7.1. If it means something else – like the message of 6.1 or earlier exhortations like 3.2 – then the recovery of coherence will have to be through some acts of inference. And the word *rather* in 7.1 suggests a contrast with 6. The doubt about the meaning of *the precept* makes the text slightly incoherent at this point. My preference is for the advance-labelling interpretation because 8.1 remains more general rather than specifically about language learning.

Doubts about the coherence of the text around this point continue with the prospective quality of *competitive* in 7.2, introducing 8.1, and having to survive a paragraph break.

There may be disagreement about how far 15.1 is a rephrasing of 14, but the case has been put and analytic readers must judge for themselves.

At present there are no standards for comparison about the levels of tolerance that are acceptable in cases of doubt. The best an analyst can do is to have clear criteria and make firm assignments and be precise about areas of uncertainty. It is not anticipated that this kind of analysis will lead to exactly repeatable results, since human beings must retain a margin of individuality, even at their most conformist. To differ about the coherence of a text is entirely justified, and the role of the analytical framework is to enable people to understand the nature of the difference.

### Double acts of reference

In the following sentences, two acts of reference were noted:

> 12.1 *So* (logical act) . . . *too* (logical act)
> 12.2 *This* (deictic act) . . . *also* (logical act)
> 13.4 *And* (logical act) *this* (deictic act)

In the cases of 12.1 and 12.2 the two acts seem to be independent. The word *also* in 12.2 indicates that *flexible response* has to be retrieved from 10; as a logical act it is not strictly necessary in the syntax, but locally supportive. In the case of 13.4 the two acts seem to be closely coupled, although they contribute separate meanings: the *And* gives the meaning of concluding a section of the text.

A double act of reference is also to be found internally in 3.2 and 10.

> 3.2 *and* (logical act) *that* (deictic act)
> 10 *and* (logical act) *this* (deictic act)

These are similar in most respects to 13.4, except that the meaning of the *and is* different. A concluding *And* needs to start a sentence or at least follow a colon or semi-colon; in 3.2 and 10 it has the status of introducing an appendage, following a dash or comma.[4]

## Conclusion

The hypothesis about coherence stands up fairly well to detailed examination. The sentence is usually adequate as a surface indicator of a coherence unit; in the cases where it is not so, there are explicit acts of either (a) encapsulation of the first part of the sentence by the second or (b) prospection of the second by the first.

The principal type of coherence is through encapsulation. It is so well established that in cases where there is no explicit link between sentences the default interpretation is encapsulation. The regularity of this mechanism lends support to the view that each successive sentence has a kind of communicative autonomy. It does not need to have elaborate connections with components of sentences before and after; these so-called 'cohesive' links are only relevant in the occasional instances of verbal echo. A text does not consist of a string of sentences which are intricately interconnected, but of a series of sentence-length texts, each of which is a total update of the one before. In addition to encapsulating the preceding text, a sentence can make a prospection about the next sentence, thus establishing a need for the next sentence to fulfil the prospection if coherence is to be maintained. The sentence fulfilling the prospection does not encapsulate the prospecting sentence.

The 36 non-initial sentences and the four internal acts of reference total 40 occasions on which a coherence choice is made in this passage. Clear cases of encapsulation join 34 of the 41 coherence units; there are two verbal echoes, one of which, in the absence of any other signal, directs the discourse. There are four overlays. One encapsulation, in addition, is allocated by default, and there are three other doubtful cases, as the section on selective references (p. 95) shows. Five encapsulations are doubly marked. There are ten cases of prospection.

There is a basis here for further study of different styles of writing, and for the study of similar phenomena in the spoken language; it is not unlikely that coherence is a common property of both modes of language, realized with some superficial differences. The main difference of the spoken language is that texts are constructed by more than one individual. Both encapsulations and prospection were first seen to be important in the study of the spoken language. It is natural that a new speaker constructs each contribution as an independent re-action to the state of the discourse, unless something specific is prospected.

It was not so clear, however, given the preoccupation of analysts with point-to-point cohesion, that similar priorities might be worth establishing for the written language, but for this sample text the analysis is simplifying, revealing and could be intuitively satisfying to many users.

## Appendix 5.1

### *British must get their tongues around 1992*

1 There is a character in an Anthony Burgess novel who reflects sadly on the typical 'monoglot Englishman' as being 'tied to one tongue as to one cuisine, and one insular complex of myths'.

2.1 The British have become less insular in some respects (cuisine is one of them) but they are still disastrously monoglot. (2.2) This is the first gener-ation in history to delude itself into thinking that because one particular language, English, seems to be very widely understood, no other language need be learned.

3.1 The foreign language requirement in the UK's National Curriculum will help to change things, but the British cannot afford to tread water until its products have fed through the system. (3.2) Those already employed in UK firms must be prepared to learn languages – and that means in-service training and the energetic use of self-study courses.

4.1 The Prince of Wales is among those who think it is high time they should. (4.2) Last week he addressed British industrialists, and his message was typically forthright:

5.1 'In two years' time, the United Kingdom will find itself part of a single market and, in effect, a single population of 320 million people, 82 per cent of whom do not have English as their mother tongue. (5.2) To all of these people, however, British firms will wish to sell their goods; with all of them, British people will wish – and need – to communicate. (5.3) And yet, how often do we see British commercial representatives at trade fairs abroad hard put to communicate with their potential customers because they speak no language other than English?'

6.1 Successful businesses, by contrast, have always been sensitive to the need to respect the language capabilities and preferences of their customers. (6.2) A Finnish manufacturer would not dream of using Finnish to market a product in Germany or France, nor would a Spanish firm rely on Spanish to attract customers in Italy or Sweden.

7.1 This very obvious ethos is not going to change with 1992: rather, the importance of the precept will be sharply enhanced. (7.2) The single market will make trading conditions even more competitive.

8.1 As the rewards for enterprise increase, so businesses will have to refine every aspect of their work to match the high professionalism of powerful rivals. (8.2) And 'every aspect' most certainly includes language skills – not just for the sales force, but for middle management to keep in touch with trends in other countries, and for personnel involved in research and development so that they can learn as rapidly and accurately as possible of new ideas and processes. (8.3) The Japanese use Western languages not merely to market their goods, but to improve their products by studying those of their rivals.

9.1 The implications are daunting. (9.2) Not merely must a business have personnel with skills in several different languages, but the particular languages and the degree of skill may vary from person to person according to his or her job within the business. (9.3) They may also vary from decade to decade as new markets open up in different countries.

10 Clearly, therefore, businesses need to develop a strategy of 'flexible response' to language requirements, and this means a workforce that includes an adequate proportion with language-learning aptitude, and the willingness, as well as the ability, to embark on in-service language training.

11 None the less, even the largest and most enterprising firms must recognise that there are far too many languages in the world (a couple of dozen in Europe alone) for every language to receive equal treatment.

12.1 So we must recognise, too, that – to paraphrase the English author, George Orwell – some languages are more equal than others. (12.2) This is where flexible response also comes in. (12.3) It is natural for two parties, a Finnish business person and one from Portugal, say, to explore what language they have in common and then use it (Spanish, perhaps, or French, or English) in their negotiations. (12.4) Within Europe, in fact, provided a firm has good facility in three or four languages, it is usually easy to agree on a common language for a given discussion with neither party perceiving itself to be at a disadvantage.

13.1 The notion of perceived disadvantage is very important. (13.2) The use of German in negotiation between a Stuttgart firm and a Copenhagen firm, may be efficient and perfectly logical where the Danes concerned are fluent in German. (13.3) But, perhaps without the Germans noticing, the Danes may well feel that they are on less than a comfortable equal footing and may harbour some silent resentment. (13.4) And this, of course, can hardly make for the most satisfactory outcome on either side!

14.1 As a result, it is precisely the native speakers of the 'major' languages, such as German and English, who have to be most assiduous in foreign language training and most sensitive about the choice of language in negotiation. (14.2) Yet these are the very people who are most liable to be complacent.

15.1 At long last, UK businesses are waking up to the realisation that, although English is the language most widely used in international trade, it should not be automatically assumed by native English speakers to be the most satisfactory choice for negotiation with clients. (15.2) To quote the Prince of Wales again: 'I see a real danger that, by putting itself at a competitive disadvantage in linguistic skills, British business will find itself left on the touchline as others challenge for Europe's industrial supremacy.'

16.1 National newspapers in the UK carried a large advertisement from the British Department of Trade and Industry on this subject in March. (16.2) It included the statement '*En el mercado único todo el mundo habla varios idiomas*', with the exhortation 'to make language training a vital part of your Single Market business plan'. (16.3) About time too!

## Appendix 5.2

| Sentence number | Type | Schedule of coherence relates to | Subtypes |
|---|---|---|---|
| 1 | | | |
| 2.1 | overlay | 2 | |
| | prospection | 2.2 | topic selection |
| 2.2 | prospected | 2.1 | |
| 3.1 | encapsulation | 2.2 | deictic: lexical |
| 3.2a | encapsulation | 3.1 | inferred qualified |
| 3.2b | encapsulation | 3.2a | logical and deictic, double internal |
| 4.1 | encapsulation | 3.2 | logical: ellipsis |
| | prospection | 4.2 | topic selection |
| 4.2 | prospected | 4.1 | |
| | prospection | 5.1 | attribution |
| 5.1 | prospected | 4.2 | |
| 5.2 | encapsulation | 5.1 | logical |
| 5.3 | encapsulation | 5.2 | logical |
| 6.1 | encapsulation | 5.3 | logical |
| 6.2 | overlay | 6.1 | |
| 7.1a | encapsulation | 6.2 | deictic: including naming |
| 7.1b | encapsulation | 7.1a | logical internal |
| | prospection | 7.2 | topic selection |
| 7.2 | prospected | 7.1b | qualified |
| | prospection | 8.1 | topic selection qualified |
| 8.1 | prospected | 7.2 | |
| 8.2 | verbal echo | 8.1 | selective |
| | encapsulation | 8.1 | logical |

| | | | |
|---|---|---|---|
| 8.3 | overlay | 8.2 | |
| 9.1 | encapsulation | 8.3 | logical: ellipsis |
| | prospection | 9.2 | advance labelling |
| 9.2 | prospected | 9.1 | |
| 9.3 | encapsulation | 9.2 | logical |
| 10a | encapsulation | 9.3 | logical |
| 10b | encapsulation | 10a | logical deictic, double internal |
| 11 | encapsulation | 10 | logical |
| 12.1 | encapsulation | 11 | logical |
| 12.2 | encapsulation | 12.1 | logical deictic, double |
| 12.3 | prospected | 12.2 | |
| 12.4 | encapsulation | 12.3 | logical |
| 13.1 | verbal echo | 12.4 | selective |
| | prospection | 13.2 | advance labelling |
| 13.2 | prospected | 13.1 | |
| 13.3 | encapsulation | 13.2 | logical |
| 13.4 | encapsulation | 13.3 | logical deictic, double |
| 14.1 | encapsulation | 13.4 | logical |
| 14.2 | encapsulation | 14.1 | logical |
| 15.1 | overlay | 14 | qualified |
| 15.2a | encapsulation | 15.1 | logical |
| | prospection | 15.2b | attribution material |
| 15.2b | prospected | 15.2a | |
| 16.1 | encapsulation | 15.2 | deictic: selective |
| 16.2a | prospected | 16.1 | |
| | prospection | 16.2b | attribution |
| 16.2b | prospected | 16.2a | internal |
| 16.3 | encapsulation | 16.2 | logical |

# 6   The internalization of dialogue

This chapter tries to tackle the origin of complexity in sentence grammar, continuing the theme of linking spoken and written language in a single description and offering evidence to suggest that much of the complexity of grammatical structure consists of internalizations of features of spoken language interaction. The paper began as a small part of my contribution to an interdisciplinary conference at the University of Bologna, and was written up for the proceedings of that conference, *Incommensurability and Translation*, edited by R. Rossini Favretti, G. Sandri, R. Scazzieri and published in 1999 in Cheltenham by Edward Elgar.

## Introduction

The hypothesis of this chapter is that much of the complexity of sentence grammar can be explained as the internalization of features of spoken inter-action. Turn-taking, performing speech acts, averring and so on is physically observable as people talk to each other, in dialogue, and it is suggested here that this kind of behaviour provided a series of models for the development of a mode of the language which could sustain long continuous contributions from a single participant. This feature was particularly important in the development of writing.

The process is presented step by step, from the largest units downward. This method of presentation allows us to show how each additional facility is in-tegrated into a grammatical description and gives rise to grammatical meaning. Thus a representation of a class of events which is observable and meaningful in the physical world is imported into the abstract system of grammar.

Any new social development or invention is likely to be modelled on some-thing else in the experience of the members of the society. Aircraft still look very like birds, with wings, tails, bodies and noses/beaks; the roofs of houses in some parts of the world still look like upturned boats. As human affairs increased in complexity it is reasonable to assume that pressure was put on the languages to maintain efficient communication by developing new features appropriate to the new communicative needs. In the case of the elaboration of the discourse of a single participant, the nearest model was dialogue, which we normally assume to have predated it.

The contextual theory of J.R. Firth provides a suitable framework for this hypothesis. Language, Firth insists, always relates to a context of situation, which consists of the verbal action, and people, things and events that are relevant to the verbal action (Firth 1957a). Participants in face-to-face interaction would find it easy and natural to work out conventions whereby aspects of the interactive structuring were represented inside the speech of a single speaker, thus losing their actual interactive meaning but creating new meaningful patterns of monologue.

Let us examine an example of this process. Writers, especially of first person fictional narrative, can perform this kind of internalization on an ad hoc basis. One of the primary assumptions of written language is that it is premeditated; the writer has had time to consider it, and is aware of what is to follow as he/she writes any particular sentence – the opportunity of revision confers a responsibility on the writer. However, to contrive particular effects, a writer may appear to amend the text sentence by sentence, as if events were unfolding as the writing was being done. Often a string of incomplete sentences is used to convey this impression. Here are some examples from a recent popular novel (Laurie 1997):

1    There can be no other answer.
     Unless.
     Unless unless unless.

2    The sort of eyes that can make a grown man talk gibberish to himself.
     Get a grip, for Christ's sake.
     'You're a liar,' she said.
     Not angry. Not scared. Just matter-of-fact. You're a liar.

3    I also wondered why I hadn't known that he was Woolf's bodyguard.
     Or even that he had one.
     But much, much more to the point, why hadn't Woolf's daughter?

From these examples we conclude that temporal succession in life and textual succession in the written language are not the same, and that there is as yet no recognized, normal way of representing sudden changes of perspective in a written text; humorous writers exploit this gap for dramatic effect, and the techniques that they use have the status of a literary convention.[1]

The conventions that are described in this chapter are much more firmly settled in the structure of the language. They are central components of the grammar, not stylistic extras that can be called upon on occasion, in certain types of writing. Unlike the quotations above, their occurrence is unremarkable, and normally unremarked.

## Dialogic and monologic language

It is very likely that the presentation below will make readers associate the description with conjecture about the origin and evolution of language, and therefore it is important that a disclaimer is given early. There are no records of the early stages of speech, and therefore no objective evidence for the hypothesis that the model for internal complexity is to be found in interaction. Even if the hypothesis is close to what happened, the steps of internalization as portrayed here are far too schematic to summarize a chronological development. Seekers of trends that support the general argument of this chapter will find some traces in recorded history; for example, in sources as different as Plato and English medieval poetry, simulated dialogue is used to present arguments; and Halliday (in Halliday and Martin 1993) shows the development of one of the steps of internalization in Renaissance texts in English and Italian.

If the hypothesis is found to be broadly satisfying, then we have to assume that each of the steps has taken place at least once in every language. There is an implication here that at an early stage of language the structure of sentences was rather simple; that is dangerously close to a 'grunt' theory of language origin, and it must be reiterated that by the time it became possible to develop a written form of a language, the structures were already capable of great complexity.

It is also natural to see the various steps as of the written language internalizing features that are characteristic of the spoken language, and although that is an oversimplification, it is a useful image to bear in mind. But it must not be forgotten that all the complexity set out here is available to both speakers and writers.

For this reason I use the terms *dialogic* and *monologic*. Dialogic language is language in an interactive mode; utterances tend to be brief and turn-taking frequent; the structure of the discourse is co-operative, and utterances from all the participants contribute towards its construction. In broad general terms, it is the mode of the spoken language.

Examples and traces of dialogic language are to be found, of course, in writing. Some types of personal correspondence are partly dialogic, and a lot of present-day forms that people have to fill in show traces of this kind of language (but only superficially, since the behaviour of one participant is predetermined). In situations where participants are present but speech is impossible or forbidden, an interaction can be developed in writing in almost exactly the same way as in speech – as shown in the way schoolchildren pass notes to each other during class.

Monologic language, on the other hand, is language that does not require elaborate contributions from other participants; a single author (or a team) constructs a text which is self-standing and has no structural dependence on any other text.

Monologic language is thus the natural mode for writing, for one of the defining strengths of the written language is that it can be communicatively effective without the principal participants (writer and reader) being copresent. The writer has to anticipate the likely contributions or reactions of a target reader, and build these into the construction of the text. Since a writer is normally denied the support of an interactive situation, the development in writing of monologic representations of interaction is an essential step in extending the scope and power of the written language.

Monologic and dialogic modes are presented as contrasting extremities of a mixed spectrum, characteristic of writing and speech respectively. But just as some writing can tend towards the dialogic, we can find plenty of monologic behaviour in speech. Wherever one participant dominates the talk, talks all or most of the time, the discourse is moving towards the monologic; wherever all the participants except one are confined to minimal expressions of discourse support, or just to nodding and smiling, their contributions have very little structural role, and the main speaker takes responsibility for the discourse as a whole. There are several types of event – lectures, talks and ceremonies – where rather strict monologic conventions are observed for all or most of the time.

## Speaker change

In each case of internalization, there is an exchange of meaning potential; something is lost and something is gained. The loss is the loss of one of the characteristic features of the independence of linguistic units, and the gain is the gain of an additional feature of structural complexity within the utterance. For example, one of the basic assumptions of discourse is that speakers associate themselves with what they say – they aver what they say unless they make it clear that they are not averring. An apparently factual statement, like:

4    Rudolph picked up the phone[2]

is not understood as a matter of Popperian objective knowledge, but as an averral; the speaker offers it as true and, by sharing it with others in a conversation, engages the other participants to accept it as true or to challenge it. If it is not challenged, it acquires a temporary local veracity according to the status of the speaker.

However, if a speaker reports an event, he or she as the person reporting avers only the fact of the report; responsibility for its contents is assigned to the person who is reported, someone who remains inside the utterance, and is not a participant in the situation in which the report is made:

5    Renata called me up . . . and said she had never cared for this Flonzaley.

The speaker avers that Renata said this, but it is Renata who is said to have averred that she never cared for Flonzaley. Since Renata is not a participant in the discourse that contains the report, the reported clause is not an averral in that discourse.[3]

Since the default interpretation of an utterance is that it is averred by the speaker, it is necessary in discourse for a speaker to maintain postural coherence throughout an utterance; successive units in an utterance must either be consistent with one another or the inconsistency must be signalled or readily interpreted. It would be absurd if a speaker were to say:

6    *Rudolph picked up the phone, he did not pick up the phone.

Posture is the internalization of speaker change, and it is quite a sophisticated feature of language, brought to a fine art in the soliloquy, where an actor talks to himself (or 'himselves', as it sometimes appears). In the first line of the most famous soliloquy in English, there are two changes of posture, and therefore three postures, presented:

7    To be, or not to be, that is the question.

(Hamlet, Act III, Scene 1)

The word *or* at a clause boundary is a reliable indicator of a postural change; the usual interpretation of these contrasting phrases is that they express the choice between maintaining a positive attitude to living and contemplating suicide. The word *that* refers to these two expressions of contrast of attitude, and therefore realizes a *plane-change* (Sinclair 1981), which entails a change of posture. *The question* also refers to the contrast. Hamlet expresses three different postures in eleven syllables; the passage continues in the same vein, and indeed there are several more 'Hamlets' to come; if we try to identify the smallest number of different Hamlets, this depends on one's interpretation of some of the passages, whether they are consistent with an earlier position or not.[4]

The ability to internalize speaker change undoubtedly adds another dimension of meaning potential to text, and is characteristic of the processes I want to describe in this chapter. Speaker change is an observable physical event which structures and advances a discourse; one of the key features of verbal interaction is that participants are separate and distinct individuals, and they are *discontinuous* (Weinrich 2000) with respect to each other; it must be assumed that their views and attitudes will differ unpredictably.

We assume, however, that an individual maintains a certain consistency of views and attitudes; of course individuals change and modify their positions, but they do so in accord with social conventions and therefore their behaviour is normally coherent and predictable. But by internalizing speaker change, a single speaker can in a single utterance represent conflicting or even unrelated positions, and thus internalize many features of an interaction:

8    There was an extension phone in the bedroom, but surely Colette had been fast asleep when he left her.

In the first clause of (8) the character is wondering if Colette had listened in to his phone call, and by drawing attention to the extension phone in the bedroom he is allowing the possibility that he was overheard; *but surely* indicates the change in posture, and the remainder of the sentence, by drawing attention to

Colette being asleep, argues against the likelihood that she listened in to his phone call. The two parts of the sentence would sound quite natural from two different speakers, provided only that the verbs are altered from the report tenses they are in:

9   'There is an extension phone in the bedroom.'
     'But surely Colette was asleep when you left her.'

On this evidence, we associate speaker change in dialogic language with this kind of sentence complexity, where different – and often incompatible – positions are expressed within the sentence. By internalizing this feature, monologic language gains the ability to build up an argument within a sentence. Sensitivity to other points of view can be shown without the speaker/writer yielding control. The correlate of speaker change within the sentence is carried by a main clause and is called a change of posture.

## Illocution

Changes of posture occur in complex sentences, defined as sentences which contain more than one main clause. Whenever a second or subsequent main clause is decided upon, the opportunity arises to choose a new posture.

There is another choice that becomes available at the same point, and that is the choice of mood – whether declarative, interrogative or imperative. This choice can easily be seen as an internalization of the *performative* or *illocutionary* aspect of discourse (Austin 1962).

In establishing posture as a linguistic category, we began with the notion that one speaker in each utterance adopts one posture, and added the complexity by internalizing speaker change, so that within one utterance a speaker could elaborate his or her discourse through behaving as if he or she moved between or among different personae. For dealing with sentences as speech acts, we mount a similar argument. The starting point is that each utterance can perform one speech act, and often does; however the meaning of a speech act can be internalized so that the notion of a complex speech act arises, where main clauses choose different moods, but only one speech act results.

In the early analysis of spoken discourse, there was a distinction made between *move* and *act*, which it is helpful to recall at this point. In Sinclair and Coulthard (1975) a move is defined as the smallest 'free' unit, meaning the smallest unit that can stand as a complete utterance. The structure of moves is in terms of one or more acts, and the choice of the name *act* was deliberately made in order to indicate their relationship to speech acts. The relation between discourse and grammar is indicated by the statement: 'Discourse acts are typically one free clause, plus any subordinate clauses' (Sinclair and Coulthard 1975: 23; see clause complex, p. 110 below).

This distinction, between the possibility of making an independent mood choice (an act, a main clause) and the actual making of one (a move) is internalized in sentence grammar. Within a posture, there can be more than one main clause, with different mood choices, but only one of them is a speech act in the ongoing discourse structure. Thus a move in discourse has the dialogic potential of being a complete utterance in itself, and the monologic potential of building longer utterances.

In classroom discourse, the following examples show how an act, in company with another one, loses its independent choice of speech act, and provides the speaker with the possibility of a greater range and flexibility at the rank of move:

> 10   *Teacher*: Those letters have special names – do you know what it is
>
> (Sinclair and Coulthard 1975: 64)[5]

> 11   *Teacher:* What's the next one mean – you don't often see that one around here
>
> (Ibid.: 67)

> 12   *Teacher:* The first quiz is this – can you fill in this sentence – see if you can do it in your books
>
> (Ibid.: 63)

In no. 10 and no. 11 the illocutionary force of the utterance is that of an elicitation, triggered by the interrogative clauses, and the declarative clauses – at the beginning in no. 10 and at the end in no. 11 – allow more detail and context for the question. In no. 12 the overall force is that of a directive, going with the imperative mood of the last clause, with the preceding declarative and interrogative clauses giving a supportive introduction to the task.

It appears that there is a tendency towards an order of precedence among the three types of initiation; if one of them has a directive force then the whole posture is directive, and the other main clauses lose their independent contribution to the speech act structure; if there is no directive, the elicitation takes precedence over the informative. This tendency is also noted in sentence grammar in the written language:

> 13   If you are not a lark, you might have to invest money in getting up: try a costly telephone alarm call or one of those weird teamaking machines.

The overall illocution of no. 13 is directive, and the declarative main clause is preparatory; it takes the edge off the 'command' force of the directive and helps to make the sentence into a rather light suggestion.

The internalization of what is illocutionary force in dialogic discourse thus extends the range and subtlety of the deployment of mood choices, and provides an open-ended set of speech acts.

## Interactive potential

Within sentence grammar, only main clauses can select mood; the order of the structural elements in subordinate clauses does not vary, and even if a subordinate clause seems to show an imperative or interrogative structure, it is not interpreted as such. So the first clause in no. 14 below is analysed as an 'inverted conditional', while the first clause in the saying in no. 15 appears to be in the imperative mood, but is interpreted as a subordinate conditional:

14   Had he been faithful, everything would have been all right.

(Jespersen 1933: 371)

15   See Naples and die!

Subordinate clauses with this kind of word order are rare, however, and by far the majority of subordinate clauses in English have the same word order as an ordinary declarative main clause.

A clause without mood choice has no interactive potential; it does not *do* (in Austin's sense) anything in a discourse, but operates within the interactive frame of the main clause to which it is attached. Many grammars treat such clauses as equivalent to elements within the structure of the main clause, calling them 'noun clauses', 'adverbial clauses' and so on, thus reducing their grammatical status to that of a single word.

The loss of postural independence was one step in losing independence, and the loss of illocutionary force another; here is a third, where the clause relinquishes any interactive role at all. Whereas the earlier steps were in complex sentences, the grammar of subordinate clauses takes us into compound sentences, the heart of sentence grammar.

There are several ways in which a subordinate and main clause can combine to extend the range of meanings available. One we have already seen, in example no. 5 above, where a subordinate clause that makes a report is protected from averral. To be able to say something without averring it is a major instance of the flexibility that is made possible by internalization.

At this point in the presentation we change from talking in terms of averring, speech acts and so on, to talking about possible worlds and truth values (Sinclair 1996). This is because discourse terminology is not relevant to most subordinate clauses, which make their meaning within the confines of the grammar of the clause. In the case of reported clauses, it is still reasonable to explain their function in discourse terms, but they can also be explained in terms of possible worlds. A report is a report of an averral (or another speech act) in a possible world, not the world in which the reporting (main) clause operates.[6]

The need to change the parameters of description as we reach subordinate clauses lends support to the idea of the sentence as at a watershed between grammar and discourse. The sentence is commonly put forward as the largest unit in grammar, and the grammars often tail off above the clause, offering very little detail about the larger units. Most grammars are grammars of the clause.

Huddleston (1984) uses the term 'clause complex' to mean one main clause plus any attendant subordinate clauses, and makes this unit the focus of attention rather than the sentence. This avoids paying much attention to sentences which are concatenations of main clauses, which in most grammars are named rather than described, and it suggests that the clause complex is the real upper limit of grammar. The viewpoint of this chapter is different from that of a pure grammarian, and begins with units of discourse rather than grammar; but it arrives at the same watershed from the other side, so to speak. Above the main/subordinate relationship of clauses, the description involves verbal interaction in a direct way; at and below that area there is an important step in abstraction taken; move becomes proposition, averral becomes truth value, and context of situation becomes possible world.

The process of internalization is the same, but the relationship to the dialogic mode has another step added, a switch to focusing attention on the content of the propositions, rather than their value in discourse. A proposition is a clause which could, if deployed appropriately in a discourse, be averred as true by the speaker. But since all but the main clauses are prevented from participating in the discourse, the discussion of their meaning shifts from the discourse to a hypothetical space where possible worlds replace the real world. It was pointed out above that averral involves the commitment of the utterer to the truth of the averral. This means that, unless challenged, the proposition realized by the averral is assigned a positive truth value – a local and provisional one, like all the assignments in discourse. Here is the link between averral and truth value. From a philosophical perspective, having a truth value is a property of a proposition; it does not matter whether it is positive or negative as long as there is a possible method for determining it. Within a discourse, averral is one method of determining truth value.

The normal way of setting out propositions in English is to use the word order of 'Subject–Verb–Object', which is the same as that used by main clauses in declarative mood, and almost all subordinate clauses. They all look like potential averrals (minus any subordinating conjunction, of course), and so make it easy to imagine possible worlds where they might be averred. The impression of a watershed between two different aspects of meaning is also reinforced by the fact that declarative main clauses are simultaneously averrals and propositions.

We have briefly mentioned above the subordinate clauses of report, which displace an utterance from averral; another type of subordination is where the subordinate clause expresses a contingency that applies to the main clause – timing and placing, conditionals, concessionals and all the other kinds of so-called adverbial clauses. This feature makes possible an improvement in precision of statement: the speech act of the main clause is not relevant to the immediate discourse in all circumstances, but only in those that fit the contingency. That is to say, there is at least one possible world where the contingency is true, and where that coincides with the world of the discourse, the speech act of the main clause takes effect; where there is no coincidence, the discourse moves into a possible world where the contingency is true.

There is thus a change in the relationship between language and the context of situation that has far-reaching consequences; instead of the context being a stable framework within which the language makes moves, the propositions – quasi-moves – define themselves with reference to other possible contexts of situation, and in the interpretation of utterances we have to examine whether or not there is a coincidence between the real world and one or more of the possible ones.

Some contingent clauses – for example, those beginning with *since, because, although, while* – indicate that there is a coincidence between the two worlds, and so the speech act of the main clause can be activated. On examination, it can be seen that there is an implication that the proposition realized by the subordinate clause has already been averred and accepted as true in the discourse. If in fact such an acceptance has not happened, then the structure can be used as a device for tucking away in a subordinate clause a proposition which would otherwise have to pass the test of averral.

The contingent clauses thus open up in language a way of communicating in hypothetical terms; one of the principal qualities of human language, distinguishing it from other communication systems, and a prerequisite for expressing science, planning and other key activities in society.

The third principal type of subordination is the elaboration of the noun group by internalizing a clause, usually called a relative clause, of which the sub-variety known as the defining relative clause is the typical case:[7]

16  Helen went across to the phone which was in the far corner.

17  A *phone-in* is a radio or television programme in which people telephone with questions or opinions and their calls are broadcast.

(Cobuild 1997)

As Halliday and Martin point out, this facility allows the formation and expression of complex concepts. This is made very clear in the conventions of definition; a normal definition has as its *definiens* a superordinate followed by one of these clauses (hence the word *defining* in the term). The speech act of definition can be applied cyclically, with the *definiendum* of one definition used as the superordinate in another. The process forms a ladder of increasing conceptual complexity without a corresponding complexity in the linguistic structure, since at the end of each act of definition there is only a simple *definiendum* standing for the whole ladder. Without this facility, the expression of knowledge would be too complicated to be achieved.

In interpreting defining relative clauses the argument is similar to that for contingent clauses; of the whole set of items referred to by the rest of the noun group, the defining property is only true of certain of them. We are no longer confined to possible worlds, because the clauses relate to noun headwords that may well have substantive reality. The defining relative clause makes distinctions, and those distinctions operate in whatever world the clause containing the noun group refers to. The truth value is the criterion for inclusion or exclusion of instances from the set defined.

## Truth value

There are other, simpler phrases which have a similar function in relation to a noun group, but which are not clauses;[8] prepositional phrases are very common:

> 18   The man on the phone said he had no idea.

The phrase 'on the phone' can easily be paraphrased as 'who was on the phone', and now it has a truth value. But before – as a prepositional phrase – it did not have a truth value, or at least not an overt one. The ease of paraphrase suggests a close relationship between clause and phrase, and it can be seen as a further stage of internalization; in the noun group, defining phrases are like clauses that have lost the expression of their truth value. Since the operation of the noun group is the same in both cases, the truth value is still used as the criterion for inclusion in the set, so it must be implicit; this is the main argument for bringing together clauses and phrases, which otherwise have quite different structural roles.

The difference between phrase and clause in the noun group is mainly one of size; phrases allow compression. Compression is not normally an important matter in language, because in turn it reduces redundancy, which is a very important matter. But in the case of the noun group, there is a need sometimes for several defining qualifiers, and if each had to be a clause, the group as a whole would become very long and clumsy to use, and the shorthand of the prepositional phrase is a great help in coping with complexity.[9]

## Semantic potential

There is one final stage in the internalization of moves, via propositions, and this is another feature of the noun group in English. Nouns can modify nouns, so that occasionally there are quite long strings of nouns one after the other in a sentence. In the case of *phone*, we find *kitchen phone, wall phone, vision phone* and *home phone number, Government cross-channel phone cable*.

The semantic properties of these combinations are not the concatenation of the semantic properties of each of the elements, but a substantial reduction of them. The component words lose some of their independence of meaning, and new meanings are made possible by our interpretation of the intersection of their meanings.

There is a price to pay for this versatile and economical structure. Like the defining phrases dealt with above, the principle of compression that is working here leads to a loss of explicitness, so that if the precise relationship between the component words is not already known, it is not retrievable from the structure.

A *vision phone* may be what it seems, a futuristic phone with vision as well as sound, but it would not be safe to define it as such – it might just mean a smart new design.

Each combination of two or more nouns is capable of paraphrase as a phrase or clause which makes the organization of the meaning explicit, so the juxtaposition of nouns can be seen as a further step in internalization. This time there is a loss of the range of meaning associated with each noun, as against the acquisition of a simple and flexible way of expressing complex concepts.

The building up of noun strings is open-ended, and can be used ad hoc, for example if one cannot remember a word. But when individual words are used very frequently with others, their co-occurrence begins to have a meaning of its own, like *phone-in* above (no. 17), or *phone call* (telephone conversation), *phone box* (telephone booth), *phone book* (telephone directory). Here there is not just restriction on the combination of meanings, but sometimes extension of one of them on a literal level – *box* – or figuratively – *call*.

Apart from the everyday, largely unconscious process of compounding, the combination of nouns is an important process used in the making of technical terms, which are ever more in demand for the recording of knowledge and the management of peoples.

## Conclusion

This chapter has attempted to trace a process of internalization through several steps, from the largest units of grammar (sentences) to the smallest (words). At each step there is a loss of independence on behalf of the unit that is internalized, and a gain in complexity in the unit to which it now relates. Here is a summary of the argument.

In the grammar of sentences, it is possible to choose more than one main clause. When chosen, a second or subsequent main clause can choose to have or not to have:

a  a new and independent choice which creates an internal representation of speaker change, called posture;
b  a new and independent choice which creates an internal representation of speech act, called mood.

With each main clause, it is possible to choose one or more subordinate clauses. These are of three main kinds:

i  the reported clause creates an internal representation of discourse, without the commitment of averral;
ii  the contingent clause creates an internal representation of an event in a possible world, without the commitment of factuality;
iii  the relative clause creates an internal representation of an event which may be factual or not, and whose relevance to the sentence is confined to the elaboration of a concept.

Relative clauses operate within the structure of noun groups. As alternatives to them, it is possible to use phrases that have the same function but are shorter. Phrases do not express full propositions, and therefore do not have an explicit truth value. Such phrases can be seen as internalizations of relative clauses.

Still further compression (and inexplicitness) can be got by juxtaposing nouns together, leaving the listener or reader to work out the precise relationship between them. Because of a paraphrase relationship that makes it possible to expand the noun strings into phrases or relative clauses, the component words can be seen as internalizations of such phrases or clauses.

In terms of loss and gain, the process can be presented as follows:

A move loses its property of constituting an independent utterance:
the sentence gains the facility of posture as a property of main clauses;

a posture loses its property of constituting an independent speech act:
the sentence gains the system of mood as a property of main clauses;

a main clause loses its property of interactive potential:
the sentence gains the subordinate clause as a property of the clause complex;

a subordinate clause loses its property of truth value:
the sentence gains the qualifying phrase as a property of the noun group;

a word loses its semantic potential:
the sentence gains the noun modifier as a property of the noun group
(leading to compounds and technical terms).

Much of the complexity of sentence grammar, and therefore of grammatical meaning and monologic discourse, can be traced by this argument to features of dialogic discourse through processes of internalization.

In developing this hypothesis, it was necessary to alter the terms of the description halfway through, in the clause complex. Whereas it is not difficult to see the reported clause as an internalization of a discourse element, the contingent clause requires a switch to a hypothetical dimension where the dynamics of the ongoing discourse are not directly affected by the interactive potential of the clauses. It is interesting that the clause complex is the unit that grammarians often regard as the upper limit of grammar, whether explicitly or in their choices of study items.

The 'top-down' approach of this chapter suggests that if so many of the features of sentence structure can be traced back to dialogic discourse, it is unsafe to separate grammar below the main clause from grammar above it.

# 7   A tool for text explication

This chapter was written as a contribution to the Festschrift of Göran Kjellmer of the University of Göteborg, Sweden. It explores the use of corpus evidence in the explication of discourse strategies, and thus brings together the twin themes of Chapter 1. It tries to avoid the pitfalls of Critical Discourse Analysis by focusing on an emotionally charged incident and describing how the language makes its meaning, without taking a stance on the moral problem involved. The Festschrift was entitled *A Wealth of English*, edited by Karin Aijmer, and published in 2001 in Göteborg: *Acta Universitatis Gothoburgensis* no. 81.

## Introduction

This chapter reviews some of the principal ways in which scholars have set about the job of describing the communicative impact of a text, and suggests that evidence of usage drawn from a large text corpus offers a new and powerful tool for the analyst. It can provide information about the meaning that was not previously available, indicate important areas for further investigation, and refine the analyst's intuitive notions – as well as confirming and supporting the impressions that a person with command of the language can access without effort.

In the second part the chapter gives a brief illustration of the application of corpus evidence, using a short extract from a long text, evaluating the phraseology using the linguistic resources of a large corpus.

The study of language text in the scholarly community seems to be responsive to an invisible pendulum, steadily swinging between subjectivity and objectivity. The basic task is the explication of text, and while some scholars reject any systematic approach, relying instead on a direct appeal to the sensitivities of their audience, many prefer to make use of descriptive schemes, claiming that they have several advantages over the self-reliance of the individual.

The application of a shared and explicit descriptive apparatus allows the treatment of one text to be readily related to others, and generalizations can be formulated that were not visible until the structures were expressed in a common terminology. Another powerful argument is that the explicitness of the description will enable analyses to be replicated by others, providing an accuracy check of the highest scientific pedigree. The public availability of the terminology and descriptive apparatus also makes for clarity of exposition, and lays a foundation for critical discussion.

Text study, if thorough, is inherently slow and laborious, and to compound the problem, one principle of the objective school is that analysis should normally be comprehensive. The reason for this is that language patterning is too rich for uncontrolled choice; if the researcher can choose only some of the language patterns, then almost anything, and its opposite, can be demonstrated. So if analysis is to be selective then the selection has to be justified and applied uniformly. In recent years the prospects of automating analysis with computers has raised the hopes of researchers, because of the potential gain in efficiency with the guarantee of objectivity that computers offer.

But ultimately the achievements of any systematic analysis will fall short of the perceived goals and standards set by the guardians of intellectual truth. Since at extremely refined levels of interpretation there is almost certain to be a personal element, no shared system of analysis will be considered adequate. This reservation, of course, applies to all areas of intellectual enquiry.

The results of systematic linguistic description fall seriously short of even the most generous view of adequacy; this despite a number of significant improvements in method and extensions in scope in the last half-century. The explication of texts, as carried out following the example of I.A. Richards (1929) in the 1950s in programmes entitled 'Close reading and composition', was commendably text-sensitive but did not refer to any external descriptive method; it was focused on literary texts. A new wave of descriptive linguists in the 1960s developed this approach using the new grammars of the time, called it 'stylistics', and extended its scope to include all textual material rather than just literary. Linguistic descriptions, especially those of grammar and phonetics, were applied to short texts and some of the mechanisms for creating meaning were identified (e.g. Fowler 1966).

Stylistics had a rather short period in fashion; it suffered from two major problems. One was that the linguistic theories of the day could not provide a foundation on which a stable descriptive system could be built that was powerful enough to cope with complex text; indeed that problem has still to be solved. The other was that linguistic descriptions, while strong on grammar and phonetics/phonology, were weak or non-existent in the areas of lexis, semantics, and discourse – hence the places where shared, fairly objective description could be presented were sporadic and unsatisfactory.

Scholars began to feel that they could get no farther along this road, and so there was a tripartite parting of the ways. Those with central literary interests incorporated aspects of linguistic analysis within an essentially subjective 'literary stylistics'. They narrowed their focus to concentrate on literary texts, and specifically withdrew from the move to extend the methodology of stylistics to make it relevant to any text; indeed one of the central tenets of the proponents of linguistic stylistics – that there is nothing unique about the literary language – was never popular among literary critics.

However, the pursuit of style and structure in non-literary texts had established itself and attracted a variety of scholars, including some from the sociological end of the spectrum, which became a clearly identifiable group. This work also assumed an essentially subjective attitude – in this case an ideological one. The use of language as a means of social manipulation became a hot topic across the spectrum from linguistic to cultural studies, giving shape to new language syllabuses in the schools. Considerable use was made of the growing kit of linguistic tools, sometimes for their own sake and sometimes to deflect emphasis from the underlying political education that was going on (Fowler et al. 1979; Kress and Hodge 1979).

At this time, linguistics was just becoming sensitive to language as interaction, and a third group of scholars was making advances in the description of text above the sentence, particularly in the study of spoken conversation and academic text.[1] 'Discourse Analysis' was the name given to the former, and it gradually broadened out; 'Text Linguistics' was used for the latter, and the areas gradually overlapped. This research thrust was a return to the more objective style of analysis, with a substantial descriptive apparatus that claimed to account for a large proportion of the meaningful patterns. Powerful toolkits were placed in the hands of a generation of researchers and substantial results obtained, with notable influences on applications such as language teaching.

Once again, though, the toolkits were not powerful enough – they did not explain everything. Inferences, intentions, strategies, etc., lurked about, slipped through the nets, and not even the refinements of prototype theory, schema theory and the like made these objectively validated systems fully acceptable. The pendulum swung again, and scholars distanced themselves from the 'elaborate hierarchical framework', the 'exhaustive structural model of discourse organization' and 'descriptivism of this sort' (Jaworski and Coupland 1999: 33–4). The emphasis of such variants as 'critical discourse analysis' was on qualitative analysis, which meant subjectivity.

Some influential figures in the subjective approach to discourse do advocate recourse to linguistic analysis; Fairclough (1992: 193), for example, says 'there is a real need for relevant models of language; for frameworks which turn the insights of linguistics into comprehensible and usable forms.'

In recent years the availability of large general corpora for consultation by the academic community has offered another dimension of objectivity. Instead of a commentator having to rely exclusively on his or her sensitivity to language, and the chances that an audience will reveal matching sensitivity, reference can be made to the huge accumulation of usage that is lodged in the corpora, providing evidence of shades of meaning and subtleties of expression that have not until now been transferable into the shared area. This is the resource that I want to examine, as a tool for the interpretation of texts. Louw (1993) has given a lead in the literary field, and Stubbs (1996) has used statistical corpus evidence in the classification of texts.

Indeed, Fairclough (1992: 217, n. 4) refers to a corpus for evidence to support his intuitions about the use of *killer* in the phrase *killer riot*. He is lucky in having as his amanuensis Geoffrey Leech, a leading corpus linguist, who consults the corpora held at Lancaster University, but unfortunately there is not nearly enough evidence because the total size of the three corpora available is but three million words and *killer* only occurs seven times followed by 'a lexical item'.

In the current version of *The Bank of English*, *killer* occurs 12,404 times, followed by a noun 4,837 times. Within this raw total there are around 3,000 which match the pattern of *killer* followed by a noun which *killer* modifies. The principal collocations are:

The main semantic grouping of the collocates is around the notion of illness – *cell, disease, bug, virus, drug, brain* (which is a further modifier of a head which is principally *disease, bug*). Sport accounts for the next group – *instinct, blow, touch, punch, goal, pass*. Animals seem to be the next, with *whales* and *bees* (and *ants* not far behind), but it should be pointed out that a number of the instances of collocation with *instinct(s)*, *whale(s)*, and *bee(s)* are the proper names of pop groups and songs, and a notable racehorse. I have not attempted to remove these in this quick survey, but they would be largely removable in a more thorough study.

*Table 7.1* Principal collocations of *killer* + noun[2]

| Collocate | Occurrences | Total |
| --- | --- | --- |
| cells | 191 | |
| cell | 34 | 225 |
| disease | 133 | |
| diseases | 56 | 189 |
| whales | 100 | |
| whale | 86 | 186 |
| instinct | 179 | |
| blow | 90 | |
| bug | 69 | |
| touch | 64 | |
| virus | 42 | |
| bees | 39 | |
| punch | 35 | |
| drug | 37 | |
| goal | 37 | |
| brain | 31 | |
| pass | 22 | |
| nanny | 18 | |

At the bottom of the list, *killer nanny* is the sole instance of reference to a person. Farther down the list of collocates will be found several more, especially in the headlines of the popular press – *nurse, nun, doc, wife, hubby, mum, dad, driver,* and *rapist,* but they refer to individuals rather than groups, and in the overall stream of language they are not very prominent.

There is one instance of *killer riot* among the 12,404 occurrences, in a headline from an Australian newspaper reporting an event in South Africa (where Fairclough's example came from):

Church torched in killer riot.

Words close to riot in *Roget's Thesaurus* (www.thesaurus.com) do not collocate with killer at all; *revolt, rebellion, mutiny, rising, uprising, insurrection, row, commotion, disturbance, commotion, tumult, uproar* do not appear next to killer. There are 13 instances of *killer strike,* which Roget lists as close in meaning to riot under the heading of 'disobedience' – however all the corpus instances are from football reporting, not industrial relations. There are two instances of *killer outbreak,* but these refer to outbreaks of infectious diseases, not gatherings of people.

The conclusion is not only that the word *riot* hardly ever collocates with *killer,* but neither do other words with similar meanings. The characteristic patterns of semantic choice of *killer,* summarized above, are very different indeed. Just possibly, since the only example of *killer riot* in *The Bank of English* refers to a similar event also in South Africa, such a phrase may be more accessible in the local variety of English, but I have no means of checking that; it is accepted in corpus research that a single instance is not evidence.

In a more recent paper, Fairclough (1999: 62) examines the 'metaphor of flexibility' in recent economic writing. This becomes 'the discourse of flexibility used within this struggle over global economy', and is summarized as the efforts of multinational companies 'to make flexibility – the new global capitalism – even more of a reality than it already is'.

Although concepts can be distinguished from words, they are closely related, if not systematically correlated. In particular, evidence concerning people's attitude to concepts and evaluation of them will mainly be found in linguistic expression, in the contexts of use of the words and phrases that express the concepts. It is difficult to conceive of a communicative process in a speech community whereby a word expressing a concept that had unpleasant consequences for the majority of citizens always occurred in benign and uplifting contexts, unless the speech community was created by George Orwell, and all communication was under strict control. So it is relevant to examine the use of the words *flexible* and *flexibility* to see the textual reflection of the way the concept is being received and handled. Fairclough's repeated phrase 'the discourse of flexibility', and his use of illustrative quotation, indicate his respect for the way people actually use language.

This is where the large and broadly based corpus can provide us with evidence beyond the capacity of any individual to inspect. For example, the flexibility reported in Fairclough's paper is represented as uniformly undesirable for those who are obliged to be flexible, and yet there are plenty of instances in the corpus of *flexible* and *flexibility* used with approval by people other than the captains of industry. In financial matters to have *flexible arrangements* and *plans* is mainly seen as a good thing, and in labour relations such things as *flexible working hours* are seen by employees as advantages; the collocation of *flexibility* and *freedom* is strong, and its expression is not restricted to any one social group.

There is of course evidence to support Fairclough's concerns; his perception of the importance of the concept carried in the words is confirmed by their frequency (13,318 in all) and centrality in a range of texts. But there is also considerable evidence of other well-informed attitudes to the concept. To give one example, the most significant collocate of *flexible*, as measured by t-score, is *more* and the top two for *flexibility* are *greater* and *more*. There are other indications (e.g. *less, degree, increased, considerable*) that the way in which flexibility is perceived is of a gradual change and not a sudden imposition. Fairclough makes no mention of this prominent feature of the use of the words, and his argument is weaker from overlooking it.

From the above it can be confirmed that citation of 'used language'[3] proves nothing in itself about language unless the process of selectivity that is inevitable in such circumstances is controlled. The way in which massed corpus evidence can show the ideological trappings of a word or phrase is very good news for those students of discourse who are prepared to accept a moderate discipline of objectivity.

## Text example: background

During the summer of 2000, the population of Britain became intensely interested in a news story that occupied the front pages again and again. It raised unprecedented moral, emotional, religious and legal issues, and had seemingly endless ramifications. This very complex story will be briefly summarized.

It concerns the birth of twin girls who were physically joined – what used to be known as 'Siamese twins' in English. Unfortunately they shared vital organs, and so could not both survive if separated; on the other hand medical opinion was united that neither would survive if they remained joined, because of the strain on the shared organs. The twins thus had conflicting interests.

The twins were given the legal names of Jodie and Mary. Jodie was the stronger one, having all the vital organs in working order; Mary was not so endowed. If the twins were separated, Mary could not survive the operation. It was thought that Jodie would survive, but there were considerable doubts about her chances of a good quality of life in the longer term.

This became a classic case of a well-known moral and legal dilemma – in what circumstances, if any, is it defensible to sacrifice one person to facilitate the survival of another? Since there was a good chance that Jodie could survive, but only if she was separated, was that reason enough to cut short Mary's life, given that she was only expected to live a matter of weeks anyway? The level of public debate was intense, and major figures of state and church became involved.

The parents resisted pressure to authorize the operation; the twins had individual legal representation and the affair went to the High Court, which ruled in favour of the operation. An appeal was made to the Appeal Court, the second highest court in England, and again the unanimous decision of three judges was to authorize the operation. The family decided not to press their case in the House of Lords, and acquiesced. The operation took place on 7 November, and was 'successful', in that Jodie survived.

### The text

In his ruling, Lord Justice Ward, the senior Judge of Appeal, set out the argument behind his decision in great detail. I would like to explicate the last few lines of the paragraph immediately before the one where the judge announces his decision.

> Mary has always been fated for early death: her capacity to live has been fatally compromised. Though Mary has a right to life she has little right to be alive. She is alive because and only because, to put it bluntly but nonetheless accurately, she sucks the lifeblood of Jodie and her parasitic living will soon be the cause of Jodie ceasing to live.

The phrase 'right to life' has already occurred in the paragraph and in the one before, and here it is subtly contrasted with 'right to be alive'. I will return to this contrast later, but would like to start with the judge's comment about his own language:

> to put it bluntly but nonetheless accurately

He distinguishes between two ways of saying – bluntness and accuracy – and these strike a chord with the ways in which linguists describe word meaning. Accuracy suggests semantic classification; correctly labelling something; bluntness draws our attention to the effect that some wording might have or be intended to have. Whereas traditional work on language description has concentrated on accuracy, recent work in discourse analysis has emphasized 'doing things with words'.[4] Current work in corpus linguistics makes the further claim that all complete *lexical items* realize an element of meaning which is the function of the item in its cotext and context. Let us briefly review these types of meaning.

### The analysis of meaning

Semantics has made a similar distinction to that of the judge by talking of *denotative* and *connotative* meaning. The former is classificatory, placing the *definiendum* correctly in relation to other words and concepts. It is the principal tool of lexicography, terminography, etc. The latter is an occasional additional feature of a word's meaning, a 'shade' of meaning, carrying perhaps a negative orientation or a feeling of informality.

A slightly different contrast is made in lexicography in the terms *literal* and *figurative* – or sometimes *metaphorical* – or at other times *idiomatic*, but whereas an item can have both denotative and connotative meaning at the same time, the other categories are mutually exclusive. *Literal* meaning, like denotative, suggests that there is a simple and direct link between the word and something in the world that it signifies – the Saussurean duality of *signifié* and *signifiant*. Literal meaning contrasts with the other terms, because for them the link between *signifiant* and *signifié* is more problematic; some imaginative act of interpretation has to be performed to make the link. While the terms each have a slightly different focus – *idiomatic*, for example, tends to be used of phrases rather than single words – they refer to the same area of interpretation.

In recent years the notion of *pragmatic* meaning has come to the fore, and is highlighted in a number of dictionaries. This is also sporadic and unpredictable, and mainly seen as an alternative way of interpreting the meaning of – usually – a phrase. Pragmatic meaning derives from Austin's (1962) *speech acts*, and is thus centrally concerned with the effect of saying something.

The problem with this tangle of terms is that the literal/denotative kind of meaning is seen as the central and obligatory one, with the others as rather unpredictable variants. It arises from the status of the word as the presumed carrier of meaning (turning a blind eye to the hundreds of common words which can hardly be said to denote anything), whereas the lexical item is characteristically phrasal, although it can be realized in a single word. I proposed (Sinclair 1998) that an element of the structure of a lexical item should be the *semantic prosody*, which is the only obligatory element apart from an invariant *core* word or words – those by which the item can be detected.

It is called a prosody because, like prosodies in phonology, there are often uncertainties about its exact realization, and it ranges over the whole lexical item, in that all the other elements are interpreted within the framework it provides, including classifying aspects of meaning. The important matter is the effect, i.e. what communicative job the lexical item performs, and that is expressed or pointed up by the semantic prosody.

## *Phraseology*

'Putting it bluntly' suggests the use of words and phrases with strong negative prosodies, whereas 'accurately' means selecting meanings that are appropriate to the objects and events under discussion, and their properties.

It is perhaps just as well that the judge warns his audience that he is going to speak bluntly, because his social image is of one who does not normally stoop to such verbal manipulation, but rather uses 'measured' language. Judges are distanced from ordinary mortals by a variety of semiotic features and rituals, and are assumed, however unrealistically, to inhabit a world of rationality, where semantic accuracy should be the only consideration. Qualities assigned to them include impartiality, restraint, and even a touch of old-fashioned other-worldliness, as when in novels they use the word 'pantechnicon' instead of 'removal van'.

In real life there is no such purity, but here the judge not only takes off his semantic gloves, but also says he is going to. He has not only to express his judgment in a legally sound manner but also, in view of the intense public interest, to persuade ordinary readers that his view of the problem is the right one.

In the first sentence of our quotation the words *fated* and *fatally* occur, words which are associated even in classificatory semantics with unfortunate consequences. In the *Encarta English Dictionary*, for example (http://dictionary.msn.com), the first sense of *fatally* is 'so as to cause death: in a manner that results in death', and in the second sense, the same thing is said for 'ruin'. Correspondingly, there are two groupings of collocates following the word in the corpus: physical – *injured, wounded, shot, stabbed* – and institutional – *flawed, undermined, weakened, damaged*. The phrase in our passage, *fatally compromised*, occurs 11 times, just enough to make a significant t-score, but in none of the instances does it refer to physical death. Things like images, judicial processes and attack schemes are fatally compromised, not lives. So although the judge uses a word that in much of its occurrence is associated with death, the particular collocation he chooses is associated with institutional ruin.

The Encarta definition of *fated* is 'apparently decided by fate: believed to be controlled or predetermined by fate'. Overwhelmingly, the corpus adds a negative prosody; over 80 per cent of the 1,462 instances are prefaced by *ill-*. The combination *fated for* is not common, but in its 13 occurrences the following word has mainly institutional reference (*custody, transportation, oblivion*) and there is a tendency to use it a little light-heartedly (*jazz*) and even ironically (*fated for success*). So at this point the judge is using the 'heavy' words *fated* and *fatally*, but using them in mild collocations, taking the sting out of them.

The other phrase in the first sentence of the passage is *capacity to live*. Again it is not a common collocation of either word; verbs such as *produce, absorb, develop* and *carry* dominate the collocational profile. There are 3,535 instances of *capacity to* followed by a verb, and in only 11 cases is this the verb *live*. Moreover, in four cases there is an adverbial following *live* and indicating how the person should live, twice there is the cognate object *life*, with an adjective in between, twice it is the phrase *live up to* once each *live with, live and let live*, and *live in*. So there is no parallel case in the corpus to the phrase in this text, and so the reader has to make an interpretation that adjusts the normal meanings of *capacity* and *live* so that they make some sort of sense.

In the last sentence, after the judge warns about his bluntness, there is some strong language by any standard. *Parasitic* is mainly used in a fairly neutral sense (living off another organism) in scientific contexts, and collocates principally with *disease(s), wasp(s), infection(s)* and *worm*. But in approximately 10 per cent of cases it has a human headword, or one which concerns human affairs and behaviour – and it is here that the unpleasantness comes in. Nouns like *alien, exploiter, excres-*

*cences, sharks and liars, useless beggars, idleness, bastards, swine* give the flavour of the semantic prosody of *parasitic* when applied to a human being. Whereas *parasitic worm* is in a scientific essay a purely classificatory description, the same phrase applied to a person is a serious insult. To call Mary parasitic on Jody is technically accurate, but since Mary is a person it is also gravely disparaging.

*Sucks the lifeblood* is also accurate, but the phraseology is again dramatic. We should first consider the choice of *lifeblood* rather than just *blood*, because they appear to have, in terms of classificatory semantics, the same referent; there is no blood that is not, ultimately, someone's lifeblood.

There are 370 instances of *lifeblood* in the corpus, and so to compare I looked at 370 of the over 40,000 instances of blood, and found collocates of both as follows:

> *blood*:        pressure, red, cells, heart, vessels, high, transfusion
> *lifeblood*:   economy, game, business, sport, city, oil, industry

Clearly *lifeblood* is used in a metaphorical sense, while *blood* remains pretty literal. And it is normal for the metaphorical sense to have a more dramatic orientation. In the various combinations of *blood*, the verb *suck* (i.e. *suck/s/ed/ing*), *life* and *lifeblood*, there are echoes of 'parasite', plenty of gloomy scenarios, and occasional occurrences of the vocabulary of vampirism. One recurrent phrase (19 instances) is *blood-sucking*, concerning usury or vampires. We are moving from drama to melodrama.

In the passage we are studying, *lifeblood* is used literally; the emotional charge remains, however, and the associations derived from the usages noted above make a powerful semantic brew, more than justifying the judge's warning of bluntness.

Less dramatically, the paragraph comes to an end on the phrase *ceasing to live*. This is a synonym of *die*, and the few instances in the corpus confirm its euphemistic semantic prosody. It might seem unnecessary, after the colourful language of the previous clauses, to quieten down so much, but there are two possible reasons for the choice of phrase. One is that, having used such emotionally charged language, not expected of a judge in a lengthy statement, he needs to return to a more measured style; the other is that he needs such a quiet segment in view of what happens next.

In the next sentence following, the first sentence of the next paragraph, he makes another blunt statement, but attributes it to Jodie.

Jodie is entitled to protest that Mary is killing her.

Both in order to give this protest its maximum effect, and to maintain a proper judicial distance from it, the judge has to make a division between it and his own 'bluntness' in the previous paragraph.

In this quiet ending of the paragraph there is a phrase that carries a definite semantic prosody of foreboding: *the cause of*. The principal collocates of this fairly common phrase (5,549 instances) are *death, crash, accident* and *fire*. Stubbs (1995) has already pointed out that the apparently neutral word *cause* is typically associated with unpleasant events, and this phrasing is a particularly clear set of evidence in support of his contention.

We now turn to the central statement. The biggest problem of communication that the judge has to overcome is to explain why, if everyone has equal rights in the matter of living, some are, in Orwell's words, 'more equal than others'. This he does in the central short sentence, which is also the pivotal element of his judgment:

> Though Mary has a right to life, she has little right to be alive.

There is a clear contrast set up, apparently between the noun *life* and the predicate *be alive*, and the reader is invited to work out the difference in meaning between what seem to be synonymous phrasings.

*A* right to something, or *the* right to something, is a matter of principle and is not directly related to events. It is due to everyone no matter who they are or how they behave; they do not have to earn it and they can only lose it under certain known circumstances. The phrases are not always glossed in this absolute way, and there are Orwells about – one citation reads:

> some have less of a right to life than others

Not so the judge, who says earlier in the paragraph from which the quotation comes:

> Into each scale goes their right to life. This right is universal: we all share it equally. The scales remain in balance.

But there is another usage of *right* that can be found in the phrases *every right to*, *no right to*. Here the sense is of what one deserves or is entitled to, rather than an inalienable right. It is a gradable notion, you can have more or less of this kind of right, and there are three examples in the corpus of *no right to be alive*. The phrase *little right to be alive* is an example of this sense.

The distinction is fine but clear. I have not found a one-volume dictionary that points it out, but the two senses are noted in *Roget's Thesaurus* as adjacent categories of moral obligations (VI/IV/1). Although there are only two instances in the corpus of *little right to*, it clearly joins *every* and *no*:

> they can feel they have little right to be wanting more.
> Those in authority have little right to complain.

So if *right* occurs in a structure where it is prefaced by an article or a definite determiner such as *her, your,* then the phrase refers to what is due to someone; if it is prefaced by *every, little* or *no,* being indefinite determiners, then the phrase refers to what someone deserves. The opposition of the noun *life* and the predicate *be alive*, which is where we started, is needed to establish that there are two different concepts, but is not integral to the contrast in meaning. The two phrasings could almost be exchanged for each other without destroying the meaning contrast.

The judge's cunning antithesis thus allows him to move one's entitlement to life/live from an absolute right to a relative one, and paves the way for later, when he says of the principle of the sanctity of life, 'This is not an absolute rule'.

Let us now summarize this detail. The passage quoted begins with (a) expressions of the inevitability of Mary not living long, using words of drama like *fated* and *fatally*, but putting them in bland contexts that take a lot of their steam away. Then after the central statement (b) which establishes that one's entitlement to live is not an absolute, there is (c) a short section of quite violent language, alienating the reader from Mary, and (d) the paragraph ends on a sombre and quiet note, contemplating the sad possibility of the death of Jodie.

During the passage the focus shifts from Mary to Jodie; Mary is named in the early part of the passage, and is the subject of five of the clauses; latterly it is Jodie who is named (twice following the proposition *of*). The next paragraph, whose first sentence is quoted above, focuses on Jodie, and the way is open to pursue Jodie's interests, which is what happens in the rest of the judgment.

## Conclusion

Whatever personal views readers may take on this extraordinary problem and the judgment made by the Appeal Court – and I have tried not to take sides – the wording of the judgment can be seen as subtle and effective. The classificatory semantic meanings are precise and the prosodic semantic meanings are highly charged, especially immediately after the 'bluntness' warning. While any competent user of English would be likely to respond to the passage in much the way the judge intended, the mechanics of its construction are not immediately obvious.

I deliberately chose a passage which was likely to engage any commentator at a personal level, and therefore where, with an exclusively subjective approach to explication, it would be difficult to remain neutral. The availability of a corpus as a point of reference gives some objectivity, not only because of the vast store of usage that it contains, but also because it allows the commentator to keep a distance between his or her own sensitivities and the job in hand. But perhaps the greatest gain is the enhanced clarity with which we can see the operation of language in the creation of meaning, not only the classificatory kind, which linguists have long been able to analyse, but also the more slippery kinds of meaning. The contrast, for example, between *blood* and *lifeblood* is crystal-clear in the concordances to the two words, but not retrievable by intuition.

Not all the effects need the computer and the concordance. The associations of *suck* and *blood* will be obvious to most. But others are not. The discovery that the combination *fated for* is often used fairly light-heartedly; that *fatally comprom-*

*ised* is usually associated with ruin rather than death, that one's *capacity to live* is an unusual phrase that needs interpretation on the spot; that the phrases *a right to* something and *little right to* something refer to different kinds of right, that *parasitic* is only insulting when applied to people, and that *the cause of* is foreboding – for most people these will all be new observations about the language they use daily without effort; facts of English that lie below the surface, usually below consciousness, that have their effect on meaning but are difficult to pin down without external evidence and appropriate tools. Those who, on reading this explication, feel sure that they had this information available all along, should beware of what Bill Louw calls '20/20 hindsight' (Louw 1993: 173).

In the passage chosen it becomes obvious that the only reason for uttering the words is to make the semantic prosodies that we have identified; first, to confirm, somewhat distantly, that Mary's fate is sealed anyway, and there is nothing that can be done for her; second to establish that no one has an absolute right to live regardless of other circumstances; third to present Mary as a malevolent pressure on Jodie, and finally to identify with Jodie's sad plight.

Finally, I would like to point out that the legal position exposed serious problems for the medical authorities, for whom the Hippocratic oath is absolute regardless of how it is realized in the day-to-day exercise of their profession. In this case they were forced into hypocrisy that was totally predictable. Lord Justice Ward made it clear in his judgment:

> The separation will result in certain death for Mary within minutes of the common aorta being severed.

*The Guardian* report of the operation on 7 November 2000 includes the following:

> 'Unfortunately, despite all the efforts of the medical team, Mary sadly died,' a hospital spokesman said.

# Part III

# Lexis and grammar

# 8   The lexical item

This chapter follows directly on from Chapter 2, and organizes the information presented there into a structural model suitable for lexis. A new example is exhaustively analysed to check the categories. The origin of the paper was a talk given at an invited seminar on semantics at the University of Münster, Germany. Papers from the seminar were published, like this one, in *Contrastive Lexical Semantics*, ed. E. Weigand, Amsterdam: John Benjamins, 1998.

## Introduction

In the early days of computational lexicology, some 40 years ago, it was felt important to distinguish between a *word* and a *lexical item*. This was a period for emphasizing the complexity of language, and proposing abstract categories of language form to escape from the confines of surface phenomena; procedural models, like Immediate Constituent Grammar (e.g. Stageberg 1966: 262 ff.) were held in suspicion because position and sequence were non-negotiable. On the other hand, Firth (1957b) made a distinction between 'sequence', the physical positioning of linguistic events relative to each other, and 'order', realized mainly by sequence, which was an abstract representation of language form.[1]

Hence an orthographic word was recognized as a string of characters lying between spaces, but the equivalent lexical unit had greater freedom, sometimes being more than a word, and possibly even less than a word in extent, with some variation and discontinuity. At the time it was felt that in most cases the physical and the formal categories would coincide exactly, but there was a small amount of superficial evidence to justify the distinction (Sinclair 1966). Words such as *another, maybe, wherever* were so obviously concatenations of otherwise separate words that little phrases such as *in order to, as if, of course* could easily be interpreted as essentially the same structures with the word space(s) retained. Compounds and (in English) phrasal verbs were so important that large sections of the morphology (for compounds) and substantial digressions in the syntax (for phrasal verbs) were regularly devoted to these in descriptive publications. The phrasal verb resisted all efforts to accommodate it in a description where word and lexical item were fused.

Idioms and other phraseological conventions were regarded as important by the powerful language teaching lobby, but as little more than a nuisance by grammarians and lexicographers. Is there any point in analysing 'Don't count your chickens before they're hatched'? On the one hand, it looks like a well-formed sentence of two clauses, but on the other hand there seem to be hardly any alternatives to the succession of word choices, and a grammatical analysis in such circumstances has little value if one believes that meaning arises from choice.[2]

At this time, computers were just beginning to cope with text rather than numbers, and they were ill-equipped for the task, both in hardware provision and suitable programming languages. One of the few tasks they could perform reliably was the identification of orthographic words, and to leave aside the distinction between word and lexical item seemed at the time an innocent simplification in practice, since the distinction had been clearly recorded for future attention.

The simplification was not challenged; in fact it was supported by two other contemporary models of language description. One was the dictionary model, which for practical reasons – ease of consultation – if nothing else, has always been based on the rough equation of a word and a unit of meaning. Phrases and idioms warrant a note at the end of some entries, but there is no attempt at all to articulate a theory that allows for them, and for the relationship between the 'independent' and the 'dependent' uses of a word (Sinclair 1987b).

The other model of the period was the lexical component of a transformational grammar (e.g. Katz and Fodor 1963), which was clearly word-based. The representation of text, for example as the output of the phrase structure component, was as a string of words, each of which became an entry in the lexicon. Although the argumentation in support of this decision was not provided, the unrecognized assumption that the word is the unit of lexical meaning remains largely unchallenged.

As a result of this insensitivity to lexis, the last generation of linguistics has seen grammar going through many stages of sophistication, whatever the theoretical model of preference, while the unit of lexis has remained fixed and concrete, pinned to the surface of language. The apparatus of grammatical description has acquired many components, levels, categories and scales, while lexical description has nothing but feeble surface categories like word and collocation.[3]

The need for a more detailed and abstract model for lexical description became clear when lexical information began to be extracted from multi-million word corpora in the early 1980s.[4] Several long-accepted conventions in lexicography were called into question – for example the idea that a word could inherently have one or more meanings. The working assumption was that when these meanings were explicated (or translated, in a bilingual dictionary) and, in the better dictionaries, exemplified, the lexicographer's job was done. This practice proved to be incapable of organizing the strong, recurrent patterns that were shown by corpus analysis to be present in the way words were used in texts; the importance of the surrounding language far outweighed the question of how many meanings there were and how they were related to each other.

A dictionary is a practical tool, and no place to introduce a new theory of meaning, even if one had been available. So the first dictionary derived from a corpus (Sinclair, Hanks et al. 1987) was conservative in its design, in relation to the disturbing nature of the evidence encountered by the lexicographers. Despite the massive organizing effect of cotext, pride of place in an entry was usually awarded to one of the meanings least dependent on the cotext. At one time in the design phase of Cobuild it was suggested that the normal pattern of an entry should be turned upside down, since the phrasal uses, which are habitually summarized crudely at the end of entries, if at all, were so important; but this was judged to be unhelpful for normal users, who might become very confused, no matter how theoretically sound the structure might be.[5]

As research progressed in the following decade, it became clear that the original distinction between a word and a lexical item was the key to a more helpful description of the vocabulary, and a more accurate account of meaning. The 'innocent simplification'[6] obscured two basic facts:

a  many, if not most, meanings require the presence of more than one word for their normal realization;
b  patterns of co-selection among words, which are much stronger than any description has yet allowed for, have a direct connection with meaning.

## Meaning

The establishment of a lexical item as an abstract category distinct from the word requires us to take meaning into account, and it is important not to overburden the argument with all the problems that the concept of meaning brings along with it. Only one problem will be tackled, a central structural problem that can be discussed without raising the others.[7]

The problem is as follows: in dictionaries, lexicons, thesauruses, etc., meanings are linked primarily with words; how can the appropriate meaning be identified in a text, at the point where a word occurs? If a word has 50 different meanings in a dictionary, how is an occurrence of the word related to just one of those meanings? And what happens if none of the 50 meanings precisely covers the case?

It is contended here that the theoretical frameworks that linguists use are inadequate to solve this problem – or even to state the problem in such a way that a solution could be attempted. So there must be adjustments made to our theoretical perspectives, after which the problem can be restated.

The initial statement of this problem of meaning has some similarity with Chomsky's well-known view of a grammar as a finite set of rules that specifies the non-finite set of sentences of a language. Chomsky was concerned primarily with syntactic well-formedness, but the same problem arises with the lexis. The problem in both cases is how to relate a finite resource to an unlimited set of applications; in the case of syntax the set of rules is finite and the set of sentences is not; in the case of lexis the set of meaningful items is finite and the set of meanings in use does not appear to be limited.

Chomsky's solution to the problem of linking the rules and the sentences was to introduce recursive rules, but recursion is not a useful concept in the lexicon. Recursion is one of the simpler types of combination; a single rule-form in the grammar[8] provides the link between finite and unlimited sets. For the combinatorial relations of the lexicon, a more complex relationship needs to be defined. That is the purpose of this chapter.

A lexicon, or a dictionary, consists of a list of words, to each of which is attached a number of statements, features, etc., which together express what can be said about the meaning of the word. The words are arranged according to the rules of grammar to make text.[9]

The problem is that a text is a unique deployment of meaningful units, and its particular meaning is not adequately accounted for by any organized concatenation of the fixed meanings of each unit. This is because some aspects of textual meaning arise from the particular combinations of choices at one place in the text, and there is no place in the lexicon-grammar model where such meaning can be assigned. Since there is no limit to the possible combinations of words in texts, no amount of documentation or ingenuity will enable our present lexicons to rise to the job. They are doomed.

However, the meaningful combinations can now be described in new ways which make them much more tractable. At the time lexicons of the familiar kind were being designed, much of the regularity of the combinations was obscured by the inadequate means of observation of the data. It was impossible to gather together a sufficient quantity and selection of data in which the underlying patterns could be identified. The application of powerful computers to large text corpora has begun to improve our methods of observation.

## Reversal

To give just one example of the inadequacies of a lexicon built by established methods, they do not take into account the common phenomenon of semantic reversal.[10] Situations frequently arise in texts where the precise meaning of a word or phrase is determined more by the verbal environment than the parameters of a lexical entry. Instead of expecting to understand a segment of text by accumulating the meanings of each successive meaningful unit, here is the reverse; where a number of units taken together create a meaning, and this meaning takes precedence over the 'dictionary meanings' of whatever words are chosen. If the two meanings (the one created by the environment and the item, and the one created by each item individually) are close and connected, the text is felt to be coherent; if they do not, some interpretation has to be made – perhaps the meanings of the items are neutral with respect to the semantic demands of the environment, perhaps there is a relevant metaphorical interpretation, or an irony, or a very rare meaning of an item, or a special interpretation because of what the text is about at this point.

Whenever the meaning arises predominantly from the textual environment rather than the item choice, it is considered to be an instance of semantic reversal. The flow of meaning is not from the item to the text but from the text to the item.

In practice, the flow is rarely in one direction only. The textual environment will nearly always have some effect on the meaning of a unit, and the accepted features of the meaning will not often be totally ignored.[11] So the problem of the description of meaning can be traced back to the rigidity and frequent irrelevance of the lexicons that supply the meanings. Not only do they (a) only supply some of the meaning, but also (b) they often supply meaning components that do not fit the particular environment; in addition (c) there is no mechanism that I am aware of for adapting a lexical entry to suit a particular recurrent set of circumstances, far less an individual instance.

The effects of reversals can be seen in dictionaries and lexicons when a word is frequently found in collocation with another, and this has an effect on the meaning. For example, *white wine* is not white, but ranges from almost colourless to yellow, light orange or light green in colour. That is to say, the meaning of *white* when followed by *wine* is a different colour range from when it is not.

Traditional dictionaries tend to obscure this point by using encyclopaedic information to explain the meaning, for example:

> (of wine) made from pale grapes or from black grapes separated from their skins
>
> (*Collins English Dictionary* 1991)

This assumes that the user already knows roughly what colour *white* is when collocated with *wine*.

Such examples are familiar enough. But when the word *holy* is interpreted as an abnormal mental state, as in the example 'The ambience borders on the holy . . .' we must assume that this semantic feature is assigned not by any lexicon. There is no lexicon that sanctions such a meaning, and indeed, if there were, it would be a distraction with reference to most of the occurrences of the word *holy*. The meaning is created in the collocation with *borders on*. Whatever follows this phrase indicates the limits of normality by specifying a mental state that lies just outside normality. When the adjective is *obsessional*, the feature of abnormality is already present in the meaning of the word, and the co-ordinated choice will be felt to be coherent; in the case of *holy*, the required feature has to be added by reversal. And if there were an instance of 'borders on the normal', this would be interpreted as fully ironical, suggesting that the normal is unexpected.

The way in which such a semantic problem is tackled is parallel to (or even identical with) a wide range of potential difficulties of interpretation; for example if in a conversation someone says 'Wasn't that awful what happened to Harry?', and if you, as the receiver of this query, do not know a Harry to whom something awful has happened (or you know more than one unfortunate Harry), you have two basic courses of action. You can either challenge the presupposition that there is no identification problem, by pointing out your ignorance and/or your interlocutor's lack of clarity, or you can use a reversal technique – try to pick up from the following conversation what you need to know. Or if you are reading a book that is outside your normal area of expertise, and come across items that the author assumes you know the meanings of – like abbreviations – you can either break off in your reading and consult a specialized glossary, or plough on with whatever understanding you can glean from reversal techniques. After a while either your interpretation will break down altogether or you will survive the particular passage because none of the unresolved meanings are critical to your overall understanding.

## Theory adjustment

'Reversal' is one of the new descriptive categories that will be required to account adequately for the data. The problem goes deeper, however, and requires some reorientation of theory. As a start, here are three hypotheses that, in various ways, cut across established theoretical norms and assumptions. Without the acceptance of these hypotheses, or their refutation, progress towards a better account of meaning will be slow.

> 1    Language text is not adequately modelled as a sequence of items, each in an environment of other items.

We normally accept an underlying model of language as 'item-environment'. At any point in a text we can interpret the occurrence of an item in terms of what other choices are possible, given the environment. Hence each item is both an item in its own right and a component of the environment of other items.

This model must be examined carefully, because it seems inherently implausible. Each item would have to be interpretable, simultaneously, as having many different meaning-relations with other items, equally multifaceted. As each item came to be processed for its contribution to the meaning of the text, every other item nearby would change not only its meaning, but also the basis of its meaning – whether central or peripheral to the node in focus.

This would lead to a huge multiplicity of meanings, and the need for a complex processor to relate them to each other, discard irrelevant ones, etc. Further, since we have no reason to believe that the interpretation will proceed on a strict linear basis, the model would become extremely complex.

Such complexity reflects the interdependence between words and their environments, and makes it clear that all the patterning cannot be described at once; some elaboration of the model is needed in order to disperse the complexity. This could take the form of a diversification of units into different types, as grammar has nouns, verbs, etc. – we already recognize 'grammatical' and 'vocabulary' words, without being able to distinguish them formally, and we use equally informal terms such as 'idiom', 'figurative' and 'metaphorical' in lexicography. It could also take the form of erecting a hierarchy of units, a *rank scale* in Halliday's terms (1961), where structural patterns of different types and dimensions are arranged in a taxonomy.

Exactly what model will emerge is not possible to predict at present; my aim in this chapter is to establish the need for it, and to put aside some well-respected assumptions about language that may be hampering our thinking – such as the imbalance at present in favour of the independence of the word, rather than its interdependence on its cotext, or verbal environment. To put these notions aside is not to discard them for ever, or to attack their intellectual integrity, or the competence of those who uphold them; it is merely to suspend their operation temporarily to see if the picture that emerges from a rearrangement is more satisfying than the present one.

This point is particularly important with respect to the second hypothesis that I would like to put forward:

2    Ambiguity in a text is created by the method of observation, and not the structure of the text.

If a word is likely to be intricately associated with the words that occur round about it, then the consequences of studying its meaning in isolation are unpredictable. Dictionaries, which have little choice than to organize their statements of meaning around the word, present a picture of chaotic ambiguity. Words have many meanings, and there is no way of working out in advance which one is appropriate in a text.

However, if we extend the viewpoint to two or three words (which is normal when lexicographers recognize a relatively fixed phrase) much of the ambiguity drops away.[12] People use this extended viewpoint so naturally in reading and listening, and language teachers labour the importance of concentrating on the broad aspects of meaning and not the particulars of a single word.

Despite almost universal accord with the position that the environment of occurrence is important in text structure, every machine lexicon I know persists in starting with the inappropriate unit, the word. When such a lexicon is applied to a text, all the possible meanings of a word are listed, including whatever phraseological meanings have been noticed, as if all were potentially relevant on each occasion of the occurrence of the word. Having created quite fictitious ambiguities, the researcher then multiplies them with similarly complex possibilities for the next word, and the next . . . leading to the most innocuous sentence having many thousands of possible 'meanings'.

Here is a superficial example.[13] In the *Collins English Dictionary*, words are assigned a number of meanings as follows, approximately:

| | |
|---|---|
| cat | 24 |
| mat | 17 |
| on | 25 |
| sit | 18 |
| the | 15 |

The number of possible combinations of meaning, on these figures and multi-plying 'the' in twice, for '*The* cat sat on *the* mat' is thus 41,310,000.

In this desperate situation, there arises a need for sensitive algorithms to filter out all the meanings that do not apply in the particular instance, all except one. The mess is so serious by now that this cannot be achieved by automatic process alone; humans must be trained and employed to clear it up.

This process must be compared with the normal linguistic activity of an ordinary person. All day long, effortlessly, this person interprets passing sentences, usually correctly, and often against a background of high levels of distraction. He or she is not even aware that any of them are potentially ambiguous.

The discrepancy that we perceive between human and machine behaviour is so gross that the model behind the machine's performance must be questioned. The human, perhaps, works with a better notion of meaningful units, and does not encounter ambiguity.[14]

This position casts doubt on the relevance to language study of all the work over many years in Artificial Intelligence and Natural Language Processing (NLP) which concentrates on the resolution of ambiguity. The ambiguity that is studied is evidenced in carefully contrived short utterances, often of a kind which would be very unlikely to occur in texts. This possible objection to them is dismissed on the grounds that grammar deals with potential utterances, and whether or not an utterance actually occurred is uninteresting.[15] Now that large corpora can provide, with growing reliability, statements of regularity and norms in language usage, the marginal status of the work on artificial ambiguity can be clearly seen.[16]

This is not the place for a thorough examination of ambiguity and associated phenomena; the aim here is merely to open a case for reorientation of our attitudes to a very firmly established viewpoint. A representative account of the current NLP positions on the topic can conveniently be found in Monaghan (ed.) (1996). Most of the types presented there can be classified as one of:

a    created by the observer's perspective – this is the commonest
b    suggested by generality or vagueness of reference; one of the strengths of human language is its ability
c    to avoid having to discriminate (Channell 1994)
d    created by reference to a formally marked distinction in another language – a genuine problem for
e    translators but not an ambiguity in any one communication system
f    created by a grammar which lays claim to too much meaning potential
   i    combinations which might be contrastive if they occurred, but are inhibited by other factors
   ii   contrasts which are not formally distinguished in the language system and therefore can only be a matter for interpretation outside the system.

In other words, none of these count as ambiguities that have to be resolved in language description. Indeed, it can be claimed justifiably that a model of language is inappropriate if it obliges the description to make distinctions in a particular text segment which are not necessary for the interpretation of the text as a whole.

3    The form of a linguistic unit and its meaning are two perspectives on the same event.

At first sight, most scholars in a structuralist tradition would not see anything exceptional in this statement. It is accepted that form and meaning are very closely related, and that variation in one normally leads to variation in the other. Even for those whose viewpoint leads them to perceive ambiguity, the close alignment of form and meaning would not be undermined; one would have to accept a lot of overlap, which is not the same as either a confusion between categories or a fusion of them.

Indeed in retrospect it is clear that the association between form and meaning has had to be somewhat loose, to allow for such notions as transformation (Harris 1957). As has been argued in the case of words, syntactic patterns may seem to vary independently of the meaning, as long as the cotext is kept to a minimum. So if active and passive constructions are presented bereft of cotext, their similarity of meaning ('who did what to whom') is highlighted, and their differences, which show in the higher organization of the discourse, are not obvious at all.

The position adopted in this chapter is intended to be in sharp contrast to the approximateness of the traditional view. It is asserted that form and meaning cannot be separated because they are the same thing. Considered in relation to other forms, a lexical item is a form; considered in relation to other meanings, it is a meaning.

It follows from this tighter statement that ambiguity must in practice be very close to zero, or the statement would have to be seriously weakened. Also, the form of a lexical item must include all the components that are realized in the example. Meaning cannot inhere satisfactorily in just a selection of the components of an item when there are other components left in the cotext, but requires them all to be assembled together, and a way of stating the structure of an item has to be devised.

It follows from the requirement that all the components of a lexical item must be included in its specification, that these genuine meaning-bearing items will have very little connection with their cotexts; all the choices that depend substantially on other choices will be grouped together in the item, and the text will be represented essentially as a succession of relatively large-scale and independent choices.

No doubt the reality will be a good deal more complicated than this sketch supposes. Discontinuity of lexical items is a strong possibility, and various kinds of embedding cannot be ruled out. The method of work, which is based on studying and processing concordances of words and phrases, draws out and highlights those choices that contain an element of coselection or conditioned selection. Other choices, which may also be structural, are less obvious in the data studied at present because they are sporadic with reference to the pattern of choices.

## The axes of patterning

In order to restate the problem of meaning, we must draw some general implications from the three hypotheses that have been discussed above. The main one, which pervades the whole argument, is that the tradition of linguistic theory has been massively biased in favour of the *paradigmatic* rather than the *syntagmatic* dimension. Text is essentially perceived as a series of relatively independent choices of one item after another, and the patterns of combination have been seriously undervalued.

It is easy to understand how this has happened; once again it depends on the nature of the observations and the stance of the observer. The difficulty has been how to cope with the large range of variation that is apparent in most uses of language. In presenting structure, traditional linguistics puts most of the variation to one side through the device of separating grammar and semantics at the outset. This then obscures most of the structural relevance of collocation, and removes any chance of the precise alignment of form and meaning. It also presents the semantic level with the kind of problems that this chapter is discussing.

The opportunity to observe recurrent patterns of language in corpora has shown how choices at word rank co-ordinate with other choices round about in an intricate fashion, suggesting a hierarchy of units of different sizes sharing the realization of meaning. The largest unit will have a similar status to the sentence in grammar (and may coincide with sentence boundaries in many instances) in that it will be relatively independent of its surroundings with respect to its internal organization (see the distinction between *rank* and *level* in Halliday (1961)).

Meaning appears to be created by paradigmatic choice; this is within the orthodoxy of most theories, whether or not it is explicit. This perception also relates meaning to the information of Information Theory. However, the mechanism of paradigmatic choice is so powerful that constant vigilance should be exercised to make sure that it is not misapplied. Sometimes in the actual use of language there is less choice than the paradigm is capable of creating, as in the example of counting chickens given earlier; in these cases to present the paradigm unqualified is to distort the description by claiming more meaning in an expression than is actually usable.

It seems that this happens as a matter of routine in most published descriptions, and that a language is characterized as having hundreds of thousands of meanings that are not in fact available, because they are constrained by the need for other choices in the environment. By giving greater weight to the syntagmatic constraints, units of meaning can be identified that reduce the amount of meaning available to the user to something more like his or her normal experience; the balance between the two dimensions will more accurately represent the relation between form and meaning.

Such a conclusion calls for nothing less than a comprehensive redescription of each language, using largely automatic techniques. Problems remain, particularly one concerning the inability of the paradigmatic and the syntagmatic dimensions to relate to each other. They have no contact with each other, they are invisible from each other, and to observe one, the other has to be ignored. The phenomenon is similar to the observational problems that led to Heisenberg's famous principle of uncertainty in atomic physics. An atom can have both position and momentum, but these cannot be observed simultaneously, because the techniques for observing one cut out the possibility of observing the other. Similarly, a word gives information through its being chosen (paradigmatic) and at the same time it is part of the realization of a larger item (syntagmatic); in order to observe either of these, however, we lose sight of the other. Unless the requirements of the cotext are precisely stated, the word as a paradigmatic choice will be invested with far too much independent meaning; on the other hand when observed purely as a component of a larger syntagmatic pattern, it can have very little freedom, and therefore can give very little information; it might be no more meaningful than a letter in a word, serving only the purpose of recognition. A means must be found of relating the two dimensions in order to give a balanced picture.

We are now in a position to restate the problem of meaning in tractable terms by means of the following hypothesis:

4    The meaning of a text can be described by a model which reconciles the paradigmatic and syntagmatic dimensions of choice at each choice point.

The model is set out in a preliminary fashion in Sinclair (1996b). Five categories of co-selection are put forward as components of a lexical item; two of them are obligatory and three are optional. The obligatory categories are the *core*, which is invariable, and constitutes the evidence of the occurrence of the item as a whole, and the *semantic prosody*, which is the determiner of the meaning of the whole, as we shall see in the example below. The optional categories realize co-ordinated secondary choices within the item, fine-tuning the meaning and giving semantic cohesion to the text as a whole.

The optional categories serve also as a means of classifying the members of a paradigm, and thus the two axes of patterning, the paradigmatic and the syntagmatic, are related; the relationship is in principle capable of automation, and is quantifiable. The three categories that relate words together on either dimension are *collocation, colligation* and *semantic preference*. The first two are Firth's terms (1951, 1957b).

Collocation (at present) is the co-occurrence of words with no more than four intervening words[17] (given the arguments of this chapter, the word is no more reliable as a measure of the environment than it is as a unit of meaning, so this measure will have to be revised, but it is at present the only measure in general use). On the syntagmatic dimension, collocation is the simplest and most obvious relationship, and it is fairly well described. On the paradigmatic dimension it is defined rather differently, because items can only collocate with each other when present in a text, and two items in a paradigm are by that arrangement classed as mutually exclusive. The relationship is that of *mutual* collocation, i.e. that they both collocate (on separate occasions, usually) with the same item or items. So whereas *manual* and *restoration* are both significant collocates of *work*, they themselves do not co-occur significantly.

Colligation is the co-occurrence of grammatical phenomena, and on the syntagmatic axis our descriptive techniques at present confine us to the co-occurrence of a member of a grammatical class – say a word class – with a word or phrase. Colligation as a paradigmatic concept is displaced, like collocation, to that of a mutual relationship; so a possessive may colligate with a particular noun, and the so-called 'periphrastic' construction, *the . . . of . . .* may occasionally occur as an alternative. So *your* (etc.) *true feelings* is the norm, but *the true feelings of people* is an example of the less common structure realized by this phrase.

Semantic preference is the restriction of regular co-occurrence to items which share a semantic feature, for example that they are all about, say, sport or suffering. This feature is relevant in the same way to both syntagmatic and paradigmatic phenomena.

The three categories are related to each other in increasing abstraction; collocation is precisely located in the physical text, in that even the inflection of a word may have its own distinctive collocational relationships. To observe colligation one has to assign a word class to each word under examination; where there is a preponderance of one particular word class, this is colligation. Within the abstraction of the word class, of course, there may be one or more collocations.

Semantic preference requires us to notice similarity of meaning regardless of word class; however there may well be found within a semantic class one or more colligations of words which share both the semantic feature and a word class. There may also be collocates, specific recurrent choices of word forms carrying the semantic preference.

### *Example*

The word *budge* in English poses a problem for dictionaries; for example:

> to (cause to) move a little
> (*Longman Dictionary of Contemporary English*)

Leaving aside the tortuous syntax of this sort of definition, it is easy to demonstrate that there is no feature of the meaning of *budge* that restricts movement. Budging is the overcoming of a resistance to movement, and so it concentrates on the beginning of movement. Even a little movement constitutes a budging, which might explain the definition above, without justifying it, because something once budged (i.e. set in motion) might move a great deal.

The point is that English does not talk much about budging at all, but about *not* budging, where the quantity of movement is irrelevant. The two examples that follow the definition above are indeed both negative, but the entry reads as if the lexicographers had not noticed this primary fact of usage, and the user, of course, has no idea how to evaluate the presence of the negatives since they are not referred to.

It would be difficult to find an instance of this word which is semantically positive. Appendix 8.1 (p. 147) gives 31 instances from a corpus, all that there are in almost 20 million words. Of these I propose to ignore one, tenth from the bottom, which is clearly written to represent the dialect of a region. Most of the indications of colligation with a negative are to be found to the left of the central, or *node* word; immediately to the left we find eight instances of words ending in *n't* and eight of *not* – together making slightly over half the total. Most of the others show the word *to* in this position, and by examining the word previous to that, there is a strong collocation with forms of the lemma *refuse* – nine in all. Although not a grammatical negative, *refuse* can reasonably be considered as a lexicalization of the kind of non-positive meaning that characterizes *budge*.

There are, then, just five remaining instances that do not follow one of the three prominent ways of expressing negativity. The eighth line has a double negative in an extended verbal group, the tenth has *determined not to*, the eleventh has a *neither/nor* construction. The two remaining instances show neither grammatical nor lexical negation; the second line expresses the refusal aspect with *has yet to* – implying that Mr Volcker refuses to budge, and the third line draws attention to a presumably long and unpleasant period preceding eventual budging (the extended cotext of this line is 'so deep with caustic dirt that skin would come off scrubbers' hands . . .').

The negative quality of the phrase centred around *budge* is thus expressed in different ways, but with a predominance of collocations *refuse to* (and inflections), *wouldn't, didn't, couldn't*. Colligation is with verbs, with modals (including *able to*) accounting for half the 30 instances.

From this point I will not attempt to describe comprehensively the two instances above that imply rather than express negativity (lines 2 and 3). I will include them when they conform to a choice pattern, and ignore them silently when they diverge. They are sufficiently conformant with the general usage of *budge* to be given low priority, so little will be gained by an exhaustive account of their minor deviations; but also I am concerned to establish a methodology that concentrates in the first instance on recurrent events rather than on unrepeated patterns. When the habitual usages of the majority of users are thoroughly described, we will have a sound base from which to approach the singularities, which may of course include much fine writing.

*Budge* is an ergative verb, in that whatever is to be moved may figure either as subject or object of the verb; subject in an intransitive clause, and object in a clause where the subject is the person or thing making the attempt to move. A guide to these alternatives can be found by looking at whatever immediately follows *budge*. Intransitive clauses may well end with the verb, so where there is a punctuation mark following *budge* we may expect that the clause is intransitive.

Twelve times there is a full stop, twice a comma and once a dash – 15 instances in all, or half of the total.

The distinction between *won't* and *can't* draws attention to two different reasons why people or things do not budge, refusal or inability. Refusal is ascribed to whoever or whatever is not budging (*won't, wouldn't* . . . etc., and *refuse* . . .), while inability is usually ascribed to someone who is trying to get something or someone to budge (can be expressed by *can't, couldn't*). Of the first type, there are 20 instances expressing refusal or interpreted as implying it, all intransitive; where the subject is non-human and the verb modal (a snake, a quotation and a thermometer) we anthropomorphize (which is a kind of reversal). Of the second type, there are four examples; the non-budging is ascribed to inability, the 'agent' is in subject position, the clause is transitive and the person or thing that is not budging is named in the object.

One instance has indications of both possible reasons; the modal cluster is *won't be able to*, and the clause is intransitive. This is a prediction of a future inability to budge, and *won't* does not indicate refusal.

There remain five instances, of which four are *didn't* or *did not*. This usage is neutral with respect to refusal and inability; the structure is intransitive and so suggests that an agent is not important, but a person energetically trying to move a physical object is apparent in adjoining clauses in three of the cases. In the fourth the subject of *budge* is a person; the cotext makes it clear that he is under pressure to move, so it is closer to refusal than inability.

To summarize this matter, we note that 25 of the 30 instances are intransitive, with the item that does not budge as the subject; where this item is animate, it strongly collocates with *refuse*, and the semantic preference of refusal is found in most of the other instances, mainly through colligation with certain modals. In the transitive instances the non-budging item is object, the agent of movement is in the subject, the semantic preference is inability and there is strong colligation with the modals of ability.

A minor optional element of the cotext of *budge* is the expression of the position from which there is to be no budging. There are eight instances, all beginning with a preposition; *from* four times, *on* twice, and *above* and *off* once each. Most are of the 'refusal' type.

At this point we may argue that most of the patterning in the cotext has been accounted for, with the possible exception of the word *even*, which occurs four times to the right of *budge*, and links semantically with *yet*. Something fairly extreme is being referred to. We consider why people use this word, why they do not just use the common verb *move*, with which any use of *budge* can be replaced. Something does not budge when it does not move *despite* attempts to move it. From the perspective of the person who wants something moved, this is frustrating and irritating, and these emotions may find expression, because this is the *semantic prosody* of the use of *budge*.

The semantic prosody of an item is the reason why it is chosen, over and above the semantic preferences that also characterize it. It is not subject to any conventions of linguistic realization, and so is subject to enormous variation, making it difficult for a human or a computer to find it reliably. It is a subtle element of attitudinal, often pragmatic meaning and there is often no word in the language that can be used as a descriptive label for it. What is more, its role is often so clear in determining the occurrence of the item that the prosody is, paradoxically, not necessarily realized at all. But if we make a strong hypothesis we may establish a search for it that will have a greater chance of success than if we were less than certain of its crucial role. For example we can claim that in the case of the use of *budge* the user wishes to express or report frustration (or a similar emotion) at the refusal or inability of some obstacle to move, despite pressure being applied. Then there is an explanation for *even* and *yet*, and other scattered phrases from the immediate and slightly wider cotext of the instances. A selection of the evidence for pressure and frustration is given below, with reference to Table 8.1.

1  the President may be out of his mind
2  should no longer . . . intervene . . . but . . .
3  stained so deep
4  she knew she couldn't
5  <prediction based on experience>
6  blows his pipe furiously
7  especially if ordered to do so . . . indignant and thunderous
8  <prediction based on present circumstances>
9  the polio faction . . . the virus fanciers
10  <decision based on prior events>
11  neither death nor disease
12  nudge it with my shoulder, but
13  stuck in his mind and . . .
14  leant against the heavy wooden door
15  even in the mating season
16  naughty . . . ignoring requests . . . forced to . . . capricious
17  It was a dismissal.
18  not even with money
19  <typicalization of experience>
20  two horses could not . . .
21  thrust himself between the duellists and . . .
22  [not considered]
23  he may lose a client
24  That's ridiculous
25  he shook it more fiercely
26  no matter how hard he tugged
27  he knew he couldn't
28  do what they might,
29  <diplomatic pressure>
30  no amount of arguing
31  I tried the idea on him

The above quotations and remarks are taken from a wider cotext than that printed in the table, but still a small one. The evidence is probably enough to convince many readers that the prosody exists and is expressed, implied or alluded to in most of the instances. But the range of expression is apparently without any limit, and the amount of inference necessary to identify it as evidence is often great; moreover in several instances there is no actual piece of language that can be quoted, but a more general appeal is made to experience.

This amorphous collection is an unlikely starter for being related to a structural category, and yet the claim is made that it is the most important category in the description. Without a very strong reason for looking, a computer would find virtually no reason for gathering this collection, but if we can predict a structural place for it, then at the very least the computer could pick out the stretch of language within which a prosody should lie, and whose absence was as significant as its presence. There is good reason to believe, also, that as the number of instances available rises, so do regularities appear that were not reliably shown in smaller sets. The occurrences of *even* are already obvious, and the phrase *he/she knew* recurs even in this small sample; there is similarity in the phrases *blow . . . fiercely, shook fiercely, hard . . . tugged*, and money is mentioned in the wider cotext of 11 (*Money would send her home when neither . . .*) as well as 18.

It is impossible to predict how much or what will be left over at the end of an extensive study of this usage, but it certainly looks unlikely to be neat and tidy; hence we need a clear and strong hypothesis about the nature and structure of the lexical item of which *budge* is the core, in order at least to search for indications of the semantic prosody. The core gives us the starting point, in the case of *budge* one that anticipates the prosody fairly clearly; the optional patterns of collocation, colligation and semantic preference bring out relevant aspects of the meaning, and the prosody can then be searched for in the close environment.

It is not surprising that this is a very common structure in language, because it allows the flexibility that was identified earlier in this chapter as essential for an adequate lexical item. The prosody is normally the part of an item that fits in with the previous item, and so needs to have virtually no restriction on its formal realization, whereas the core, often in the middle or at the end of an item, is buffered against the demands of the surrounding text that it can remain invariable. An item of this shape and structure makes it possible for the lexicon to have finite entries which are adequate to describe the way the meaning is created by the use of the item.

In this lengthy description of the lexical item whose core is NEG *budge* I have not had reason to make a distinction that most lexicographers would regard as primary – the literal and figurative uses of the word. For example:

> (cause to) move very little, make the slightest movement; (fig.) (cause to) change a position or attitude
>
> (*Oxford Advanced Learners Dictionary*)

## Appendix 8.1

| | | | |
|---|---|---|---|
| 1 | ight be out of his mind and refuse to | budge | . In that case, the Vice-President |
| 2 | ergencies. But Mr Volcker has yet to | budge | on changing his controls over domest |
| 3 | off scrubbers' hands before it would | budge | . It was rumoured to be make-work to |
| 4 | to do so, but she knew she could not | budge | me from my view. We spent several v |
| 5 | he recognizes it, he'll refuse to | budge | off that stool where he's sitting n |
| 6 | side, but still the snake will not | budge | . He keeps banging it on the head wi |
| 7 | away louder than ever. I wouldn't | budge | either, or come back, till a boy w |
| 8 | now. We won't none of us be able to | budge | tomorrow. 'They sat at their tea |
| 9 | blow. The virus fanciers refused to | budge | . Whatever the diagnosis, my recove |
| 10 | sat in a corner; I determined not to | budge | from it until closing-time. I also |
| 11 | hen neither death nor? disease could | budge | her. She wrote a cheque for more th |
| 12 | it with my shoulder, but it will not | budge | . I go to the backdoor. I find that |
| 13 | ng the following months and would not | budge | – 'What's done cannot be undone |
| 14 | ooden door of the museum. It didn't | budge | . Hastily, I looked round for a bel |
| 15 | another snail near him he refused to | budge | , even in the mating season. I ofte |
| 16 | me into the dining room, refusing to | budge | , so that no one else budged, and s |
| 17 | It was a dismissal. Bonasera did not | budge | . Finally, sighing, a good-hearted |
| 18 | 9o caliber pezzonovante. You can't | budge | him, not even with money. He has b |
| 19 | fternoons when the thermometer won't | budge | above minus twenty. 'And those |
| 20 | be so heavy that two horses could not | budge | it even in moist earth. Although Wa |
| 21 | between the duellists and refuse to | budge | . Often to everyone's great relief |
| 22 | the coroner himself are gawn t' | budge | on that. In the first place, d |
| 23 | omise up to a point but he refuses to | budge | on design principles he knows to be |
| 24 | The humanity here just refuses to | budge | . 'That's ridiculous,' says |
| 25 | out of the packet. When it did not | budge | he shook it more fiercely like 'a t |
| 26 | ed at the doorknobs the doors didn't | budge | or even rattle. 'Oh, my God!' |
| 27 | and hesitated. He knew he couldn't | budge | Ben Canaan. He walked to the alcove |
| 28 | at they might, the British would not | budge | from their immigration policy. In m |
| 29 | pressure any delegation. They won't | budge | from that position. 'What a ti |
| 30 | the wings of the eagle and refused to | budge | . after three thousand years of wait |
| 31 | tried the idea on him. He wouldn't | budge | . He seemed to have already faded aw |

It is easy enough to go through the examples and pick the 11 that show the figurative use, where views, opinions, policies, principles, etc., occur instead of doors, stools and thermometers. Where the option to express position is taken, the preposition *on* seems to be restricted to the figurative use, though *from* occurs with both. In a few instances the distinction hardly seems necessary, because both the literal and figurative aspects of the meaning of other words are also relevant; for example the wider cotext of the first instance, about the President being out of his mind, includes the use of *office* and *sitting*; moving the President from his office simultaneously requires his physical relocation and the cancellation of his authority.[18]

## Conclusion

I have tried to show that there is a seriously weak point in the automation of language description in the design of a lexicon. Current models do not overcome the problem of how a finite and rigidly formalized lexicon can account satisfactorily for the apparently endlessly variable meanings that arise from the combination of particular word choices in texts. I have suggested that the word is not the best starting-point for a description of meaning, because meaning arises from words in particular combinations.

The term *lexical item*, used to mean a unit of description made up of words and phrases, has been dormant for some years, but is available for units with an internal structure as outlined above. Elements in the surrounding cotext of a word or phrase are incorporated in a larger structure when the pattern is strong enough. The lexical item balances syntagmatic and paradigmatic patterns, using the same descriptive categories to describe both dimensions.

The identification of lexical items has to be made by linguists supported by computational resources, and in particular large general corpora. The impact of corpus evidence on linguistic description is now moving beyond the simple supply of a quantity of attested instances of language in use. It is showing that there is a large area of language patterning – more or less half of the total – that has not been properly incorporated into descriptions; this is the syntagmatic dimension, of co-ordinated lexicogrammatical choices. Because of the great range of variation in realization, the regularities of this dimension have been overlooked, whereas from the perspective of a computer they become both more obvious and easier to describe.

# 9   The empty lexicon

The origin of this chapter was an invited seminar at the Istituto di Linguistica Computationale in Pisa in 1994, which concerned the structure of the lexicon. It has been substantially changed in revision for the first issue of the *International Journal of Computational Linguistics*, 1996. It picks up a recurrent theme of several papers, the inadequacy of a finite, word-based lexicon for application to text.

Let me contrast two views on the analysis of language. Both are perfectly respectable, and both are intellectually sound. But although they each encompass a broad spectrum, they contrast quite sharply, and divide professionals throughout the language sciences.

In one view, language is primarily a carrier of messages. The propositional content of the sentences in a text – or most of the content of most of the sentences anyway – can be retrieved and symbolized in a knowledge base. The form of the sentences is only of value insofar as it does its job properly and allows the messages to be transmitted efficiently. The components of language text – words and phrases – have known meanings (such as are explained in dictionaries), and the process of construction of text is the selection and arrangement of these components according to the meaning that is to be delivered, and within the prescribed rules of construction – the grammar of the language.

The metaphor of 'coding' is characteristic of this view of language, and is much used in the writings of its adherents. A code is a transliteration convention, which has no effect on the meaningful segments of a language text, while altering their surface realizations. A code is 100 per cent reversible. The notion of language text as an encoding of meaning implies (a) that meaning has the segmental quality of the text, and (b) that the 'text-to-meaning' process is a simple reversal of the 'meaning-to-text' process.

This view is sharply distinguished from another. In that view, language is a means of communication that deals in much more complex communications than messages, although it recognizes that messages are important, even though very difficult to define. The form and the message cannot easily be separated, and the particular selections in a text interact with each other to such an extent that it is impossible to sustain the position that they deliver a stable unit of meaning on all occasions.

I shall first build up a broad picture of the first position by sketching out representative attitudes on a number of issues, namely:

- terminology
- sublanguages
- lexicons
- selectiveness
- sentences
- information

Then I shall contrast the two views more specifically, and examine their different attitudes to:

- interaction
- written language
- semantics

The paper concludes with an expression of hope that the newly available evidence from language corpora may help to reconcile these views.

## Terminology, and the fixing of meaning

The first point of view fits in very well with the way in which terminology is normally conceptualized. The invention of writing made it possible, after some time, to isolate the word as an orthographic unit, and the next stage was to give special treatment to the meanings of selected words, using them as terms. In disciplines that rely on terminology, attempts are made to insulate terms from the normal effects of the usage of words. In ordinary language, the meanings of most words gradually change in time, while in terminology every attempt is made to keep the meaning of terms constant. What changes are made are motivated by considerations external to the structure of language, but have to do with clarifications or advances in the disciplines.

Also, it is clear that, left to themselves, the meanings of words change by their frequent association with other words – Louw (1993) has revived Darmsteter's (1887) notion of 'contagion' to describe this effect; so, for example, while in English *enormous* can be used of both pleasant and unpleasant things, *enormity* is restricted to crimes, scandals and heavy burdens.

Furthermore, with frequent usage together, words form syntagmatic associations with others round them, so that instead of merely taking on some of the meaning of their surroundings through contagion, they form a new unit of meaning which requires the presence of both words (or more than two in many cases) to be instantiated (Sinclair 1996b). Corpus work has already called into question the way lexical and semantic studies have been dominated by single words.

There is also in the creation of language text the requirement of expressing unique, unrepeatable meanings by means of a syntax and vocabulary which must retain a high level of rigidity so that the texts can be understood by all the users of the language. Inevitably, meanings are flexed as far as possible, and an ad hoc phraseology is put together to cope with difficult circumstances. But words and meanings that are protected by the conventions of terminology exclude as far as possible any variation that is specific to the occasion.

So on the one hand we have a picture of ordinary words that, through usage, change their meaning in a variety of ways, as against terms, which are protected as far as possible from the effects of usage. In practice the line is not easy to draw; on the one hand there are many nouns – the names of flora and fauna, for example – whose behaviour is very close to that of terms, and where there is a considerable overlap, while on the other hand there are many words that have a specialized and 'protected' meaning in a discipline without necessarily being granted the status of terms. These quasi-terms include for example the distinctive meanings and uses of *mouse* and *window* in computing; these words do not have the status of standardized technical terms, and may never acquire it, but are nevertheless specialized. *Window* is a fashionable word at the present time, and has another specialized meaning in telecommunications, again without reaching the status of a term.

For scientific, technical, legal, and some bureaucratic language there is a well organized terminology industry, that seeks to maintain the semantic isolation of the terms, and to counter the natural pressures of usage.

In ordinary, non-technical language the institution of terminology is not established, but similar attitudes to meaning are shown in comments on language change in the national press, in politics, and in the education profession. It is recognized that words change their meaning through time, but this is a process which frequently attracts criticism. It is claimed that the language is constantly being degraded, that fine words are losing the edge of their meanings and newer, more pompous expressions are replacing the pungent phraseology of the common people and the received usage of the educated. There is a lot of affinity between this popular perception and the stance of the Protector of Terms in a scientific community.

## Sublanguages

The view that language is primarily a carrier of messages fits well also with the notion of sublanguages. Here the underlying assumption is that users of a language accept on certain occasions a set of voluntary restrictions on their expression. The restrictions normally occur in connection with specialized topics, particularly scientific and technical topics and the usual language variety that is studied in this connection is the written variety, at a formal or near-formal level.

It is assumed that the topic controls the vocabulary selection, and studies show that this is partly true (e.g., Roe 1977; Yang 1986). Keeping to a single text type may simplify the grammar. Further restrictions arise from the function of the communications, which in the case of normal scientific writing is assumed to be almost exclusively the provision of information. Structures that are overtly interactive, questioning, requesting, cajoling, etc., will not often be found in the kind of texts that are usually picked out for study as sublanguages.

Hence the position arises that limitations in the messages of some varieties will lead to simplifications in the structure of the language used; as if there were a direct relation between the complexity of the language used and the content and function of the messages.

The specification of a sublanguage is controversial, and so is empirical confirmation of their existence. To demonstrate the existence and importance of sublanguages, there are several possible strategies. One is just to look for them. A user community that kept clearly separate the language that was used in a particular subject-matter area, and whose usage in that area differed markedly from its other usage and the usage of comparable communities, while remaining largely within the rules of the general language – such conditions would identify a sublanguage.

Societies that support attempts to establish sublanguages of this kind need to protect them in a similar way to the activity of the terminologists. Rules must be explicit, of the kind found in style guides for scientific and technical journals. However, the control is only very partial, sporadic, and superficial.

Another way of identifying sublanguages is to imagine that they are embedded within less disciplined, more liberated text. Only certain sentences, in this approach, are examples of the sublanguage in action, and the rest are ordinary language sentences.

Genre Analysis (Swales 1990) provides broad general guidance as to where prime specimens of a sublanguage are to be found, and the structure of chosen sentences could be checked against the rules of the sublanguage. Harris (1988) is quite straightforward about this; as a procedure, it risks the charge of circularity. Such a charge can be answered if the procedure leads to clarification of the whole text, but is questionable if the sentences which are deemed not to be part of the sublanguage are not accorded full status in the description.

The principles of limitation, restriction, selection, and simplification are central to the notion of sublanguages. There are many reasons why sublanguages have been popular in Natural Language Processing. There is the practical matter that smaller problems can be solved more quickly than bigger ones, which means that applications can be mounted and results achieved while only a fraction of the complexity of human language is tackled analytically. This has led to early applications of Natural Language Processing being confined to highly specialized areas such as medical records. Language for carefully controlled routine communication among narrowly trained professionals is indeed likely to vary less than that used by everyone for most purposes.

The priorities that researchers have observed for some years suggest an underlying notion that certain hypothetical sublanguages encode the most important matters of human knowledge. The search for sublanguages includes stripping off most of the interactive signals and context-dependent variation, leaving the bare propositions of science. Much of the effort centres on the key issue that the sentences of a proper sublanguage might in principle be relatable to a finite knowledge base in a way that would allow for traffic between them. This relationship would be a kind of encoding of knowledge in language. Sentences which performed this function would be considered very important.

Again we see attempts to assign high value to some sentences over others on the basis of their structure, to protect this chosen set of patterns, to fix the relationship of text to meaning so that it is independent of the occasion of usage.

## Lexicons

The view of language that I am characterizing is consonant with the creation of computerized lexicons. Typically, in such a lexicon, there is an entry for each word, listing its morphological, syntactic, and semantic characteristics. In the morphological component, the various forms of a word are associated together, and each with its grammatical function; in the syntactic component, such patterns as transitivity and modification are dealt with. Between them, there is usually a morphosyntactic component which assigns each word to one or more word-classes.

In the semantic component, the meaning of words is analysed typically in terms of features, for example, Typed Feature Structure (TFS). Terminology provides an appropriate model for a lexicon of this kind because the meaning of each term is clear and terms can be related to each other by, for example, being placed in hierarchies and inheritance chains. The lexically rich and stable part of the vocabulary is the most amenable to this analysis, and that is the closest to terminology.

The success of this kind of work, which commands a lot of interest and resources at present, depends on several assumptions about the nature of language and usage. It assumes that, when realizing a single identifiable sense of a word, the word behaves consistently, and is not adapted in meaning by its surroundings. It further assumes that people use words with attention to the logic of their relations with other words, so that none of the features that are claimed for them are incompatible with the content of the utterances in which they are used. It assumes that the task of attaching an adequate set of features to a word is a possible procedure, and not one of Abercrombie's pseudoprocedures (Abercrombie 1965). It assumes that where the word is not in fact the appropriate unit of meaning, and perhaps a multi-word unit or a subword unit has to be identified, reliable criteria can be found to do this job.

Although sometimes claimed to be a procedure that can be applied to every word, it appears that in practice many of the commonest words in the language have to be excluded from this analysis – probably in most cases more than half of the words in running text. These are all the instances of the 'grammatical' or 'function' words. We must postulate two further assumptions, namely (1) that there are two kinds of words in a language, one for which an explicit, permanent lexical profile is appropriate – the so-called 'vocabulary words'; and

(2) that objective, scientific criteria can be stated for deciding on the dividing line between these words and the rest; without such criteria, there is an arbitrary act of expediency at the heart of the analytical system.

## Selectiveness

We have touched on selectiveness before, in considering sublanguages, and we return to it again to make a more general point. An approach to language description that focuses on the message is going to find that some sentences are more interesting and important than others. Those that appear to have clear, detachable messages will be prioritized. Further, it is likely that the notion of a sentence will be subtly redefined to support this prioritization. The primitive notion of a sentence is that it is the largest textual segment with a coherent grammatical structure. All text would divide into discrete sentences. But if further criteria are developed to support the equation 'sentence = message', then it could follow that some stretches of text are not deemed to be sentences. Texts, then, would be divisible into sentences and 'others'.

In this view, the analyst is entitled to evaluate sentences for the purpose of study, and to select those that are of an approved variety, rejecting the rest. This is an application of the notion of 'well-formedness'; only those sentences are interesting that respond well to the analysis.

It is a short step from this position to one in which the text is altered to fit the analysis. A strong theory projects clear criteria for defining its basic unit of description; however, such units are not easy to find intact in running text. Most texts are not an uninterrupted string of such sentences. However, with minor amendments the number of qualifying sentences can rise sharply. Often the amendments required are merely clarifications of sentence boundaries.

If this policy sounds unscientific, it can certainly be justified by hallowed practice in language study, and by the present state of computational linguistics. The traditional grammar and many subsequent versions of grammar are only operative on certain classes of sentence, and those sentences that do not fit the analysis are put to one side, or adapted, or just ignored. This is part of the everyday routine of many linguists, and is unremarkable.

Further, when attempts are made to computerize the analysis, the difficulties are severe, and message-oriented linguists find it necessary to impose on a text a strictly defined notion of a sentence, and to reject text that either does not conform to the definition, or cannot be adapted, using accepted procedures, to the definition.

Computational semantic analysis is not nearly as far advanced as syntactic, but there are already clear indications of general policy directions in the model of the lexicon outlined above.

The obvious place to start a computer-oriented semantic description will be with sentences in which the words are used in accordance with the way they are specified in a pre-existing lexicon, and to leave the other sentences for attention later, if ever. For it can be argued that there is likely to be such a huge amount of work in dealing with these prioritized sentences that there may never be an opportunity for delving into the murky areas of idiom, interaction, speech, and other places where words do not always mean what they are supposed to.

This policy goes along well with a terminologically influenced model, since the stability of meaning of the words is an essential constituent of an analysis that depends on a predetermined lexicon. It also obviously fits well with the notion of sublanguages. Sublanguages in their purest form may be expected to consist largely of sentences which conform precisely to the predictions of the syntax and the lexicon, which in turn have to be specially devised for the restricted but specialized features of the sublanguage.

There is clearly a risk here that the various kinds of 'pre-processing' – as it is often called – might when taken together constitute a substantial change in the nature of the language data. Instead of describing naturally occurring text, the descriptions might apply only to texts which had been selected or adapted so that they fitted the description.

This is the unavoidable risk that arises when a formal system meets raw data. A formal system defines what it can describe, and is restricted to that; since what it can describe is never exactly co-extensive with naturally occurring data, the fit, and the relevance, must be only approximate. The nature of the approximation, the way in which the rigorously defined categories are related to the data, is one of the central issues in linguistic theory.

The prevailing view of this relationship is the one which has been sketched out above, centering on the notion of well-formedness. Sentences that do not meet the structural requirements of the formal system are not described, whether or not they occur. While this policy reduces the problems encountered, it makes the descriptive apparatus less useful in practical projects; as one group of practitioners reports 'perhaps the largest . . . Definite Clause Grammar anywhere . . . was able to parse completely and uniquely virtually no sentence chosen randomly from a newspaper' (Cunningham, Gaizauskas and Wilks 1996).

## Sentences

One of the lines of selectivity that is relevant here is the central interest in the sentence. Text is primarily seen as a string of sentences, with semantic links and occasional logical links, but not structurally related. The sentence is the traditional watershed between grammar and what lies beyond – rhetoric, argument, story, etc., just as the single isolated word is usually regarded as the basic lexical unit. Again the relationship between language and message is preserved in this model, for underlying the sentence is the proposition, the minimal constituent of the message, the building block of organized content. Sentences, of course, can contain many clauses, but the traditional grammar offers the simple, or one-clause sentence, as the prototype, all the subordinate clauses are added as ancillaries, and other main clauses, making complex sentences, are simply concatenated.

## Information

Messages are sentences in statement form, and thus tend to be informative; that is to say, they fit the pervasively popular information model of communication. That is a one-way model, which works under two basic assumptions, both of which we have met already – that the message can be separated from the medium, and that it can be transferred from one individual (or machine) to another without losing its integrity.

The pros and cons of the information model of communication is not a topic that can be pursued in this chapter; all that is required at this point is a recognition that there are no likely problems of alignment between the message-oriented perspective on language and the information model of communication. They fit well together.

## Academicians and Thespians

We have, thus, sketched out in broad outline this major perspective on language, the orientation towards the message. From a practical point of view, it offers the possibility of reducing the truly daunting uncertainties of natural language to a set of problems which, if not finite, at least give the impression of being manageable. Many end users of language services at the present time have interests which are limited to their own professional areas, and often have needs for automation which are very tightly defined even within a small area of discourse. They need to process language which is highly technical, and full of terminology – language to which the sublanguage/lexicon/selective approach is well suited; language that does not threaten the information model.

I would like to offer a name for this general approach to language – the Academy approach. No single word will capture all the strands of preference and priority that link the many proponents of this approach, but the notions of precision, prescription, science, and content that can be associated with an Academy make it an adequate mnemonic.

Once again, let me emphasize that to be an Academician you do not have to espouse all the causes outlined above. You may not care about sublanguages, or even know about them. You may be indifferent to strolling on the information highway, but still mainly oriented to the message in communication, and to data which is mainly couched in the form of written statements. It is enough that your intellectual inclinations point in that general direction.

The alternative, contrasting approach can be called the Thespian. Here, the message is regarded as only one of the facets of a communication, and one which can only be distilled from the rest by a complex and ill-understood process. It is contended that there is no such thing as 'the' message in a verbal interaction, whether spoken or written, since each participant may (if not must) create his or her own message, according to circumstances which are particular to each individual.

## Interaction: message and utterance

There is a very broad formula that can be used to relate the putative message to the interaction as a whole:

message = utterance − interaction + inferences

That is to say, some of the linguistic choices realized in any utterance have as their main function negotiating the interaction, although the elements of which they are a part nearly always contribute to the content as well. Because of this syncretism, it is not possible in practice to remove the traces of interaction, but we must assume that in some manner a listener/reader does just that, in order to derive the message from the utterance. But in addition to this, there are always a number of inferences to be drawn from the timing and placing and wording of the utterance in relation to the unique set of circumstances that constitute the context of the utterance. An adequate listener/reader will convert these inferences, again by a process that we cannot describe, into additional features of the message. Thus, in broad terms, if you discard from the utterance those features which are relevant only to the immediate interaction, and add in the inferential information, you will be left with the message.

This analysis fits the Thespian approach, since both (a) aspects of the interpretation of the interaction, and (b) some of the kinds of inference, are, in our present state of knowledge, inextricable from the individual reaction. If Weinrich is right (2000) and there is a fundamental *discontinuity* between individuals, shakily bridged by language, then the notion of a stable, detachable message has to be abandoned.

Indeed the opposition of message and utterance could be considered as yet another of the false dichotomies that cloud our vision of how language works. It is convenient, for many applications, to assume that utterances encode messages, and that since messages are inherently less complex than language they can be substituted for the utterances. However, if we accept a model of language that puts discontinuity inescapably at the heart of communication, then the notion of message must be seen as incompatible with the model. We have to choose.

The uncertainty and indeterminacy of an axiomatic position like this one is hard for Academicians, as has been noted in many scientific disciplines in recent years. The same utterance will mean something different to each person who hears it. An artefact like a book or a newspaper will have as many interpretations as readers – in fact, from a communicative point of view, the solidity and singularity of the physical objects are highly misleading.

The message-oriented model has a way round even such a disturbing realization. This is the relation of reference, whereby language is able to use the stability and permanence of the world outside it to steady its inner waywardness. The twin assumptions of objective knowledge and people's ability to share it provide a reliable set of reference points, reinforcing the reliance on propositional content.

By contrast, the holistic, dynamic model makes no assumption about shared knowledge. It sees language in use as essentially and fundamentally interactive; the product of more than one participant. Interaction is not merely a set of behaviour patterns which have developed as part of the transfer rituals – it pervades the organization of language itself.

## Written language

Most written language, it is conceded, is composed by one author without any other participant being present, but the competence of an author rests on his or her ability to take into account the range of reactions to be expected of target readers. The other participants in a written 'conversation' are merely displaced in time.

In the Thespian approach, the propositional content of an utterance may on occasions be of minor interest compared with other aspects of delivery of the utterance – its relation to the previous utterance, for example, or its prospection of the next one. The student of verbal interaction is fairly eclectic about variety, but is inevitably drawn towards those varieties where the interactive element is prominent. Spoken interaction is a favourite, because on occasions the message element may scarcely be articulated at all, and the exchange of subtle interactive signals may dominate the conversation.

Written language, being insensitive to the passage of real time, or the presence of the participants, is less likely to depend on interactive signals, but it has no less of a discourse structure than its spoken counterpart. Parts of the structure may not be as obvious as they are in spoken interaction, particularly the prospection of future events, but they can be shown to play an important part in the organization of the material.

On the surface, the least interesting kind of language for the interaction specialist is the deadpan expository prose of scientific writing. Because it attempts to prioritize its message, it relies hardly at all on interactive signals. Where there is a connection expressed between one sentence and another, it is a logical connector, and even those are not common. The reader is normally assumed to be sufficiently informed to construct a discourse out of the barest linguistic clues.

This compositional strategy appears to give the message element the best chance of stability, so that it can be understood accurately and consistently by many readers, who have no chance of conferring. What it relies on, as is apparent from the previous paragraph, is stability, consistency and a high level of shared information among the readership. The responsibility for the reliability of the message is passed to the community, and there are only scattered clues in the text.

Language which is sensitive to interaction makes frequent evaluations of the state of the discourse; whereas the specialized language of scientific exposition contains very little overt evaluation, normal everyday language is full of it. Hunston (1989) has done a detailed and sensitive study of evaluation in science text, and shown that even the most objective scientist cannot avoid it; although well-hidden, it is there. However, without faith and a model of language that expects to find frequent evaluation, it will stay hidden, and is not referred to in conventional descriptions of scientific exposition.

There is a parallel to be drawn between words and sentences in the focus of the message-oriented approach. The terminological tendency isolates words by trying to avoid the 'contagion' of their contact with other words; where a term consists of more than one word, the phrase tends to be fixed and isolated. Parallel to this is the relative isolation of sentences in this approach, by various means including:

a  the very fact that sentences are seen as the largest grammatical structure isolates them. Any process that links and organizes sentences with respect to each other is of secondary importance.
b  as a consequence, structural features such as cohesion and interaction are downgraded in the descriptions.
c  mirroring the theoretical stance of (a) and (b), the cohesion considered necessary in 'scientific' communication is severely limited as compared with non-specialized text
d  similarly, there are hardly any indications of interaction in such writing.

At word level, isolation helps to preserve the pretension of a pure terminology, and to impose a similar conservatism on the general use of vocabulary; at sentence level, isolation opens up interpretative space.

Scientific prose written for fellow members of a community in a given field is likely to show a heavy concentration of terminology. The words do not adapt to their verbal environments; the words are as isolated as the sentences, and the phraseology is in constant danger of becoming ritualized. By contrast, language using ordinary vocabulary is constantly making fresh combinations, extending the phraseology, using genuine creativity in adapting itself to unique occasions.

Major developments in science – scientific revolutions – do indeed call for changes in the language, as Halliday has demonstrated, both in his studies of language change (1993) and in his own practice of writing (e.g. *a social semiotic, wording, texture*). Such evolutionary processes that initiate conceptual shifts move on a dimension well beyond the mundane focus of this chapter. For most, conformity is the watchword, and there are a large number of scientific writers whose competence is only achieved through rigid conformity.

Many of what are expected to be recognized as sublanguages come from varieties of highly specialized scientific and technical writing. The essentially restricted nature of a sublanguage ensures its relative rarity in everyday life, where people are not as disciplined or compartmentalized as they would need to be to use sublanguages as a matter of course. Scraps of sublanguage abound, of course, and they may well be found in unexpected places, as for example in the language of dictionary definitions (Barnbrook 1995; Sinclair, Hoelter and Peters 1995). Conversations with computers on the telephone, or indeed under any circumstances, are in a sublanguage, often one that is distinct on the surface from any natural language.

## Semantics: the empty lexicon

We shall concentrate mainly on semantic aspects of the lexicon in this section; syntactic aspects are secondary and are a consequence of the meaning distinctions. The idea of a lexicon from a Thespian perspective is quite unlike the conventional one. There is no familiar set of properties permanently attached to each word, there is no discernible starting-point for a word, there are no preconceptions, no prerequisites; only a format for how the lexicon entry will be built up through examining the usage of the word.

To justify the normal form of a lexicon, with its rigidity, its discreteness, and its determinism, we would have to construct a pseudo-historical notion that at some early time the words in a language were all tidily related to meanings; in this linguistic paradise, presumably before anyone started using the language, the meaning or meanings of each word were all distinct from each other, and discrete. Through the brutal clash of usage over the centuries, words have moved in meaning, and units of meaning have been forged consisting of more than one word.

In a synchronic view of language, the origins of meaning are not under scrutiny. But some of the processes of change are inescapably obvious. New meanings are constantly being created, mainly through gradual movements of collocation, and occasionally a word/meaning relationship is given the status of a term, and thus a measure of protection within the discourse of a specialized genre.

To build an adequate lexicon, we must start with usage. As speakers of the language, even as experts in its lexical structure, we cannot reliably anticipate usage, and so we have to study large samples of the language to uncover the regular patterns. It does not really matter what the dictionaries say, or even the term banks; a dictionary is a retrospective summary of usage, and if it does not agree with usage then it is inadequate, out-of-date or both. A term bank is a prospective imposition on usage which may be respected in whole or in part, and, therefore, may be more or less relevant to usage. Both are put together with massive subjective intervention, and so are not very useful for internalization in machines; recently some dictionaries have considered corpus evidence, though mainly keeping it at arm's length, but on the whole terminologists do not find textual patterns very interesting.

The lexicon is considered empty at the start because nothing appears in it except what is gleaned from the study of the language in use – nowadays, through the study of corpora. There is no assumption that meaning attaches only to the word; it is anticipated that meanings also arise from the loose and varying co-occurrences of several words, not necessarily next to each other. It is, thus, not possible to compile a list of entries in advance of analysing and interpreting the evidence, because the lexical items are not always words, and each word may enter into a variety of relationships with others to realize lexical items.

The format of this type of lexicon is familiar in principle to linguists, because it consists of three components – a form of a lexical item, an environment, and a meaning. A word becomes associated with a meaning through its repeated occurrence in similar contexts. The distinction between the item and its environment is not clear-cut, because the choice of a meaning has a profound effect on the surrounding text, one which is not suddenly cut off at a boundary, but which is correlated with adjacent meanings. Similarly, the domain of meaning does not consist of discrete entities, 'meanings', to each of which can be linked a form; it is assumed to be an amorphous area that is ordered by the number and type of lexical items. Hence the construction of the lexicon requires us to vary all three components against each other, in ways outlined in Sinclair 1996b.

Most words in common use can be associated with several meanings, and consequently meaning differentiation (sometimes misleadingly called dis-ambiguation) is a major issue in the structure of computational lexicons. In the ordinary language, multiple meanings of words are unavoidable; no matter how clear is the meaning in its context, with our present language models the machine has to compare exhaustively a given citation with all registered meanings before making a decision. The simplifying prospect of 'one word– one meaning' is unattainable unless one is able to place a restriction on the language so that just one meaning per word is permitted. While this last restric-tion might well be found in a sublanguage (Barnbrook 1995) and is a necessary condition of technical terminology, it is impossible to imagine in free text.

What happens in everyday language is that the meaning of the word and parts of its immediate context become inseparable. Repeated usage actually fuses the sense and the expression, and when this involves the recurrence of certain sequences of words, it is said to be an idiom. But the repetition may not always be obvious; the repeated pattern may be a step or two in generalization away from actual forms; such patterns are not normally thought of as idioms, but as senses of the central word.

Other kinds of spillover of meaning beyond the word are well documented, and many technical terms involve more than one word. The compound noun is a particular favourite among terminologists. But there is an important difference between such acknowledged multi-word units of language and the lexical struc-tures that are regularly created in ordinary text. The difference lies in the variability of the units of the 'live' lexicon. They adapt to the ever-changing, never-quite-repeated circumstances of communication, and as such cannot, in principle, be fully prescribed in advance.

It has often been remarked how rare are actual instances of the fixed-phrases that are logged in the textbooks and solemnly taught to the learners; it has more recently been pointed out (Sinclair 1991; Moon 1994) that idioms in use are prone to massive variation.

It is clear that there is a lot in common between the 'fixed phrases' in all their variations, and the senses of a word that are only realized under certain contextual conditions. They are in fact different ways of describing the same phenomenon, and both are distinct from technical terms, fixed phrases, and preordained lexicon entries.

From the discussion so far, it seems that there may be two lexicons used by speakers of a language. One is essentially an extended term bank, containing words and phrases which have fixed meanings and clear meaning differentiation. Entries to this lexicon are fixed in advance and remain accurate regardless of how much text is encountered. For most non-technical texts, this will be a small list.

The lexicon built on a terminological model is not of great linguistic interest, being largely part of an intellectual game where one group of experts identifies and defines a term, and another group tries to represent this information in terms compatible with a computer. Its relevance is confined to the margins of the vocabulary, dealing with rare and specialized words, words at their least characteristic. Understandably, though, it catches the attention of the Academician, and attempts are made to capture the whole lexical structure of a language in this model. The attempts are laborious, voluminous, and not flexible enough.

The other type of lexicon is usage-based – the 'empty' lexicon. It learns about vocabulary from the texts, and is constantly being updated. No part of it is absolute or permanent, because the boundary between item and environment is likely to move with new evidence, and meanings may merge or diverge. This is the lexicon of the living language, which reaches beyond an individual's intuition and tackles the lexical description of the central core of the vocabulary. Its comprehensiveness, provisionality, and heuristic orientation appeal to the Thespian.

Although undoubtedly attractive, such a model of the lexicon is likely to raise concerns among the Academicians. With lexical units such moving targets, how will precise and reliable lexicons ever be created? What will happen to the tidy genus-species hierarchies that allow words to be related to each other in simple ways, easily represented in a computer?

The most probable answer is that lexis does not stay still, and so no completely stable lexicon will give an adequate performance in practice. New models for lexicons will have to be devised, more opportunistic, more flexible, and more receptive to the evidence of usage. Lexical relationships there are in abundance in texts, and little has been done as yet to capture them in lexicons; there is no reason to believe that they will not form the basis of reliable lexicons.

These lexical relationships – collocations, etc., – are rather different from the familiar features and hierarchies, but there are also many indications of features and hierarchies in the texts (Pearson 1998). One of the characteristic properties of a natural language is the ability to talk about itself (Harris 1988), and particularly in specialized texts, there is a lot of such activity. The growing mastery of text by parsers should enable researchers shortly to turn this activity into evidence for a lexicon.

## The holistic orientation

In summary, the view of language that contrasts with the Academician's orientation to the message is a holistic view. Messages are not initially separated from the particular expressions used in the interactive circumstances of the utterances. In line with this position, the information model of language that is so popular and prevalent at the present time is rejected as quite inadequate for the subtleties of human communicative needs and skills, because it is insensitive to human interactive discourse structures.

Specialized varieties also are not detached from the rest of the language. Instead, they are seen as sharing the core of the language with ordinary varieties, but with individual peripheral differences. The sublanguage model implies that they are radically distinct from the ordinary language.

The emphasis on people communicating that characterizes the Thespian perspective means that Thespians do not stop their grammars at the sentence, but assume that discourse has a structure too. This insistence, plus the strong position on the importance of data, goes against selectiveness, or evaluating some kinds of language as more important than others.

The data orientation is the basis of the Thespian position on terminology and lexicons. For them, the text is the only authority on the way words are used and, therefore, the way they make meaning. The dictionary comes after the linguistic events and tries to interpret them.

The drawback to the Thespian perspective is that everything does not quite fit together as neatly as the prevailing language models predict. To the Thespian, this is not just a reflection of the early state of computer-orientated data research, but is an inalienable feature of natural language; attempts to force descriptions into tidy little boxes will not pass the acid test of computer replicability.

In the case of language, scholars are faced with indeterminate evidence of a complex organization. The question is whether it is the evidence that is indeterminate or the organization itself. Academicians feel that underneath all the detail there must be an order of mathematical-logical purity, and the job of the linguist is to find it; Thespians feel that indeterminacy is an inevitable consequence of the variety of individuals and their experiences, and the nature of language must reflect it.

While it is to be expected that the development of an adequate model based on corpora will clear up a lot of our present confusions, the inherent dynamic variation of language will continue indefinitely to defy static descriptive apparatus.

# 10  Lexical grammar

This is a discussion of the relations between lexis and grammar and whether they need to be kept separate from each other. This chapter and Chapter 12 were commissioned by the COSIH project (Corpus of Spoken Israeli Hebrew) for presentation at the project's inaugural seminar at Emory University in Atlanta, Georgia. Unfortunately I took ill and could not attend, so I made video recordings of the talks, and these were shown instead. They were then transcribed, and I edited them into the present form. Their original publication was in B. Hary (ed.) *Corpus Linguistics and Modern Hebrew*, published by the Chaim Rosenberg School of Jewish Studies, Tel-Aviv University, Israel, 2003. This chapter has also been published in M. Gellerstam, K. Jóhanesson, B. Ralph and L. Rogström (eds) *Nordiska Studier I Lexicografi 5*.

## Introduction

This chapter concerns the relation between the two types of pattern that are mainly recognized as the means whereby language creates meaning. The terms *grammar* and *lexis* will mainly be used for these, but instead of grammar you will sometimes find *syntax* or *structure*, and instead of lexis you may find *semantics* or *vocabulary*. But there is always this basic distinction, of a component which produces patterns of organization and a component which produces items that fill places in the patterns; the items tend to be chosen individually, and with little reference to the surrounding text.

The title of the chapter is *Lexical grammar* and not *lexico*-grammar. Lexico-grammar is now very fashionable, but it does not integrate the two types of pattern as its name might suggest – it is fundamentally grammar with a certain amount of attention to lexical patterns within the grammatical frameworks; it is not in any sense an attempt to build together a grammar and lexis on an equal basis.

When a dichotomy is firmly established in a culture, it is difficult to find a name for it or to talk about it as a unified whole and not two different things; that is the problem here. Recent research into the features of language corpora give us reason to believe that the fundamental distinction between grammar, on the one hand, and lexis, on the other hand, is not as fundamental as it is usually held to be and since it is a distinction that is made at the outset of the formal study of language, then it colours and distorts the whole enterprise. It is worth considering how far, using modern techniques, we can get in describing a language without resorting to such a distinction.

## Grammar and lexis

The distinction between grammar and lexis is a very basic model of language; there would be no motivation to reconsider it unless new evidence gave rise to concern about its accuraccy. One reason for such a model becoming so well established could be simply that before the computer age linguists were unable to describe all the complexity of language at once; since it could be represented as a framework and a set of choices to fit the frames, one of those elements could be held steady and the other varied against it. So we could forget, temporarily, about the patterns of semantic choice while we look at the organization of the structures; and then the process could be reversed, and when we came to look at the words and their meanings, then we did not consider at that point whether they were subjects or objects of clauses or objects of prepositions, if they were noun phrases, because that part of the overall organization was suspended.

In other words, we can put forward for consideration the suggestion that this initial division of language patterning may not be fundamental to the nature of language, but more a consequence of the inadequacy of the means of studying language in the pre-computer age. When the linguist had nothing but his or her five senses, memory and internal awareness, it was difficult to analyse such a complex matter as language; consider phonetics, for example, before the sound wave could be slowed down and divided into its components. Without the ability to manipulate language externally, the observer/analyst has to leave some things steady, or hope they stay steady while other aspects of the whole are examined. And the problem is, in language, that they don't stay steady. So we should at least question the wisdom of dividing the meaningful patterns of language into two at the outset.

## Abstractions

There is a related point to be made separately, but also a consequence of the position of the human observer. It is generally recognized that the meaningful patterns of language are of an abstract nature, which is one reason why they are so difficult to explain, and to use in teaching; from the perspective of grammar they are more abstract than they seem to be at first sight. It is possible that the reason for their unexpected level of abstraction is that grammar typically is realized through the common words and morphemes – that is, they seem to be familiar, but in fact many of them are multiply ambiguous and in a complex relationship with the categories that they realize (Sinclair 1999a). So grammar is superficially easy to observe but much more abstract than appears at first sight.

In contrast, the lexical patterns are very difficult to observe because they are realized by a large vocabulary of infrequent words, and so it is not easy to work out the recurrent patterns that lie beneath the massive variation. The patterns are patterns of combination, and this compounds the problem; whereas in grammar the recurrence of frequent words makes it fairly easy to notice patterns of combination, in lexis the combinations had only been seen in a few hundred idiomatic expressions which were so remarkable that they had to be accounted for separately. With large corpora and powerful computers we are at the frontiers of a new view of language, where we can appreciate its full complexity without getting hampered by the detail.

It is thus no accident that linguists up till now have developed grammars much more than dictionaries and lexicons; we tend to have very elaborate grammars, which contain intricate apparatus with ranks and hierarchies and structures and all sorts of categories, with many different kinds of organization and in contrast we have very, very simple models of lexical structure, which are mainly one-dimensional, based on the word. There is an ad hoc set of terms for multi-word units like idiom and cliché and saying and proverb, but all these are ill-defined terms, and there is no other network of interconnections between one word and another.

Again this disparity in our descriptions does not necessarily reflect the nature of language, but rather it reflects our collective inability to process language with sufficient power and understanding to see that the complexity of the language as seen from a lexical point of view is just as great as the complexity of the language as seen from the grammatical point of view. So we may expect that simple artefacts like dictionaries will give way to more complex lexical architectures – indeed the development of dictionaries with an influence from corpus research has begun to move in this direction.

## Meaning and structure

There is one consequence of the initial separation of language patterning into two contrasted types that could be very important. To bring it out clearly we will use the terms *meaning* and *structure*. In brief, the point is that if we ignore the meaning while we are describing the structure, then of course we have removed the meaning and will not be able to get it back while we are focused on the structure. That is one way of expressing the problem of grammar, and it has been obscured from careful examination by a kind of meaning substitute. This is the curious terminology that we use, things like positive/negative, singular/plural, active/passive, and so on. If we look at them carefully, these terms are of course quite substantially inaccurate. 'Singular' does not always mean 'one,' and 'plural' does not always mean 'more than one'. 'Present' does not always refer to the time of the utterance, and 'past' certainly does not always mean some previous time. We have learned as part of our culture to suspend disbelief when we encounter these terms, and apply a rough criterion of *mutatis mutandis* to their interpretation; 'singular' means 'not more than one, if whatever it is is countable, otherwise general reference'. The point is that because these terms are not sensitive to the meaning, then they cannot actually be used directly to elucidate the meaning of text. The distinctions could have any labels at all, and at best they have a mnemonic function (this argument is well supported by the retention in current grammars of terms like 'finite' or 'voice', which bears little relation to meaning in current English).

The only meaning that grammar provides is differentiation. From the *valeur* of Saussure to the systems of systemic linguistics and the choices of transformational grammars, then, the only way in which grammar creates meaning is by setting up mutually exclusive choices, and it exists purely as a record of the choice itself; the significance of the choice – whether a past tense verb relates to past time or present or future time or modality – is determined elsewhere.

If we now view the structure/meaning divide from the other perspective, and look at semantics without structure, then the typical way of presenting the meaning is the dictionary. A dictionary simply lists in an arbitrary order, which we call alphabetical[1] the items that it regards as being meaningful, which are usually the words of the language, and it tries to assign one or more meanings to each of the words. That is the characteristic model of a dictionary. The meanings are denied access to the structural organization that can put them together and show how they work. For example one meaning given in a recently published dictionary for the word 'white' is 'counterrevolutionary, very conservative, or royalist'; if this meaning is still current it would take some ingenuity to specify the structural circumstances under which it could occur.

So therefore substitutes, again, are offered, this time standing in for the linguistic organization that has been discarded. There are in semantics two major types of organization that have been imported; one of these is referential semantics, and the other is logical semantics; let us consider them in turn. The assumption of referential semantics is that meanings are organized with reference to the world outside; words have meanings which can be understood by indicating objects, events and attributes in the world to which they refer; for abstract entities there is the 'figurative' mode which works analagously. This is simple and seems to be broadly usable for a very large range of phenomena, and is widely used in education, but from a theoretical point of view it is absurd. Consider the proposal for a moment – on the one hand there is language, which we know is a highly organized phenomenon that operates under major constraints such as linearity, and on the other hand there is the world, which after thousands of years of research we still see as pretty chaotic, exceptionally complex and totally unable to be encompassed in a simple description. We are asked to accept that reference to the world can elucidate the structure of language? We have some reason to believe that language can elucidate some aspects of the world, but hardly the other way round. At best the referential links can help in, for example, supporting the acquisition of language by a child, before the child can cope with semantic abstractions.

The other type of imported semantic structure that is popular is logical semantics. It seems to have some advantages, being rigorous and much of it being quite close to the patterns of natural language (as well it might be, being derived from them). But it is crucial to the understanding of natural language that the organization is *not* exact, and is not reliable as an indication of logical relationships. As with the definition of terms in grammar, there is again the problem of the partial fit, the inexact fit.

Here is a brief example to show the problems of relying on logical analogies too closely. Many commentators have noted that the 'conditional' *if* does not always have its logical force, for example in the following instances culled from a large number of candidates in just one category of the BNC Sampler (spoken business)

> . . . which is obtainable from Christian Aid if people want . . . .
> I'm just thinking for the meeting if we could photocopy some Yes
> I'll be actually chairing the meeting for him. So so if you'd like to kick off . . .
> Mm. Yes. Mm. Erm Mm I could if I could just pick up one other point about you know . . .

And another one noticed casually in reading:

> If you believe me, I swung along that road whistling.
>                              (John Buchan, *The Thirty-Nine Steps*)

And one which has already occurred in this chapter (one of two):

> If we look at them carefully, these terms are of course quite substantially inaccurate.

## The axes of language patterning

We now move our perspective to a closely related dichotomy that has long been recognized in language description – the two fundamental axes of language patterning, the paradigmatic and the syntagmatic. They are usually depicted as horizontal and vertical, with the syntagmatic axis on the horizontal, because the languages of modern Europe are written in horizontal lines, and the paradigmatic on the vertical.[2] The paradigmatic axis specifies the possible choices at a particular position on the syntagmatic axis, and the syntagmatic axis controls the structure which is being elaborated. So what we observe in language text is the syntagmatic; the paradigms are the total of what might have been chosen instead.

Now, one of the interesting things about these two axes is that they cannot be simultaneously observed; you must hold one of them steady in order to look at the other. We shall return to this point, but no doubt this is the reason why we have had the division into grammar and lexis from an early stage. It is important to notice that the theoretical development of grammars in recent years has moved across this divide. If we were to map the 'grammar' composite (including syntax, structure) and the 'lexis' one onto the two axes, then the

obvious pairing would be grammar on the horizontal axis and lexis on the vertical – a model of language often called the 'slot-and-filler' model, the one
presented at the outset of this chapter. The syntactic structures form a series of
slots, and these are filled with choices from the dictionary. The well-known
models of transformational grammar are partly structured in this way, for
example at the interface between the phrase structure and the lexicon, where
the phrase structure specifes the features that any word must have in order to
make a well-formed sentence, and the lexicon associates each word with a
bundle of features. However, other influential models insist that they are primarily, if not exclusively, paradigmatic – notably Systemic-Functional Grammar
(see Halliday 1995: 15).

The syntagmatic patterns of language are not given meaning in a paradigm
grammar, nor, of course, are they given meaning in a dictionary type of lexis.
The syntagmatic patterns in a grammar are either offered as related through a
common node, or they are simply declared. The syntagmatic patterns of lexis
only appear in the byway of idiomatic phrase, where they are offered as joint
realizations of a single meaningful unit, indicating that they have no meaning in
themselves.

Let us consider the grammatical positions a little more. In phrase-structure
rules like

S → NP  VP

the only relationship between NP and VP is that they are both derived from S
in the same operation; their sequence is also determined in this single step. In
the early days of generative grammar there was a plus sign in between NP and
VP

S → NP + VP

but this signalled a quite spurious relationship pertaining on the syntagmatic
axis, and became unfashionable.

Where syntagmatic patterns come into being by declaration, there is no
explanation of where they come from or how they are to be deployed. The structure of an English clause is said to involve subject–predicator–object–adjunct, for
example, but these categories are mutually defining, and do not have meaning
until they are mapped into sets of choices, for example that a transitive clause is
one without an object. So, neither in the study of the lexis of the language nor in
the study of the grammar of the language are the syntagmatic patterns given
meaning. This is to a great extent because there is no framework within which
they can be shown to have meaning, because meaning is largely held to reside
either in the grammatical choice – on the paradigmatic axis – or in the lexical
choice of a word to deliver a meaning.

## Syntagmatic meaning

There is no effort, let us say in summary, to discover or create meaning on the syntagmatic axis; it is the responsibility of a paradigm grammar to build in all possible syntagmatic meaning as constraints on the paradigmatic choices. But such a venture would be remarkably complex, so in practice those grammars fail to describe carefully enough the *combinations* of choices that are just as central and meaningful and rule-governed as the single paradigmatic choices. They give tacit approval to the well-formedness of millions of sentences which range from the odd to the bizarre, and – by claiming as a series of choices phrases which we know to be a single choice – they claim large amounts of meaning which we know those choices do not create.

In corpus linguistics, by contrast, we have to work on the assumption that meaning is created on both axes; for want of more accurate information we may assume that they contain equal meaning potential. There is no reason why one should have a priority in meaning potential over the other. We assume a rough balance between what I have called (Sinclair 1996b) the *phraseological tendency*, the tendency of a speaker/writer to choose several words at a time, and the *terminological tendency*, the tendency of language users to protect the meaning of a word or phrase so that every time it is used it guarantees delivery of a known meaning. As we get to know more, these assumptions may well be revised.

Above we have presented a model of language as a balance between opposing forces related to the two axes of language patterning, and above that is an assertion that the two axes cannot be simultaneously observed; these sound like good reasons for keeping them apart, and describing them separately. However, the argument of this chapter is that if pattern and meaning are to be aligned, then the two axes have to be inter-related for as long as possible in the description. Consider, for example, the classic model where a choice is made on the paradigmatic axis which will lead to a particular word appearing in the text. Now it is an axiom of the present approach to corpus linguistics that meaning and cotext are inter-related in such a way that involves at least partial co-selection; so the knock-on effect of a paradigmatic choice will be felt on the syntagmatic axis. If we start from the other axis, then any existing or proposed pattern of choice on the syntagmatic axis provides a framework for the interpretation of any choice to be made on the paradigmatic axis.

## Practical consequences

The remainder of this chapter gives some indications of the direction in which this argument is heading and the kind of consequences it is likely to lead to. First we will re-examine the nature of choice and meaning, then look further into the 'meaningful' terminology of grammar, and finally pose a question about an important type of meaning that is largely ignored by both the grammatical and lexical traditions.

## Meanings from nowhere

Let us begin by revisiting the information-theoretic model of paradigm grammar which says that choice equals meaning, that the number of choices determines the amount of meaning available in each case, and the precise positioning of the choice in the structural framework determines much of the type of meaning that will be created by the choice. A description within this model must take great care that each set of choices is actually relevant and applicable at each point. Because if it is not – if another factor in the environment is affecting the range of choices on offer – then, unless the grammar is revised, it is creating more meaning than is in fact available.

If this manufacture of illusory meaning is institutionalized throughout a complex grammar, there are two obvious consequences. One is that the grammar (and the grammarians) are misled into thinking that their apparatus is more powerful than it actually is; the other is that there is little meaning left over to be assigned by the lexical structure of the language. Now that it can be demonstrated by corpus evidence that a large proportion of the word occurrence is the result of co-selection – that is to say, more than one word is selected in a single choice – every time that this can be demonstrated there is one less item of meaning to be allocated to the grammar. If you have two words that are selected in the same choice, then they cannot be independently selected. Early estimates were that up to 80 per cent of the occurrence of words could be through co-selections, which would leave, of course, only 20 per cent for the sort of independent paradigmatic choices of the grammar. A recent paper by May Fan (1999) gave hard evidence for this in regard to one of the common verbs in English.

Let us work through a characteristic example. There is a phrase in English, a common recurrent phrase, 'out of the corner of my eye', as in 'I saw something out of the corner of my eye'. There are seven words in the phrase, and they all simultaneously choose one unit of meaning to do with peripheral vision. Within this primary meaning, there are one or two variants of individual words, and this is where the corpus is essential, because the intuition cannot be relied on. 'Out of' can sometimes be replaced by 'from', and 'my' is a possessive adjective that can have other, but probably only singular forms; people do not collectively see things out of the corners of their eyes, so I think 'their eyes' is going to be very unusual. This is the full extent of the variation associated with this phrase; the remaining words are fixed, and do not realize any choice beyond the first, overall choice of meaning. So neither of the occurrences of *of* above are the normal occurrence of the preposition, because *of* is fixed in this phrase,[3] and so are 'the', 'corner' and 'eye'. The word 'my' can be alternated with other possessive adjectives. So here we have a seven-word phrase which realizes one overall choice and at most two subsidiary choices. The choice between 'out of' and 'from' here is a stylistic choice rather than a choice that delivers a totally different type of meaning – there are not two different places, and 'out of' and 'from' are just different ways of expressing the same basic position.

These single choices can consist of seven words with ease; the phraseology of

English quite frequently produces co-selections of five, six and seven words, and there are even some of up to twelve. In this connection Miller (1956) comes to mind. Miller showed that for most people the short-term memory handles seven items with ease.

## Cross-border categories

Corpus evidence consistently shows that the ways in which a meaning can be realized extend well beyond the definitions of grammatical categories. In pointing out above that grammatical terminology did not correspond to semantically coherent categories, we did not tell the whole story. Consider a term like 'negative', which will contrast with 'positive' in a two-term system of 'polarity'. There are a number of realizations of grammatical negatives in English, 'no' and 'not' and so on. There are also semi-negatives like 'hardly' and 'scarcely', which share a number of features with true negatives, but not all; these are not normally considered as grammatical negatives.

But there are also morphological negatives like the prefixes 'un-' and 'in-', which are not recognized in a clause grammar, so that 'I am unhappy' is positive and 'I am not happy' is negative. We also find that negation as a concept can be lexicalized, so that the verb 'refuse' for example has a negative force; 'he refused to go' is the same as 'he would not go' and yet it is a positive clause in the grammatical sense.

It is easy to understand the grammarian's wish to keep negation pure and simple; to accept lexicalized negation is a slippery slope, and no one knows what lies at the bottom of it. But if we are intent on elucidating the meaning of running text by analysis, then all these different ways of indicating negation are perfectly acceptable realizations, and if supported by corpus evidence we can take them all together, straddling the borders between grammar and semantics. This straddling is an important feature of lexical structure; lexis is not the residue of a grammatical description, but a different way of describing the same events; it is not bound by the conventions of grammar, and it can recognize a wide variety of realizations of meaningful choices.

The grammarian is left in a dilemma; the more sensitive grammars recognize that categories of meaning like 'negative', 'modal', 'possessive' can readily be lexicalized – or to be more neutral, can occur in grammatical or lexical or morphological realizations – so a complex realization route is devised for them. The particular way in which they are realized is then of secondary importance compared with the primary creation of meaning, which is the operative process. The question must arise of the relevance of, for example, the grammatical choice between positive and negative to the study of meaning when negative meaning can be created in so many alternative ways; and, more fundamentally, how valuable is it to be able to point out that there are many clauses which are grammatically negative but in relation to meaning, positive, and vice versa?

## Semantic prosody

Another important point to be made in the study of lexical grammar is the emergence of many latent categories of meaning, which have not been recognized in published grammars, and only occasionally in the very latest dictionaries. The first to be noticed were of the type 'something nasty' or 'something worrying' or 'disturbing'; later others like 'something magnificent', 'socially appropriate', 'positively constructive', etc. These are showing up as repetitive categories that are neither completely grammatical nor completely lexical but are nevertheless very important from a structural point of view. So once again we have to allow for the meaningful categories not to be confined within the grammar as it is normally presented, and if we divide language into these two major categories, then we will never be able to get them satisfactorily together again; also we have to add that the grammar cannot be trusted to set up such essential categories of meaning because it is not sensitive to them.[4]

Here it has to be said that the perceptions of native speakers are not to be trusted either; the referential element in meaning is frequently assigned a priority over the attitudinal, for reasons that are not justifiable; clearly an awareness of both aspects of meaning is necessary for accurate deployment of the lexical item, and if this is not available it is arguable that more difficulty may arise from a mistake on the pragmatic side than on the referential. To give a real-life example, in the preparation of a dictionary for native speakers of English by the Cobuild team, there was a strong feeling among editors and publisher that whereas for learners of English it may be necessary to state the attitudinal meaning, this is already available to native speakers. So the Cobuild definition (1987) for *scrawny* is 'unpleasantly thin and bony', while in *Today's English Dictionary* (1995) it is 'thin and bony'; the two dictionaries define *prattle* identically but Cobuild adds 'an informal word, often used showing disapproval'.[5]

## Word class

Professional linguists should not be surprised to experience a rather disturbing effect from the massive surge in the availability of evidence and the growing sophistication of the tools for examining it and testing hypotheses against it that corpus linguistics has brought. Some of the vague but useful categories of traditional language analysis, which have served humans well for centuries, are not easily replicated in computational routines; for example 'parts of speech' or 'word class' labelling. Human beings have little difficulty assigning words to a dozen or so word classes, but machines have exposed just how untidy a categorization this is. For English, which has had a lot of attention over many years, there is little or no consensus about how many labels there are – the variation from one analysis to another is very large – or how they are defined. The persistence of researchers has resulted in a significant movement of focus, so that the process is now called 'morphosyntactic tagging' – in other words it was found necessary to use some syntactic information in order to complete what was originally a morphological analysis.

This movement of focus is well recognized in corpus linguistics – the need to examine the context of an item in order to determine its function or meaning. But nothing seems able to shake belief in the underlying assumption that all the words of a language naturally fall into a small number of classes. The information from a computer examination of a corpus suggests quite otherwise, as I have argued on several occasions.[6] Since few inflections survive into modern English, and since one of the most productive areas of development in the modern language is the ability of words to move across word classes, it may be preferable to accept what the corpus seems to be signalling, which is the need for a major overhaul of the notion of word class.

In general, we must move toward a theory that reconciles the paradigmatic and the syntagmatic dimensions and allows the description of the language to remain sensitive to both dimensions for as long as the correlation is productive; no doubt there will be some residue of specifically grammatical and specifically lexical information after that stage, but we must wait to see what it is, and what categories and processes are best used to describe it.

## Lexical structure

At present, the lexical structure is presented separately, insensitive to the grammar in the same way as the grammar is, traditionally, insensitive to the lexis. It is probably a valuable exercise to prioritize the lexical patterning and to push a lexical description as far as it is reasonable to do so; the justification is that so little research has been done in this area, especially as compared with the immense attention that the grammar has had over the centuries. But such an effort should not be misunderstood; it must be seen simply as an interim step towards an eventual holistic description, and there is no imperialistic dimension to lexical description.

In the meantime, there are structures of a particularly lexical nature that are worthy of attention, and which are introduced in recent publications, particularly Sinclair 1998. These begin with *collocation*, the co-occurrence of words, and go on to *colligation*, which in this work is defined as the co-occurrence of words with grammatical choices, then *semantic preference*, which is the co-occurrence of words with semantic choices, and *semantic prosody*. The semantic prosodies express attitudinal and pragmatic meaning; they are the junction of form and function. The reason why we choose to express ourselves in one way rather than another is coded in the prosody, which is an obligatory component of a lexical item.

The ways in which the prosody is expressed are extremely varied, and seem to have no limits as to position or shape; we can thus anticipate severe technical problems in retrieving them computationally. This is the central problem in analysing open text and one of the principal reasons that the performance of devices which depend on some kind of language understanding is so poor.

At the present time the goal of the machine understanding of language is far more difficult than it needs to be, because we are not using appropriate theories – once the meaning created by lexical structures becomes available, and integrated with what we already know through grammar, then theories will be articulated that predict the prosodies and the computer will then know where to look for them. These theories will be developed from the kinds of hypotheses that are taking shape in corpus-driven linguistics.

## Example

Let me give as a conclusion an example of the kind of semantic prosody that I am talking about. Consider the English word *effort*; it is a countable noun and so it has a plural, *efforts*. And one of the most notable collocates of *efforts* is the word *to*, which follows *efforts*, and which is the infinite marker. So essentially we are focussing on a structure which has a core of *efforts* plus an infinitive. In *The Bank of English*[7] in Birmingham, which is the reference corpus that I normally use, the one that lies behind the Cobuild publications, there are 9,617 instances of *efforts* followed by *to*. For Appendix 10.1, the computer has selected 21 by the simple expedient of picking the first one in text sequence, then dividing 9,616 by 20 (= 480 in round figures) and then selecting the 481st, 961st, etc. instance through the corpus.

If we examine these, it becomes fairly clear that we use this phrasing – we talk of 'efforts to' do something – when someone appears to be very unlikely to succeed, to be heading for failure, or already unsuccessful. In other words, the prosody that appears in almost every example is the speaker/writer's prejudgement of the efforts, that they are heading for failure. So when we are discussing the machine understanding of language, if we were to talk of the 'efforts' of computational linguistics 'to' comprehend natural language, we would imply that they are doomed to failure. There are a number of adjectives, for example, like *hysterical, frantic, futile, strenuous*; verbs like *blunder, hamper, were overwhelmed*; people *close ranks against* efforts, or achieve things *despite efforts*; efforts *exhaust* us, and so on. So if this is a representative sample of the behaviour of the word, we can expect to find in the left-hand cotext of *efforts to* some indication of the likely failure of the efforts.

In a contrast which is almost ironic, we can expect to find in the right-hand cotext a set of verbs which are creative, which talk about creative action, like *please, revive, work together, protect, support, gain, raise, activate, kindle (a debate), help, give (the city something good), save*, etc. So before a reader/listener discovers that the efforts are to do something constructive and beneficial, they are already sabotaged. Our first draft of the lexical item that has as its core *efforts to* will thus contain three elements of structure – the core, the semantic preference for a verb of constructive action, and the semantic prosody of anticipated failure. The selection of the item is controlled by the prosody, because the whole point of expressing oneself in this way is to pre-evaluate the actions, which would otherwise be positively evaluated by the reader/listener.

It is likely that other expressions with structural similarity to this tentative item will be found; *attempts to* may be similar,[8] etc. The singular forms, *effort*, *attempt* may show some tendency in the same direction. A set of forms sharing similar meanings could be a further step in the mapping of an organizational framework for lexis. This work is only beginning; a few probes have been made into the lexical structure of the language, and some tentative hypotheses have been formulated.

## Conclusion

Despite the recent rush to welcome corpora into the resource collections of many students of language, we must note that the vast majority of work with corpora still takes place under the assumptions of pre-corpus linguistics, and is thus insensitive to the possibilities put forward here. It is clear that the first step towards a new view of language has now been taken by the linguistics profession in recognizing that corpora are relevant and useful; this has been effectively completed approximately 30 years from the advent of electronic corpora. It is only natural that to begin with scholars will appreciate the security of familiar concepts in engaging with such a total revolution in the availability of evidence of usage, and only gradually will they accept that some of those concepts are sorely in need of being revised and updated.

The initial separation of grammar and lexis in language description, and the subsequent prioritization of grammar at the expense of lexis, is one of the most firmly held positions among theoretical and descriptive linguists, and it will take some time before it is held up to scrutiny and approached with an open mind.

## Appendix 10.1

| | | |
|---:|:---:|:---|
| the Hungarians would continue their | efforts | to please on the football pitch. |
| made love parsimoniously.' Gaspard's | efforts | to revive their passion exhausts |
| to support poor people in their own | efforts | to work together. Development |
| at the plan and that farmers' | efforts | to protect their livestock, crops |
| difficulties, and to increase their | efforts | to support Eastern Europe. At the |
| last Thursday and could hamper their | efforts | to gain access to Polly Peck's |
| arts companies, at their continuing | efforts | to raise additional funds from the |
| First Division, made more serious | efforts | to activate their attack. Smith |
| heroes for their – albeit futile – | efforts | to prevent the countryside from |
| office, due to their own hysterical | efforts | to keep their seats. <p> Yours |
| broke through police lines in their | efforts | to get on to the Garvaghy Road |
| new weapons. <p> Despite their | efforts | to kindle a debate in France – and |
| were likely to make strenuous | efforts | to help their employees get to |
| workers were overwhelmed in their | efforts | to deal with thousands of refugees |
| Assistens Kirkegaard. In their | efforts | to give the city still more green |
| close ranks against government | efforts | to control their work. Indeed, it |
| joined neighbours in their frantic | efforts | to save the family. Later, |
| while just possibly making some | efforts | to get their feet on the bottom |
| and WRC officials will suspend their | efforts | to sign players to contracts until |
| the attack yesterday switched their | efforts | to a murder inquiry. <p> Mrs |
| blunder desperately in their | efforts | to contain the uncontainable. |

# 11 Phraseognomy

This is a short piece making one small point only – it started off as introductory remarks to my paper at the Fourth International Seminar on Phraseology, which took place in Rome, at the Università di Roma Tre, and was extended for publication in S. Nuccorini (ed.) *Phrases and Phraseology – Data and Descriptions*: Bern, Peter Lang (2002).

## Introduction

There has to be a grave-sounding word for discussing the phraseology of 'phraseology', and I offer the one in my title, which arrives with impeccable etymological credentials, if little evidence of usage.

After three interesting and successful conferences on the topic of phraseology, a society was founded to promote the study of the phraseological perspective on language. Figure 11.1 is the letterhead of the society; being European it uses the three main languages of western Europe.

Notice that the preposition used in the English version is *of*, and when I first encountered this I felt it was, if not ungrammatical, certainly uncomfortable. In French the preposition is *de* and in German *für*. The regular translation of *de* in English is indeed 'of', but of *für* it is 'for'. I wondered, does:

1    European Society for Phraseology

sound any better? Yes, I think it does, but I have no idea why.

English is in origin a Germanic language, not a Romance one, and I remember learning that one of the ways this shows is that the syntactic base remains Germanic, no matter how heavy are the borrowings of Romance vocabulary. This might lead us to expect the *for* structure rather than the *of* one.

However, there are surely plenty of examples of Societies *of* something.

2    European Society of Phraseologists

sounds fine as a phrase, but it is understandable why it was not preferred as the title of the society. There is not (as yet anyway) a recognized profession of

Europäische Gesellschaft für Phraseologie
European Society of Phraseology
Société Européenne de Phraséologie
(EUROPHRAS)

*Figure 11.1* Trilingual letterhead

*Phraseologist*; people do not go around calling themselves phraseologists in the same way as they may call themselves linguists or phoneticians or (perhaps with a certain uppishness) grammarians.

There is also a difference between building an institution around a subject rather than around the practitioners of the subject. In the former case it suggests that some of us are phraseologists and some are not, whereas by naming the society by its topic of interest it suggests that anyone who shares this interest is welcome. One has an orientation of exclusivity, and the other of openness. For a topic like phraseology, which is just beginning to define itself in among grammar, lexis and idiom, clear boundaries would probably be counter-productive at this stage.

So *Phraseology* is preferred to *Phraseologists*, and so why not *for* rather than *of?*

## Usage

Let us review the evidence of usage. In *The Bank of English*, at the time of writing, there are 4,026 instances of *Society of* and 2,504 instances of *Society for*, so the numbers at first sight favour *of*.

Citations 1 (Table 11.1) gives a selection of instances with *of*, chosen by arithmetic selection at regular intervals throughout the corpus. The suggestion above that a professional group might regularly be the noun or noun group governed by *of* is borne out by the fact that just over half of the instances show this feature. The only other usage of note is where *of* governs a place name, and there is an adjective modifying *Society* which identifies the topic. A quarter of the instances are of this kind.

Citations 2 (Table 11.2) gives a similar selection of instances of *for*. Here the most prominent pattern is just a noun group governed by *for* and identifying the area of concern or activity of the society. The noun groups fall into two distinct groups according to whether we interpret the objective as the promotion of whatever is named or the alleviation of it – *Clean Air* versus *Epilepsy*. Academic subjects such as *Microbiology* – and *Phraseology* – presumably belong to the first group.

This three-way distinction into an academic subject, a cause worth promoting and an unfortunate state of affairs that should be eradicated, alleviated or supported according to circumstances is not always clear-cut. For example, *music therapy* must be a subject in some curricula, and it can simultaneously be a focus of enthusiastic promotion. Since the notion of therapy presumes that some

*Table 11.1* Citations 1. Society of . . .

| | | |
|---:|:---:|:---|
| in Bulletin of the Seismological | Society | of America Vol. 61, pp. 1073– |
| have been elected fellows of the | Society | of Antiquaries of London: Stephen |
| make cheques payable to 'SOLIHULL | SOCIETY | OF ARTS'. |
| in the summer of 1991 that the Royal | Society | of Arts first started to think |
| a luncheon hosted by the Economic | Society | of Australia (Queensland) Inc. |
| 1953–57; and chairman of the | Society | of Authors of Scotland, 1966–72, |
| Engineering Planetary Environments ( | Society | of Automotive Engineers, |
| justice conference, organised by the | Society | of Black Lawyers, the |
| to blame people. 'But for the | Society | of Black Lawyers and the |
| Lloyds; the RYA; the YBDSA; The | Society | of Consulting Marine Engineers and |
| education. The 30th International | Society | of Education through Art (InSEA) |
| through unity. Otherwise why had the | Society | of Friends endured? Caporelli |
| books, or visit the shop. | Society | of Homeopaths, 2 Artizan Road, |
| actually published, they founded the | Society | of Individualists. The 'Liberty |
| said he would appeal. The Zoological | Society | of London admitted liability. |
| survey was presented by the American | Society | of Newspaper Editors during the |
| S. Pinafore' by Gilbert and Sullivan | Society | of San Jose, Oct. 28–29, 8 p.m. |
| For serv the commty, especly the | Society | of St Vincent de Paul |
| let us all be like the branch. The | Society | of the Missionaries of Charity is |
| The Catholic Church Extension | Society | of the United States of America |
| association has formed the | Society | of Voluntary Control of Fair and |

people are in need of it, the instance might even be seen as referring to an unfortunate group of people.

The next most numerous pattern echoes my glossing precisely; societies for the *-ion* of something. The first noun is usually derived from a verb, as *Prevention, Protection, Suppression,* and makes explicit whether the area of concern is desirable or not.

Together these instances so far account for all but a few which are commented on below. The way in which the titles of societies express their interests is summarized in Table 11.3.

Let us now examine more carefully the left-hand side of the instances. We have already noted that the area of interest of the society can be identified in a structure preceding *Society*, usually an adjective, but on occasion a mouthful like *The Catholic Church Extension [Society of the United States of America].* There are other adjectives in this position, which indicate not the topic of the society but its provenance – often its status, e.g. *Royal*, or the community that it represents, e.g. *European*. In our small samples it is clear that the distribution of such adjectives between the two prepositional structure is far from even; only three from Citations 1 are of this kind, as against 17 from Citations 2. This is further confirmation that the preposition *for* is more appropriate than *of* in our original example.

As always in any concordance sample, there remain a few cases that require special comment. One is:

3   The Royal Society of/for Arts

*Table 11.2* Citations 2. Society for . . .

| | | |
|---|---|---|
| into Tomorrow's Company by the Royal | Society | for Arts. The RSA looked at what |
| Tim Brown, of the National | Society | for Clean Air, said last night: ` |
| soreness. Contact the British Dental | Society | for Clinical Nutrition |
| of Valerie Solanas' man-hating Scum ( | Society | For Cutting Up Men) manifesto. |
| of those are children. The National | Society | for Epilepsy has now launched a |
| of Boston, told the International | Society | for Exercise and Immunology |
| Ingram, president of the American | Society | for Microbiology, says biologists |
| music therapy, contact the British | Society | for Music Therapy, 69 Avondale |
| and founder of the International | Society | for Ordained Scientists. |
| president in 1933. (Mary Evans/ | Society | for Psychical Research) |
| field ambulance for the Commonwealth | Society | for the Deaf at Buckingham Palace. |
| agency last year. The National | Society | for the Prevention of Cruelty to |
| made arrangements with The National | Society | for the Prevention of Cruelty to |
| active supporters than the National | Society | for the Prevention of Cruelty to |
| euthanasia organizations, the | Society | for the Right to Die, not by some |
| been to Jamaica for the Commonwealth | Society | for the Deaf to look at how much |
| and Richard Ryder of the Royal | Society | for the Protection of Animals. |
| outcry was immediate with the Royal | Society | For The Prevention Of Accidents |
| of Secularization (Storrs, Conn. | Society | for the Scientific Study of |
| over his report to the International | Society | for the Suppression of Savage |
| long service in the International | Society | for the Study of Behavioural |

The normal usage for this ancient body is with *of,* and as such it is somewhat anomalous. Of the various categories of 'topic' that we have identified, this one fits best with *Microbiology*; although *Arts* is not a recognized academic subject, it is a recognized category of subject classification. According to this argument, *for* would be the preposition to use, and indeed there is one instance of it. This is akin to the language-learner's sin of overgeneralization. Another relevant instance, *Solihull Society of Arts*, follows the 'Royal' model.

To complicate matters, the name by which the *Royal Society* is normally known by – apart from its initials, *RSA* – is itself a contraction from the original, which is set out in Figure 11.2 and dates from 1754. In the second line as printed it is clear that whoever contracted this title had the choice of either of our prepositions, one of which occurs at each end of the line. At first sight the choice of *for* seems the natural one, but I personally would feel uncomfortable with *Royal Society for Arts*. I feel the need for *The Arts*, which has no precedent in the full name of the society.

The *RSA*, as a venerable institution, can assume a status above the conventions of everyday usage. Of the remaining instances in our tables there is little of interest.

> The Royal Society
> for the encouragement of
> Arts, Manufactures and Commerce

*Figure 11.2*

*Table 11.3*

| | Society | | |
|---|---|---|---|
| | **of** | **for** | |
| PREP+PROFESSIONAL GROUP | 11 | 1 | Society of Automotive Engineers |
| MODIFIER+*SOCIETY* +PREP+PLACE NAME | 5 | 0 | The Seismological Society of America |
| PREP+PERSONAL NAME | 1 | 0 | Society of St Vincent de Paul |
| Subtotal | 17 | 1 | |
| PREP+-*ING* | 0 | 1 | Society for Cutting Up Men |
| ALLEVIATION | 0 | 1 | The National Society for Epilepsy |
| PROMOTION | 0 | 3 | National Society for Clean Air |
| PREP+TOPIC (inc. Arts) | 3 | 5 | American Society for Microbiology |
| PREP+*THE*+NOUN (inc. The Deaf) | 1 | 10 | The Royal Society for the Prevention of Cruelty to Children |
| Subtotal | 4 | 20 | |
| Total | 21 | 21 | |

4    The 30th International Society of Education through Art

This instance joins *Phraseology* in choosing the less frequently preferred preposition, and so does:

5    Society of Voluntary Control of . . .

The full name of this society is *The Society of Voluntary Control of Fair and Exhibition Statistics*, and it was originally set up by the *German Fair Organisers Association*, so a *for* might have been expected.

6    The Society of Vincent de Paul

This is a charitable foundation named after a suitable saint, and other instances of a similar structure are readily found in the corpus; the first few are:

7   The Royal Society of St George
8   The Society of Jesus
9   The Society of St Dismas
10   Society of St Francis
11   the Benevolent Society of St Patrick

It seems that although only a single instance of this kind of title appeared in our small sample, it is fairly common.

Among the *for* instances,

12   The British Dental Society for Clinical Nutrition

follows the pattern of 'promotion' societies, with the additional identifier of *Dental*.

13   Commonwealth Society for the Deaf

This is an example of the 'alleviation' group.

14   International Society for the Study of . . .

The object of study is *Behavioural Development*, and as such this can be classified with the 'promotion'.

We are left with the whimsical *Society for Cutting Up Men*, where the acronym *SCUM* may have influenced the choice of name.

## Conclusion

The choice patterns are set out in summary in Table 11.4, with the *for* structures first, to make the diagram simpler. I have used ad hoc terms in capital letters to refer to categories that are elaborated above:

The lack of numerical support for our original example does not mean that it is wrong; it is obviously not alone, and there may be other factors beyond the scope of this short note that could have influenced the choice of preposition – the *of* structure may be going up in the popularity stakes, or may be more common in, say, Antipodean English than in Anglo-American English, which predominates in *The Bank of English*. The strongest claim that can be made as a result of this analysis is that the choice of *for* would have been the safer one.

The last step in the argument is to dip again into the corpus, which has been substantially changed in an update since Citations 1 and 2 were extracted a year ago. Because the patterns are strong, I have only extracted a small number of instances, to be found in Citations 3 (Table 11.5). Again there is no bias in the selection.

*Table 11.4* Summary of structures

| Pre-head | Head | Preposition | Noun (group) | | No. |
|---|---|---|---|---|---|
| COMMUNITY | **Society** | **for** | TOPIC | PROMOTION | 1 |
| | | | | ALLEVIATION | 2 |
| | | **of** | PROFESSIONALS | | 3 |
| | | | PATRON | | 4 |
| TOPIC | | | COMMUNITY | | 5 |

*Notes:*

TOPIC is short for the area of interest or activity of a society,

COMMUNITY is short for the social group, geographical or political provenance, or status of the society,

PROFESSIONALS stands for groups of people who share a topic,

PATRON stands for a saint or similar whose name has been chosen to indicate the attitude and concern of the society,

PROMOTION and ALLEVIATION have already been used to refer to the two orientations of TOPIC.

The instances in Citations 3 fit the analysis in Table 11.4 quite well. Among the *of* instances, only the last does not quite fit; I presume that *Cincinnati* is both the 'topic' and the 'community', so provision should be made for the merging of these categories. All the *for* instances are concerned with 'topic promotion'. It seems that the tendency of the choice of 'community' to go with the *for* structure is no accident of our first samples; only one of the six with *of* shows this choice (*Royal*), whereas all except one of the five with *for* are so marked.

So the quick final check supports the analysis in detail. Successive sampling of this kind, especially with very small numbers, is not always as tidy, but here it shows the solidity of the evidence provided by a corpus.

I began by reporting my personal reactions to the various phrasings, as a native speaker contaminated by a career studying the language. The corpus evidence largely supports my position, suggesting at least that the corpus is a good sample of the kind of English that seems natural to me. There are, however, many kinds of English, and an area like the titles of societies may be more influenced by the globalization of English than others. Where English is an instrument of communication for millions of speakers of many languages, we cannot expect the niceties of Table 11.4 to be maintained, and perhaps the *of* structure – already numerically predominant – will become acceptable for all cases.

*Table 11.5* Citations 3. Society of/for . . .

| | | |
|---|---|---|
| salvation came just in time. The Preservation | Society | of Newport County, set up to maintain one |
| and to be elected a Fellow of the Royal | Society | of Literature (1977). As a critic, |
| former president of the Voluntary Euthanasia | Society | of Queensland, Dewick has made a voluntary |
| Ralph L. Harding, Jr., president of the | Society | of the Plastics Industry, dismissed |
| for five years; a Bencher of the Law | Society | of Upper Canada during five four-year |
| all during the 1891 to 1913 period. The | Society | of Cincinnati was organized in 1783 by |
| Greenwich, London SE10, for the National | Society | for the Prevention of Cruelty to Children |
| Richmond, Surrey; Pounds 2,000 to the | Society | for the Protection of Birds; Pounds 1,000 |
| muscles featured at a meeting of the | Society | for Cell Biology in San Francisco. |
| ALEX CHADWICK, NPR reporter: There is a | Society | for Computer Simulation, started 40 years |
| particularly dog and snake. The Royal | Society | for the Prevention of Cruelty to Animals |

# 12 Current issues in corpus linguistics

For the original provenance of this chapter, see the note at the beginning of Chapter 10. 'Current' means in the year 2000; there seemed to be some problems which were holding back progress and contributing to a gloomy prospect for the new millennium. While technology often helps problems to diminish, these ones are still with us, and the rosy future is still far off. This chapter has also been published in *Linguistica e Informatica*, ed. R. Favretti; Rome: Bulzoni Editore (2000).

## Introduction

When I looked into the present state of corpus linguistics, I became a little reluctant to talk about this title. It is an exciting subject at present – arguably the most interesting and fastest-moving area in all linguistics – and personally I am very pleased to be working in the field; for the first 30 years that I spent working in corpus linguistics, hardly anyone noticed, and it is particularly pleasant to have so many colleagues with similar interests pursuing such a variety of research topics.

The reason for my reluctance was a realization of how important it is to design corpus research according to principles that are likely to lead to good results, and not to get caught in using corpora just to tell you more about what you know already. There is an understandable feeling particularly in the community of so-called 'Natural Language Processing' that a great deal is now known about language, and it is time to reap the harvest of these decades of research in a wide range of descriptions and applications, making use of corpora as powerful aids in the various projects. The technology is sophisticated, the classic problems of language text, like ambiguity and anaphora, have been extensively studied, and great progress is being made in key applications like machine translation.

Sadly, I cannot go along with this euphoria, nor watch with equanimity the large amounts of research funding that is applied to maintain it. My own view of the current state of language and computers is that it is disappointing in terms of achievement, and unpromising in terms of prognostication. Corpus linguistics offers a fresh start without the baggage that has accumulated over the years, and instead it is being held down within intellectual schemas that are not aligned with it, and do not allow it to reveal what it has to offer. So to begin with I will mention some rather depressing features of the present state of the art, and then go on to the better news. But make no mistake – just having a corpus isn't going to save anyone; more likely it will eventually expose poor research.

## Raising hopes

I'm afraid that most of the brave claims that have been made over the years for the use of computers in the study of languages are still a very long way off. To give an example, just a couple of years ago in an official publication of the European Commission, it was said that very soon, I think it said even next year, which would have been last year, you would be able to talk into a telephone in one language, and your interlocutor would hear another. This is the kind of claim that is made from time to time – first to my knowledge made in the middle 1960s by a lecturer in the BBC's prestigious Reith series in Britain, and very much in the same terms some 40 years later. And we are still a long way off such a facility, despite notable advances in the area of speech recognition.

On the whole, language has proved so far to be pretty impenetrable. There are virtually no useful operations yet devised that can be carried out automatically on open text. By 'open text' I mean unrestricted text, any text that you find that is a reasonable sample of a particular language in use; indeed in the way in which language research has developed there is clear evidence that the study of open text is frequently avoided – I'll return to this point because it is central to my argument.

The research community has worked out an impressive range of processes that can be applied to carefully selected text, many kinds of 'added value' in terms of analytic tags, and a range of statistical tools are available, but in terms of useful operations, applications that are really valuable for society, that can do things and improve people's quality of life and so on, there are at the moment virtually none. There are, to be sure, some useful facilities in the area of text formatting, but the various mark-up languages and the bewildering variety of formats require laborious attention to very crude and out-of-date systems, and each needs a special process to be converted into another.

I get the impression that the main concerns of computational linguistics of recent years are gradually and quietly being abandoned. Nobody talks about fully automatic translation any more. In fact, only some kinds of translation support are regarded as being feasible. Very large efforts have been made in the last decade to produce machine lexicons that work, that actually can be applied to text. And the realization is gradually dawning that this is a pseudo-procedure, this is not a venture that is going to succeed; there is no such thing as an adequate lexicon; the reason, derived from compelling corpus evidence, is that quite a lot of meaning is produced by the combination of choices at the time/place when the choices are made. In a language, which has many thousands of words, the idea of there being meaning in combinations is bad news, because the possibilities are multiplied – but see below. The impact of this argument in the lexicon factories is that while more and more are being produced, in all sorts of different ways using all sort of different hypotheses, the 'smart money' is moving away. The idea of a very large lexicon, which contains somehow the lexical information of a language is not a claim, I think, that would be confidently made as we start the new millennium.

Sublanguages are dead. Sublanguages arose from the idea that you could find within natural language text substantial continuous stretches of a much simpler type of language. The search has consistently focused on trying to isolate absolutely deadpan scientific statement with no overtones and with a very precise use of terminology; all in all a variety which a machine would have a decent chance of processing. Meanwhile discourse analysts (Hunston 1993) were pointing out that scientists were far from objective and non-evaluative when they wrote, and language teachers were pointing out that it was the evaluations that were (a) crucial to understanding and (b) difficult for the learners to identify and process.

Sublanguages are now, I think, officially dead. But arise controlled languages. Controlled languages are languages which are halfway to being artificial, which are more or less carved out of the total possibilities, manipulated and processed, so that the computer can handle them; and they are more computer-oriented than human-oriented. The human being does most of the work, keeping to the tight limits of the controlled language. Similarly, there are suggestions that one of the ways of avoiding problems of translation is, first of all, to process the source text starting-point to make it easier for this translation (Somers 1997).

Anything will do, indeed, to avoid open text, because that is the really outstanding problem. So that's why I feel that it's a rather depressing picture we get at the moment, and there are opportunities and there is a great potential, but at the present time I don't think that we can resolutely claim that we have a good success ratio.

## Current issues

So what are the issues? The issues that are current and that are needing to be resolved, that could lead us astray or could lead us to breakthrough? I'd like to think of one or two within corpus linguistics itself and then one or two outside corpus linguistics in the wider area of the information sciences.

First of all, within corpus linguistics there is the question of *size*. As some of the big reference corpora get bigger and bigger – half a billion words is well within the sights of *The Bank of English*,[1] for example, and many projects are considering ultimately a billion or more words in a corpus – then there is a sort of backlash growing to defend small corpora, corpora that are, in a way, deliberately small. This is something that I want to consider briefly below.

Second is the question of the *annotation* of corpora and the way in which we – as it's sometimes said – enrich a corpus with all sorts of mark-up, and as part of the annotation drive the attempts to provide standards for document structure and formatting so that we can all make sure that our documents conform to a uniform standard. Those are the two issues within corpus linguistics that I would like to look at in turn.

Outside corpus linguistics proper there is the question of the handling of language as *information*. Information technology, of course, is one of the most important and sensitive and fast-growing areas of activity in the world at the present time; the questions are how does it handle language and how could it handle language? It seems as if the particular nature and structure of language is unnecessary and redundant in the handling of documents as information, and I want to look at that briefly.

Lastly, the big issue, the big question: can computers be made to *comprehend* natural language? Rather than try to answer that question by doing it, I think there are stages before that where you can examine what kind of a problem it is and see if it appears to be a tractable problem at all, because if it is we are not attending to it in a purposeful way, and if it is not we are wasting a lot of resource working on the assumption that it is.

### Small corpora

First of all, within corpus linguistics, what about small corpora? Are small corpora just little big ones, are they just big corpora in the making, or is there anything important about keeping them small? There are of course some kinds of corpora which are by their nature small; they simply cannot get bigger as far as we know. There are many dead languages of which all we have is a small finite corpus, and that is all we will ever have unless someone happens to stumble across lost texts. The collected works of a major author is another example – even the most prolific authors rarely reach a million words, which is small fry among today's corpora.[2] Again, there may be a disputed text here and there, there might be an occasional discovery of a lost manuscript, but to all intents and purposes, the corpus will not get any bigger. So some corpora are inevitably small and we cannot do anything about them; we just have to make the best job we can of those. But when somebody says their corpus does not *need* to get any bigger, there is enough information already here, and they do not need anything more, then I begin to wonder.

I think we should look at what distinguishes a *corpus* from a *text*, the assumptions behind the terms and the means by which we study and analyse the two. A text, even quite a long text, is something that you can get to know, something that you can analyse thoroughly, possibly exhaustively, that you can parse it 100 per cent, unless it is particularly long or you do not have the resources to do it. You can look at the beginning and the middle and the end of it; it has a structure; it has some kind of organization to it; it has a unity in the classical sense that you can discover and that you can talk about. You, the analyst, are in control. You can locate all the phenomena in this text accurately and you can, even if it is quite big, have it totally at your fingertips. These are characteristics of the way in which we prepare texts for study and of the way in which we actually study them.

Now as you build up a collection of these texts, each of which you are able to handle in this way, then you may begin to think of this collection as a corpus. And that entails a change of methodology; a corpus in its characteristic mode lies almost by definition outside this level of close reading and control. And the beginning, middle, and end of a corpus is arbitrary. The order of texts in a corpus is usually arbitrary and the whole point of making something a corpus rather than a collection of texts is in order to observe things which cannot be directly observed because they are too far apart, they are too frequent or infrequent, or they are only observable after some kind of numerical or statistical process.

The essence of the corpus as against the text is that you do not observe it directly; instead you use tools of indirect observation, like query languages, concordances, collocators, parsers and aligners. There is a considerable variety of toolkits around now, and users can take their pick – the important point is that they have either to use existing tools or write their own programs to retrieve the information that they want. This means in turn (a) that they must formulate at least in a preliminary fashion the question that they want answered, and (b) that they require other levels of interpretation beyond what they are accustomed to using when they are looking at text.

This seems to me to be the crucial distinction between text and corpus,[3] the crucial distinction is not the amount of language it contains, nor is it the nature of the content, but the methodology, the way in which you approach it. In principle you could take a very large single text as a corpus and handle it using corpus techniques rather than textual techniques; ultimately the size of a small corpus is not particularly relevant.

There is no virtue in being small. Small is not beautiful; it is simply a limitation. If within the dimensions of a small corpus, using corpus techniques, you can get results that you wish to get, then your methodology is above reproach – but the results will be extremely limited, and also the range of features that you can observe. The main virtue of being large in a corpus is that the underlying regularities have a better chance of showing through the superficial variations, and there's a lot of variation in the surface realization of linguistic units in a corpus. If similar events are repeated with variation, then the more often they are repeated, the more you are able to see the regularity, the repeated element of the event, rather than the individuality that accompanies every use of every word in a text.

Another compelling reason for a corpus to be as big as possible is that a lot of the research concerns recurrent combinations of words rather than individual words, to phraseology and beyond phraseology. Now we know from Zipf (1935) that most words do not occur very often, and if you add to this the likelihood of the occurrence of pairs of words, triplets of words, and so on, then it becomes clear that we have to have very large corpora indeed, in order to look at phraseology in any systematic way. To give one example, I once looked deliberately in several corpora for the phrase 'fit into place.' I looked at it first of all in a good general corpus of two million words, and I found that there were no examples at all.[4] There could have been one – it was rather an arbitrary fact that there weren't any at all. But if you take the likelihood of 'fit' and multiply it by the likelihood of 'into' and multiply it by the likelihood of 'place,' then even though those are all three quite common words in English, you are multiplying fractions, and therefore you are going to end up with a very, very remote possibility of occurrence. So I then multiplied my corpus by a factor of ten to 20 million and looked, and I got no examples at all, and that was a very reliable small corpus of 20 million words, the base corpus on which the first corpus dictionary was made, and there wasn't a single example of 'fit into place'. 'Fit into place' is a perfectly reasonable and normal expression; it is purely the fact that it consists of three words that makes it so unlikely. So I went up to 200 million words, another factor of ten, and this time I got half a dozen examples. From a purely statistical point of view I still had only a very slight chance, but of course words don't follow the laws of chance; some combinations are far, far more likely than their statistical probability predicts. What was particularly interesting about these instance of 'fit into place' is that this combination clearly controlled other choices in its environment – for example the word 'jigsaw' suddenly appeared as a persistent. Now 'jigsaw' is not a common word in English, and it is quite amazing from any statistical point of view that this phrase, which occurs only half a dozen times in 200 million words, should on so many of these occasions have the word 'jigsaw' as a collocate.[5] This is an example, if a striking one, of what happens all the time, which is that as you combine words together on the basis of their frequent occurrence, then each step you take brings up a further ordering that you had not envisaged at all in the original; the co-selection of words is an ordering device in text.

### Mark-up and annotation

I now turn to the matter of indirect observation, and look a little more closely at it. It is an essential step in the methodology of corpus linguistics. But there are different kinds of indirectness, and I would like to caution against the overuse of one kind in particular – the addition by hand of what are called 'tags' – to indicate aspects of formatting or analysis that are not apparent on the surface of the text. Where appropriate tagging can be a helpful procedure, but there are several drawbacks to its almost universal use that members of the corpus linguistics community should be aware of, and because of which they should be seeking alternatives.

Tagging is readily understandable in historical terms; it arose originally maybe 35 years ago when the early computers and, particularly, the early operating systems and software were quite unable to process text as text, and formatting options almost did not exist – the first corpora did not even have a distinction between upper and lower case. But the computers could be trained to recognize tags, and mark-up languages came in to help in transporting texts from one machine to another, as they still do, and gradually more and more aspects of the language, content, etc. of the texts were captured in tags.

Now one of the key problems of the 'language and information' issue that I will mention briefly again later is that the techniques of information science allow the handling of documents without engaging in the interpretation of the language that they contain. This is an unfortunate legacy from the early years; as long as a text is marked up with tags, the computer can work with the tags and ignore the language – and this is what they do, without, as far as I know, a single exception.[6] From this it is clear that the indiscriminate use of tagging is an alternative to studying the language – one studies the tags instead, and all tag users should be careful to use the tags en route to the language, and not just stop there.

The interspersing of tags in a language text is a perilous activity, because the text thereby loses its integrity, and no matter how careful one is the original text cannot be reliably retrieved. Thankfully it is no longer necessary to mix the two except for specific moments of application, and in *The Bank of English*, for example, the tag strings are always kept apart from the text itself in parallel data streams. But one of the enduring problems of tagging is the perceived necessity for human intervention. Because the analytic models from which the tag sets arise are human models and pay no attention to the clarity of the categories in the data, the machines struggle to sustain usable results.

Of course, one cosy consequence of using tagged text is that the description which produces the tags in the first place is not challenged – it is protected. The corpus data can only be observed through the tags; that is to say, anything the tags are not sensitive to will be missed.

And, ultimately, as a side-effect, text becomes grossly overstuffed with tags, and the processing speed is affected. This is what in general Tognini-Bonelli (2000) calls 'corpus-based linguistics', where you refer the categories that you use to describe the corpus to a description which is protected; that is contrasted with 'corpus-driven linguistics,' which is the variety which she and I both do. In corpus-driven linguistics you do not use pre-tagged text, but you process the raw text directly and then the patterns of this uncontaminated text are able to be observed. You manipulate the actual text units, and I'm glad to say that there is a growing family of software tools that operate directly on raw text and produce impressive results. In the fairly near future I hope to present on our website (www.twc.it) a list of such software, arranged so that each program operates either on ordinary ascii text or on the output of another program on the list; in this way the connection is kept with the data in its simplest form, and the processing and analysis is exclusively automatic.

### Information science and the utility of linguistics

I have now discussed, very briefly, the two points within corpus linguistics that are important at the present time, the size of a corpus and the methodology of tagging corpora. Now I would like to mention even more briefly the question of information science and the incompatibility at present between the way in which the information sciences see language text and the way linguistic sciences see it. To information scientists, text is unstructured and of low quality in terms of information, and so they ignore the particular patterns and structures of language and make an expensive job of marking it all up. This is an extension and a growth of the tagging principle but applied in a much more general way; no account is taken of the structure of language in the huge industry of information retrieval. One of the main reasons for this unfortunate state of affairs is the poor track record of Natural Language Processing, and that in turn is the result of relying on demonstrably inadequate theories. I have dwelt on this point in other papers[7] and will not repeat myself here.

My final point grows out of this one and concerns the longer-term utility of linguistics in the world of digitization, webs and nets, and information generally. Either we can eventually persuade computers to behave as if they understood open text in natural languages, or we cannot. I believe that we should first consider how likely we ever are to reach a position of being able to rely on the machines for even simple tasks involving the understanding of open text. If it appears to be a tractable problem, then, I think, we should go for it, and the whole corpus linguistics community should go straight for solving this problem in a series of blue-sky attacks; almost anything would be worth considering in order to make inroads on this problem, because the rewards are so great. Imagine being able to interact with your computer in ordinary language, and not via menus, clicks and pathetic help functions – imagine if you could trust the messages, apparently in a natural language, that emanate from the machine, and which nowadays we just laugh at.

If on the other hand we discover that there are some totally intractable issues concerning natural language that the computer cannot handle, as many authorities suggest, then I think we have to reconsider our entire position as regards what as a community we claim to be able to do at any time in the future, and what we are able to offer the wider community in terms of our expertise in the handling of language. We should reconsider that position and perhaps be a little less ambitious.

## Conclusion

To summarize, I would like to point out that the four issues that I have raised are interrelated quite intricately. Unless we are prepared to welcome very large corpora, we will not get access to the information that we need about the languages in order to pick up the challenges of information retrieval. As long as we rely on tags we are forcing the attention (and the resources) on pre-corpus models of language which require only small corpora anyway. Tagged corpora will not meet the requirements of the information society because they are not sensitive enough; if they had been adequate they would have become indispensable in applications long ago since they have had all the attention so far. They have proved particularly unsuccessful with open text, which is an essential part of whatever prescription will be set down for programs that understand human language.

Corpus-driven linguistics demands extremely large corpora because of its need for multiple occurrences of all the items it handles; it rejects manual tagging and invites a complete rethinking of the methods of on-line analysis; it opens up new avenues of research which may help with information retrieval and other applications, and it may get closer to the goal of the machine understanding of language, though extensive testing is recommended before assaults on this goal are attempted.

# Notes

## 4 On the integration of linguistic description

1 In the tables that follow, I make the distinction between actual utterances, in italics, and the underlying explicit structure, in capitals.

## 5 Written discourse structure

1 In this initial reliance on the sentence, no claim is made about the physical or psychological facts of language processing. The actual behaviour of a writer when writing and a reader when reading will no doubt be in some steady relationship with the recurrent patterns of written text, such as punctuation, paragraphing and layout in general. It would certainly be strange if we discovered that the process of interpretation concerned units of a different character and dimension from those with which we are familiar.

However, not enough is known about such matters to give clear support for or against our starting point of the sentence. It is the unit on the surface of written language which provides at least an initial procedure for dividing a text into interpretable segments. Also, it has the advantage of being very close to the surface, so that computers can locate the sentence boundaries without much trouble, thus giving us access to extensive surveying of long texts.

If we find evidence that more than the current sentence or less than the current sentence is occasionally processed instead of just the current sentence, this does not threaten our position. Only if evidence were forthcoming, perhaps from eye-movement studies, that the reader's attention jumped back and forth over the text and never seemed to dwell on a specific word string for any length of time, would some of the assumptions in this chapter need to be more cautiously framed.

It is instructive to compare this description of a sentence with those collected and discussed in, say, Fries (1957). They are all unsatisfactory because there is always at least one imponderable in them, such as 'a complete thought'; however, the best of them can be appreciated as moving in the direction of the present position, while fettered by unreliable assumptions about grammar.

Later in this chapter it is suggested that some sentences – those containing colons and semi-colons – may be divided at the punctuation mark using the same criteria as are established for sentence coherence. Following previous studies (Tadros 1985; Sinclair 1992c), it is conceded that the sentence may ultimately prove to be a unit of interpretation rather than of structure, and may show no more allegiance to the coherence conventions proposed here than it does to grammar.

2  I remember Winter saying just this, but I have not been able to find it in his published work. The nearest I can find is the following: 'We noted that using the clause to settle for saying less than everything was systematic in the sense that we, as communicators with one another, had a linguistic consensus about the form it should take. Example 9 demonstrated one of its common forms. We noted that the clause was affected closely by the relevance of choices for the immediately preceding clause(s) of its clause relations' (Winter 1986: 107) [JMS 2003].

3  This structure has affinity with Hazadiah's (1991) focus *exchange* in conversation.

4  There are many meanings of *and* in text structure, because it is the neutral mark of a logical act. No doubt the shades of meaning that are attributed to it are derived in some measure – perhaps a large measure – from inferences about the relationship between the new sentence and the one it encapsulates. Until we have studied a large number of cases it will not be easy to distinguish between the contribution made by its position in the text structure and that made by inference. The notes in this analysis about shades of meaning and the paraphrases of the introductory words and phrases are intended to be quite informal, based on an individual reading of the text.

## 6  The internalization of dialogue

1  The technique is occasionally used by journalists, but is regarded as marginal in reportage. Sinclair (1988) discusses the following case:

> But the quake never came, and people soon forgot the warnings.
> That is, until July 28th. On that day, at 3.42 a.m., a massive quake registering 7.5 on the open-ended Richter scale hit Hebei Province . . .
> The statement ' . . . the quake never came . . . ' is contradicted by the
> next paragraph, and is factually untrue.

2  The examples are all taken from corpus data. Some are curtailed or otherwise edited in order to exemplify the point at issue, but their use as examples is consistent with their use in their original texts, and omissions are signalled. This policy is preferred to inventing examples.

A good example should combine authenticity with representativeness. The only sure way to achieve authenticity is to cite from language that has already been spoken or written, and even then only a small proportion of actual occurrence is suitable for citation, because of other discourse factors that intervene. A good example should be acceptable to a reader without puzzlement or doubt. Any editing of an example (including stripping off the surrounding text in the first place) threatens its authenticity to some extent, and ultimately it is the reader who judges whether the example performs its task adequately or not.

3  Further discussion of averral can be found in Sinclair 1996d.

4  Some background on planes and postures can be found in Sinclair 1981, 1985a which are Chapters 3 and 4 in this collection [ed.].

5  The original orthographic transcription of these examples added sentence punctuation for legibility; it is omitted here to stress that each of the examples could be made into a single sentence, with the dash as the characteristic punctuation mark where the mood choice changes.

6  It is possible to report a conversation as it is taking place, thus making the worlds of

the two clauses appear to coincide; only the time difference between an utterance and the report of it separates them.

7 The other type of relative clause, the non-defining relative, is a device for adding relevant but secondary information to a sentence and relates very naturally to an underlying interactive model. This type is very close to the contingent variety beginning with *since*, and so on, because the implicit relevance of the clause to its main clause can be paraphrased in that way.

8 Some grammars broaden the category of clause to include what are otherwise called infinitive and participial phrases, and the boundary between clause and phrase becomes a little problematic. These expressions can be paraphrased as finite verb clauses and as such acquire a truth value, but it is not clear whether they have one in their original expression. This is not a problem I want to tackle here, so I will concentrate on the distinction between finite veto clauses and phrases without a verb, and pass over this controversial area.

9 There are other kinds of phrase which could in principle be linked into the argument at this point and traced back to interaction through a loss of truth value; the non-defining relative clauses (see note 7) have phrasal equivalents. But this chapter does not seek to cover all the grammatical phenomena; it is sufficient to indicate that there is evidence at every rank in the grammar.

## 7 A tool for text explication

1 At this time – some 30 years ago – there was also an important group of scholars in the USA working on spoken recordings from a sociological perspective; associated particularly with the names of Schegloff and Sacks (e.g. 1973).

2 This list is ordered by t-score, the most useful measure of statistical significance in corpus work. In fact it follows the raw frequencies very closely, the only word out of frequency order being *punch*.

3 The late David Brazil's neat phrase.

4 In the words of the philosopher J.L. Austin, (1962) who paved the way for the study of discourse.

## 8 The lexical item

1 The problem is still with us in the attempts to write grammars that are explicit enough to drive machine applications. Chomsky (e.g. 1965) managed to combine freedom from 'surface structure' with a procedural model of sentence generation. This was appealing on presentation, but when attempts were made a few years later to build in some of the complexities it exposed, the problem of the ordering of rules became one of the main preoccupations of the period; present-day grammars in this tradition are notoriously incapable of analysing open text.

2 Now that the behaviour of such phrases can be studied in large corpora, it is clear that there is a substantial amount of variation, but of a lexicosemantic or phraseological nature rather than a grammatical one. Of the 16 instances of *chicken* and *count* in a corpus of 200 million words, only one instance of the presumed canonical form is to be found. Two others have the *before* clause, and three have another timing expression; 11 have a possessive adjective in front of *chickens*, and there is one instance each of *no* and *any*; the remaining three are in the structure *of counting chickens*, which refers to the idiom rather than quoting it.

3   I do not refer here to the theories and descriptions of semantics, which have often been richly complex; however, since they are not systematically related to language in use, they are therefore not relevant to the present stage of this argument.

4   See Sinclair 1987a for a detailed account of the way in which this problem was encountered and dealt with in lexicography. Chapter 4 is particularly relevant.

5   That early response to corpus data has since been repeated many times as more lexicographers encounter corpus evidence.

6   There was more than one parameter of simplification; for example the organization of meanings around 'headwords' – lemmas in computational linguistics – carries an assumption that, by and large, the inflected forms of a word do not have distinctive meanings. This view is now regarded as rather suspect (Tognini-Bonelli 1995), and it is to be expected that a new generation of dictionary will arise where the indexing is through the form and not the lemma.

7   In particular, this chapter does not address the general matter of what is meant by stretches of language; where it is necessary for presentation of the argument to indicate meanings or distinctions of meaning, the statements are quite informal. Only when the meaningful units of a language have been reliably identified will it be useful to examine this matter thoroughly, and then, since the links between form and meaning will not have been broken, the task of description will be different from current work in semantics.

8   One where the same symbol appears on both sides of the operator, like 'X → XY', meaning 'rewrite X as XY'. Obviously the second X can also be expanded, and introduces another X, and so on indefinitely. See Bach's treatment of recursion (1964).

9   It is conceded throughout this argument that occasionally a multi-word phrase may be used as an item in the word list. However this raises a further problem – when two words appear together in a text, how do we know whether they realize one meaning or two? The process known as *tokenization* in computational linguistics is a relatively straightforward matter when the orthographic word can be trusted, but expands infinitely as soon as multi-word units are recognized.

10  Reversal at a propositional level is introduced in Sinclair 1987c but not given a name.

11  Presumably the often invoked and rather vague criterion for a compound or idiom, e.g. Cruse (1986) 'an expression whose meaning cannot be inferred from the meanings of its parts' applies to the more extreme cases of the effect of the textual environment.

12  This can be made clear in a bilingual context; see Sinclair et al. (eds) 1996, pages 173–4, for a practical demonstration.

13  I hope nobody actually does this, because I have deliberately exaggerated the problem to show how close it is to absurdity.

14  Here as elsewhere one cannot make absolute statements. Accidental ambiguities, that may be irresolvable even when the viewpoint is extended to the limits of practicality, are bound to arise, but very occasionally indeed; linguistic communication would be severely strained if it was more common than the sort of coincidence that happens once or twice in a lifetime. Ambiguity above the phrase – at propositional or pragmatic levels – is no more common than ambiguity at word level, but needs separate treatment which would not be appropriate here.

15  Monaghan (1996) goes as far as to say that the cases where corpus evidence does not work 'will probably be the most interesting and most crucial ones, since these will be the rarest in most corpora'.

16  Marginal for the theory of how language works, that is. There may be relevance, for example, to research in cognitive psychology.

17  The calculation of the optimal size of the collocation *span* was first published in Sinclair, Jones and Daley (1970; ed. Krishnamurthy 2003). At that time corpora were very small, so the figure was recently recalculated with reference to a much larger corpus, and with surprisingly little change. Oliver Mason programmed the recalculation, and calls it *lexical gravity*; it is a function in the CUE system of corpus query language.

18  W.E. Louw (personal communication) argues that 'literal' and 'figurative' are points close to the extremities of a continuum of *delexicalization*. Words can gradually lose their full lexical meaning, and become available for use in contexts where some of that full meaning would be inappropriate; this is the so-called figurative extension. Louw points out that a writer, especially a literary writer, must exercise vigilance so that the meaning of each word is interpreted at the intended point on the continuum. Such features as collocation are part of the control mechanism available to the writer. So in this example the use of several other words that could be interpreted literally keeps available the physical meaning of *budge*, while the overall interpretation of the passage will be institutional.

## 10  Lexical grammar

1  Alphabetical order is an order whose only virtue is that it is taught to all literate members of societies which use it. The fact that it is the only means of organizing the vocabulary of a language merely emphasizes the failure of linguists to find a better one.

2  The most available instance of this mechanism in some societies is the fruit machine, which used to be found in almost any public house in the UK. A fruit machine consists of three revolving cylinders, each of which bears a number of drawings of fruit. The player pulls a handle at the side which causes the cylinders to spin independently of each other, and come to rest in a chance combination. A row of three fruit thus appears in a central grille, and if the row corresponds to one of those in a list on the side of the machine, (e.g. banana banana banana) then the player wins, and receives several times his or her stake. The central row corresponds to the syntagmatic axis, and the cylinders contain the paradigmatic choices; a well-formed structure is one of those that wins a prize.

3  It would be a digression to argue here that *of* is not a preposition in such structures; for that see Sinclair 1991.

4  Here the new 'Pattern Grammars' (Francis, Hunston and Manning 1996, 1998; Hunston and Francis 2000) take the innovative step, guided by corpus evidence, of associating some of these meanings with structural patterning.

5  This was one of the few arguments that I, as Editor-in-Chief of Cobuild, lost; but I am still puzzled at the conviction that native speakers may need to know the referential meaning of a word but not its attitudinal/pragmatic one.

6  (a) in Tickoo (ed.) 1989, reprinted as Chapter 6 of Sinclair 1991, I showed that the second commonest word in English, *of*, had very little in common with other prepositions, and was mainly used in a unique syntactic function.

(b) I followed this up in Sinclair 1999, where I argued that most of the common words in English have individual patterns of occurrence, and do not fit into the general word-classes.

(c) As a contribution to the NERC Report (1996), I pointed out that in English, as well as words which function as nouns, and those which function as verbs, there is a substantial class which function as both (I called them *norbs*). This is a kind of under-specification which postpones a very difficult set of decisions until perhaps the analytical system is better able to deal with them..

7  At the time of retrieval the Bank contained almost 350 million words of broad general English text, from native speakers in many parts of the world, their spoken and written expression. The corpus is jointly owned by publishers HarperCollins and The University of Birmingham, and access to it can be arranged via the Cobuild Home Page, <http://www.cobuild.collins.co.uk>.

8  The appearance of *despite, failed, unsuccessful, desperate, repeated, several,* as very significant collocates of *attempts to* suggests considerable similarity, but measures have not yet been devised to compare collocational profiles.

## 12  Current issues in corpus linguistics

1  *The Bank of English* is a corpus of current English, frequently updated and now (early 2004) containing 524 million words. It is jointly owned by the University of Birmingham and HarperCollins, publishers of Cobuild. At the time this paper was written it contained approximately 400 million words.

2  As an example from English, Anthony Powell died as this paper was being written; hailed as the most prolific author since Proust, his monumental sequence *A Dance to the Music of Time* totals around a million words.

3  See Tognini-Bonelli 2000 for a detailed comparison between text and corpus.

4  This is the size of the BNC Sampler (1999) for example, and sure enough, there are no examples there either.

5  The picture today, in a larger Bank of English, is not quite as striking – *jigsaw* is a collocate in three out of eight instances – but still extremely unlikely from a statistical point of view.

6  There are indications in some of the more sophisticated search engines and document support tools of attention to a few rather obvious features of linguistic meaning, like collocation; but they are still applied from the outside, so to speak, with no awareness of their integration with other patterns of language.

7  Sinclair 1999c, 2001.

# References

Abercrombie, D. (1956) 'Linguistics and the teacher' in *Problems and Principles*, London: Longman.

—— (1965) 'Pseudoprocedures in linguistics' in *Studies in Phonetics and Linguistics*, Oxford: Oxford University Press.

Aijmer, K. and B. Altenberg (eds) (1991) *English Corpus Linguistics*, London: Longman.

Alatis, J. (ed.) (1991) *Linguistics and Language Pedagogy: The State of the Art*, Georgetown University Round Table on Languages and Linguistics, Washington DC: Georgetown University Press.

Allen, C.M. (1998) 'A local grammar of cause and effect: a corpus-driven study', unpublished MA dissertation, University of Birmingham.

Austin, J.L. (1962) *How to Do Things with Words*, Oxford: Oxford University Press.

Bach, E. (1964) *An Introduction to Transformational Grammars*, New York: Holt, Rinehart and Winston.

Baker, M., G. Francis and E. Tognini-Bonelli (eds) (1993) *Text and Technology*, Amsterdam: John Benjamins.

Barnbrook, G. (1995) 'The language of definition: a Cobuild sublanguage parser', Ph.D. thesis, University of Birmingham.

Barnbrook, G. and J.M. Sinclair (1994) 'Parsing Cobuild entries' in Sinclair, Hoelter and Peters, *The Languages of Definition*, pp. 13–58.

Bazell, C.E., J.C. Catford, M.A.K. Halliday and R.H. Robins (eds) (1966) *In Memory of J.R. Firth*, London: Longman.

Berry, R. (1992) *Articles*, Cobuild Guides no. 3, London: HarperCollins.

——, B. Asker, K. Hyland and M. Lam (eds) (1999) *Language Analysis, Description and Pedagogy*, Hong Kong: Language Centre, HKUST.

Bickerton D. and M. Gotti (eds) (1999) *Language Centres: Integration through Innovation*, Plymouth: CercleS (Conféderation Européenne des Centres de Langues de l'Enseignement Superieur) Secretariat, Department of Modern Languages, University of Plymouth.

BNC Sampler (1999) Release 1.1 (CD-ROM), Oxford University Humanities Computing Unit.

Bolivar, A. (1984) 'A linguistic description of newspaper editorials', unpublished doctoral dissertation, University of Birmingham.

Burton, D. (1980) *Dialogue and Discourse: the Sociolinguistics of Modern Drama Dialogue and Naturally Occurring Conversation*, London: Routledge.

Carter, R.A. (1987) *Vocabulary*, London: Allen and Unwin.

—— and M. McCarthy, (1988) *Vocabulary and Language Teaching*, London: Longman.

Channell, J. (1994) *Vague Language*, Oxford: Oxford University Press.

Chomsky, N. (1957) *Syntactic Structures*, The Hague: Mouton.

—— (1965) *Aspects of the Theory of Syntax*, Cambridge, MA: MIT Press.

Clear, J.H. (1987) 'Computing' in Sinclair J.M. (ed.) *Looking Up*, pp. 41–61.

—— (1993) 'From Firth principles – computational tools for the study of collocation' in Baker et al. (eds) *Text and Technology*, pp. 271–92.

Cobuild (1989) *Collins Cobuild Dictionary of Phrasal Verbs*, London: Collins.

—— (1995) *The Cobuild English Dictionary*, London: HarperCollins.

—— (1997) *New Student's Dictionary*, London: HarperCollins.

Cole, P. and J.L. Morgan (eds) (1975) *Syntax and Semantics 3 – Speech Acts*, New York: Academic Press.

Cook, G. (1998) 'The uses of reality: a reply to Ronald Carter', *ELT Journal*, 52, 1, pp. 57–63.

Cooper, M. (1983) 'Textbook discourse structure: an investigation into the notion of predictable structuring in the discourse of scientific textbooks', unpublished doctoral dissertation, University of Birmingham.

Coulthard, R.M. (ed.) (1986) *Talking about Text* (Discourse Analysis Monographs no. 13), Birmingham: ELR, University of Birmingham.

—— (ed.) (1992) *Advances in the Analysis of Spoken Discourse*, London: Routledge.

—— and M.M. Montgomery (eds) (1981) *Studies in Discourse Analysis*, London: Routledge and Kegan Paul.

Cruse, D.A. (1986) *Lexical Semantics*, Cambridge: Cambridge University Press.

Cunningham, H., R.J. Gaizauskas and Y. Wilks (1996) *A General Architecture for Text Engineering*, Sheffield: University of Sheffield Department of Computer Science.

Darmsteter, A. (1887) *La Vie des mots etudiée dans leur significations*, Paris: Librairie de la Grave.

Davies, M. and L. Ravelli (eds) *Advances in Systemic Linguistics: Recent Theory and Practice*, London and New York: Pinter Publishers.

Dik, S.C. (1978) *Functional Grammar* (North-Holland Linguistic Series no. 37), Amsterdam: North-Holland.

Emmott, C. (1997) *Narrative Comprehension: A Discourse Perspective*, Oxford: Clarendon Press.

Fairclough, N. (1992) 'Linguistic and intertextual analysis within discourse analysis', *Discourse and Society*, 3, 2, pp. 193–217.

—— (1999) 'Global capitalism and critical awareness of language', *Language Awareness*, 8, 2, pp. 61–73.

Fan, M. (1999) 'An investigation into the pervasiveness of delexical chunks in authentic language use and the problems they present to L2 language learners' in Berry et al. (eds) *Language Analysis*, pp. 162–75.

Firth, J.R. (1951) 'Modes of meaning' in *Papers in Linguistics 1934–1951*, London: Oxford University Press, pp. 190–215.

—— (1957a) *Papers in Linguistics 1934–1951*, London: Oxford University Press.

—— (1957b) 'A synopsis of linguistic theory 1930–1955' in *Studies in Linguistic Analysis*, special volume of the Philological Society, Oxford, pp. 168–205. Reprinted in Palmer (ed.) *Selected Papers* (1968), pp. 168–205.

Fish, S.E. (1970) 'Literature in the reader: affective stylistics', *New Literary History*, 2, 1, pp. 123–61.

Foley, J.A. (ed.) (1996) *J.M. Sinclair on Lexis and Lexicography*, Singapore: Singapore University Press.

Fowler, R. (ed.) (1966) *Essays on Style and Language*, London: Routledge.

——, R. Hodge, G. Kress and T. Trew (1979) *Language and Control*, London: Routledge and Kegan Paul.

Francis, G. (1985) *Anaphoric Nouns*, Birmingham: University of Birmingham, ELR Monographs no. 11.

—— (1991) 'Nominal group heads and clause structure', *Word*, 42, 2, pp. 144–56.

——, S. Hunston and E. Manning (eds) (1996) *Cobuild Grammar Patterns 1: Verbs*, London: HarperCollins.

——, S. Hunston and E. Manning (eds) (1998) *Cobuild Grammar Patterns 2: Nouns and Adjectives*, London: HarperCollins.

Fries, C.C. (1957) *The Structure of English*, London: Longman.

Garside, R., G. Leech and A. McEnery (eds) (1997) *Corpus Annotation*, London: Longman.

Genette, G. (1980) *Narrative Discourse*, Oxford: Blackwell.

Ghadessy, M. (ed.) (1993) *Register Analysis: Theory and Practice*, London: Pinter.

Grice, H. P. (1975) 'Logic and conversation' in Cole and Morgan (eds), *Syntax and Semantics*, pp. 51–8.

Grimes, J. (1975) *The Thread of Discourse*, The Hague: Mouton.

Grishman, R. and R. Kittredge (eds) (1986) *Analysing Language in Restricted Domains*, Hillsdale, NJ: Lawrence Erlbaum Associates.

Gross, M. (1993) 'Local grammars and their representation by finite automata' in Hoey (ed.), *Data, Description, Discourse*, pp. 26–38.

Halliday, M.A.K. (1961) 'Categories of the theory of grammar', *Word*, 17, 3, pp. 241–92.

—— (1966) 'Lexis as a linguistic level' in Bazell et al., *In Memory of J.R. Firth*, pp. 148–62.

—— (1985; 1994) *Introduction to Functional Grammar*, 1st and 2nd editions, London: Edward Arnold.

—— (1992) 'Language as system and language as instance: the corpus as a theoretical construct' in Svartvik, *Directions in Corpus Linguistics*, 61–77.

—— (1993) 'Professional literacy: construing nature' in Halliday and Martin, *Writing Science*, pp. 51–133.

—— and J.R. Martin (1993) *Writing Science: Literacy and Discursive Power*, London and Washington, DC: Falmer.

Hanks, P.W. (1987) 'Definitions and explanations' in Sinclair, *Looking Up*, pp. 116–36.

Harris, Z.S. (1952) 'Discourse analysis', *Language*, 28, pp. 1–30.

—— (1954) 'Distributional structure', *Word*, 10, pp. 146–62.

—— (1957) 'Co-occurrence and transformation in linguistic structure', *Language*, 33, 2, pp. 283–340.

—— (1988) *Language and Information*, New York: Columbia University Press.

Hasselgård, H. and S. Oksefjell (eds) (1999) *Out of Corpora: Studies in Honour of Stig Johansson*, Amsterdam and Atlanta: Rodopi.

Hazadiah, M.D. (1991) 'The structure of topic in conversation with special reference to Malaysian discourse', Ph.D. thesis, University of Birmingham.

Hockett, C.F. (1954) 'Two models of grammatical description', *Word*, 10, pp. 210–34.

Hoey, M. (1979) *Signalling in discourse*, Birmingham: University of Birmingham, ELR Monographs no. 6.

Hoey, M.P. (ed.) (1993) *Data, Description, Discourse: Papers on the English Language in Honour of John McH. Sinclair on his Sixtieth Birthday*, London: HarperCollins.

Hofland, K. and S. Johansson (1982) *Word Frequencies in British and American English*, London: Longman.

Hofstadter. D.R. (1981) 'Metamagical themas', *Scientific American*, January 1981.

Holm, J. (ed.) (1967) *Essays on the Verbal and Visual Arts*, Seattle, WA: University of Washington Press.

Huddleston, R.D. (1984) *Introduction to the Grammar of English*, Cambridge: Cambridge University Press.

Hunston, S. (1982) 'Text and sub-text: an investigation into the viability of sub-text creation as a means of revealing the complexity of written texts', unpublished MA dissertation, University of Birmingham.

—— (1989) 'Evaluation in experimental research articles', Ph.D. thesis, University of Birmingham.

—— (1993) 'Evaluation and ideology in scientific writing' in Ghadessy, *Register Analysis*, pp. 57–74.

—— (1995) 'A corpus study of some English verbs of attribution', *Functions of Language*, 2, 2, pp. 133–58.

—— and G. Francis (2000) *Pattern Grammars*, Amsterdam: John Benjamins.

—— and J.M. Sinclair (1999) 'A local grammar of evaluation' in Hunston and Thompson (eds) *Evaluation in Text*, pp. 74–101.

—— and G. Thompson (eds) (1999) *Evaluation in Text: Authorial Stance and the Construction of Discourse*, Oxford: Oxford University Press.

Jakobson, R. (1960) 'Linguistics and poetics' in Sebeok, *Style in Language*, pp. 350–77.

Jaworski, A. and N. Coupland (eds) (1999) *The Discourse Reader*, London: Routledge.

Jefferson, G. (1972) 'Side sequences' in D. Sudnow (ed.) *Studies in Social Interaction*, pp. 294–338.

Jespersen, O. (1933) *Essentials of English Grammar*, London: George Allen and Unwin.

Johansson, S. (in collaboration with E. Atwell, R. Garside and G. Leech) (1986) *The Tagged LOB Corpus User's Manual*, Bergen: Norwegian Computing Centre for the Humanities.

Johns, T.F. and P. King (eds) (1991) 'Classroom concordancing', *ELR Journal*, n.s. 4.

Katz, J.J. and J.A. Fodor (1963) 'The structure of a semantic theory', *Language* 39, 2, pp. 170–210.

Kress, G. and R. Hodge (1979) *Language as Ideology*, London: Routledge and Kegan Paul.

Krishnamurty, R. (ed.) (2003) *English Collocation Studies*, Birmingham: University of Birmingham Press.

Labov, W. and J. Waletzky (1967) 'Narrative analysis, oral versions of personal experience' in J. Holm, *Essays on the Verbal and Visual Arts*, pp. 12–44.

Laurie, H. (1997) *The Gun Seller*, London: Arrow Books.

Lehrberger, J. (1986) 'Sublanguage analysis' in Grishman and Kittredge (eds) *Analysing Language*, pp. 19–38.

Lodge, D. (1980) *How Far Can You Go?* London: Secker and Warburg.

Louw, W.E. (1993) 'Irony in the text or insincerity in the writer? The diagnostic potential of semantic prosodies' in Baker et al., *Text and Technology*, pp. 152–76.

McVie, J. (1951) *Robert Burns – Some Poems, Songs and Epistles*, Edinburgh: Oliver and Boyd.

Marcus, M., B. Santorini, and M. Marcinkiewicz (1993) 'Building a large annotated corpus of English: the Penn treebank' in *Computational Linguistics*, 19, 2.

Miller, G. (1956) 'The magical number seven, plus or minus two: some limits on our capacity for processing information', *The Psychological Review*, 63, pp. 81–97.

Monaghan, A. (1996) 'Do we need to resolve ambiguities?', in Monaghan (ed.), *Proceedings of the 5th International Conference on the Cognitive Science of Natural Language Processing, Dublin City University, 2–4 September 1996*, Dublin:, Dublin City University NLP Group, pp. 1–16.

204 References

Moon, R. (1994) 'Fixed expressions and text', unpublished Ph.D. thesis, University of Birmingham.

—— 1998) *Fixed Expressions and Idioms in English*, Oxford: Clarendon Press.

Nakamura, J. and J.M. Sinclair (1995) 'The world of *woman* in the Bank of English: internal criteria for the classification of corpora', *Journal of Literary and Linguistic Computing*, 10, 2, pp. 99–110.

NERC Report (1996) *Network of European Reference Corpora Project Report*, Pisa: Giardini.

Palmer, F. (ed.) (1968) *Selected Papers of J.R. Firth 1952–59*, London: Longman.

Pascal, R. (1977) *The Dual Voice*, Manchester: Manchester University Press.

Pearce, R. D. (1977) 'The analysis and interpretation of literary texts, with particular reference to James Joyce's *A Portrait of the Artist as a Young Man*', unpublished Ph.D. thesis, University of Birmingham.

Pearson, J. (1998) *Terms in Context*, Amsterdam: John Benjamins.

Phillips, M. (1983) 'Lexical macrostructure in science text', unpublished Ph.D. thesis, University of Birmingham.

Quirk, R. (1990) 'British must get their tongues round 1992', *The European*, 1–3 June 1990.

—— and H.G. Widdowson (eds) (1985) *English in the World*, Cambridge: Cambridge University Press.

Ravelli, L.J. (1991) 'Language from a dynamic perspective: models in general and grammar in particular', unpublished Ph.D. thesis, School of English, University of Birmingham.

—— and M. Davies (eds) (1992) *Advances in Systemic Linguistics: Recent Theory and Practice*, London: Pinter.

Renouf, A.J. and J.M. Sinclair (1991) 'Collocational frameworks in English', in Aijmer and Altenberg (eds), *English Corpus Linguistics*, pp. 128–43.

Richards, I. A. (1929) *Practical Criticism*, London: Kegan Paul, Trench, Trubner.

Rinvolucri, M. (1997) 'Fields that feed EFL methodology', *Journal of the Materials Development Association*, Folio 4/2.

Rizvi, S.N.A. (ed.) (1981) *The Twofold Voice: Essays in Honour of Ramesh Mohan*, Salzburg Studies in English Literature no. 53, Salzburg: Institut für Anglistik und Amerikanistik, Universität Salzburg.

Robins, R.H. (1959) 'In defence of WP', *Transactions of the Philological Society*, pp. 116–44.

Roe, P. J. (1977) 'The notion of difficulty in scientific text', Ph.D. thesis, University of Birmingham.

Schegloff, E. (1972) 'Notes on conversational practice: formulating place' in Sudnow (ed.), *Studies in Social Interaction*, 75–119.

—— and H. Sacks (1973) 'Opening up closings', *Semiotica*, 7, pp. 289–327.

Searle, J.R. (1969) *Speech Acts*, Cambridge: Cambridge University Press.

Sebeok, T.A. (ed.) (1960) *Style in Language*, Cambridge, MA: MIT Press.

Siciliani, E., A. Cecere, V. Intoni and A. Sportelli (eds) (1996) *Le Trasformazioni del narrare*, Brindisi: Schena Editore.

Sinclair, J.M. (1966) 'Beginning the study of lexis' in Bazell et al. (eds) *In Memory of J.R. Firth*, pp. 410–30.

—— (1981) 'Planes of discourse' in Rizvi (ed.), *The Twofold Voice*, pp. 70–91. (See also this volume, Chapter 3.)

—— (1985a) 'On the integration of linguistic description' in Van Dijk (ed.), *Handbook of Discourse Analysis*, pp. 13–28. (See also this volume, Chapter 4.)

—— (1985b) 'Selected issues' in Quirk and Widdowson (ed.), *English in the World*, pp. 248–54.

—— (1987a) 'Collocation: a progress report' in Steele and Threadgold (ed.), *Language Topics*, pp. 319–31.

—— (1987b) 'The dictionary of the future', Collins Dictionary Lecture given at the University of Strathclyde. Reprinted in Foley (ed.), *J.M. Sinclair on Lexis and Lexicography*, pp. 121–36.

—— (1987c) 'Fictional worlds' in Coulthard, *Talking about Text*, pp. 43–60; revised version published as 'Fictional worlds revisited' in Siciliani et al. (eds), *Le Trasformazioni del narrare*, pp. 459–82.

—— (ed.) (1987d) *Looking Up: An Account of the Cobuild Project in Lexical Computing*, London: HarperCollins.

—— (1988) 'Mirror for a text', *Journal of English and Foreign Languages*, 1, pp. 15–44.

—— (1989) 'Uncommonly common words' in Tickoo (ed.), *Learners' Dictionaries*, pp. 135–52.

—— (1990) 'The nature of lexical statements' in Yoshimura et al., *Linguistic Fiesta*, pp. 183–97; revised version, entitled 'Words about words', in Sinclair, *Corpus, Concordance, Collocation*, pp. 123–37.

—— (1991) *Corpus, Concordance, Collocation*, Oxford: Oxford University Press.

—— (1992a) 'Priorities in discourse analysis' in Coulthard, *Advances in the Analysis of Spoken Discourse*, pp. 79–88.

—— (1992b) 'Shared knowledge', paper presented at the Georgetown Round Table Conference, 1991.

—— (1992c) 'Trust the text' in Ravelli and Davies, *Advances in Systemic Linguistics: Recent Theory and Practice*, 1–19. (See also this volume, Chapter 1.)

—— (1992d) 'Written text structure', in Sinclair, Hoey et al., *Techniques of Description*, 6–31.

—— (ed.) (1995) *Today's English Dictionary*, London: HarperCollins.

—— (1996a) 'Fictional worlds revisited' in Siciliani et al. (ed.), *Le Trasformazioni del narrare*, pp. 459–82.

—— (1996b) 'The search for units of meaning', *Textus*, 9, 1, pp. 75–106. (See also this volume, Chapter 2.)

—— (1996c) 'The empty lexicon', *International Journal of Corpus Linguistics*, 1, 1, pp. 99–119. (See also this volume, Chapter 9.)

—— (1998) 'The lexical item' in Weigand (ed.), *Contrastive Lexical Semantics*, pp. 1–24. (See also this volume, Chapter 8.)

—— (1999a) 'A way with common words' in Hasselgård and Oksefjell (eds), *Out of Corpora*, pp. 157–79.

—— (1999b) 'New roles for language centres: the mayonnaise problem', in Bickerton and Gotti (eds), *Language Centres*, pp. 31–50.

—— (2001) 'The deification of information' in Thompson and Scott (eds), *Patterns of Text*, 287–313.

—— and D.C. Brazil (1982) *Teacher Talk*, London: HarperCollins.

—— and R.M. Coulthard (1975) *Towards an Analysis of Discourse: The English Used by Teachers and Pupils*, Oxford: Oxford University Press.

—— and A. Renouf (1988) 'A lexical syllabus for language learning' in Carter and McCarthy (eds), *Language and Vocabulary Teaching*, pp. 140–60.

——, M. Hoelter and C. Peters (1995) *The Languages of Definition*, Studies in Machine Translation and Natural Language Processing, vol. 7, Luxembourg: The European Commission.

——, M. Hoey and G. Fox (eds) (1993) *Techniques of Description*, London: Routledge.

——, S. Jones and R. Daley (1970) *English Lexical Studies*, report to the Office of Scientific and Technical Information.

——, S. Jones and R. Daley (1972) *English Lexical Studies*, report to the Office of Scientific and Technical Information.

——, J. Payne and C.P. Hernandes (eds) (1996) 'Corpus to corpus: a study of translation equivalence', *International Journal of Lexicography*, 9, 3, pp. 171–8.

——, I.J. Forsyth, R.M. Coulthard and M.C. Ashby (1972) *The English Used by Teachers and Pupils*, Report submitted to the Social Science Research Council.

——, P. Hanks, G. Fox, R. Moon and P. Stock (1987) *Collins Cobuild English Language Dictionary*, London: Collins.

——, J.H. Clear, et al. (1995) *Cobuild on CD-ROM: Collocations*, London: HarperCollins.

Somers H. (1997), 'A practical approach to using machine translation software: "post-editing" the source text', *The Translator*, 3, 2, pp. 193–212.

Stageberg, N.C. (1966) *An Introductory English Grammar*, New York: Holt, Rinehart, and Winston.

Steele, R. and T. Threadgold (eds) (1987) *Language Topics: Essays in Honour of Michael Halliday*, Amsterdam: John Benjamins Publishing Company.

Stubbs, M. (1995) 'Collocations and semantic profiles', *Functions of Language*, 2, 1, pp. 23–55.

—— (1996) *Text and Corpus Analysis*, Oxford: Blackwell.

Sudnow, D. (ed.) (1972) *Studies in Social Interaction*, New York: The Free Press.

Svartvik, J. (ed.) (1991) *Directions in Corpus Linguistics: Proceedings of Nobel Symposium 82, Stockholm 4–8 August 1991*, Trends in Linguistics, Studies and Monographs 65, Berlin and New York: Mouton de Gruyter.

Swales, J.M. (1990) *Genre Analysis: English in Academic and Research Settings*, Cambridge: Cambridge University Press.

Tadros, A. (1981) 'Linguistic prediction in economics text', Ph.D. thesis, University of Birmingham.

—— (1985), *Prediction in Text*, Discourse Analysis Monograph 10, English Language Research, University of Birmingham.

Thompson, G. and M. Scott (eds) (2001) *Patterns of Text: In Honour of Michael Hoey*, Amsterdam and Philadelphia: John Benjamins.

Tickoo, M. (ed.) (1989) *Learners' Dictionaries: the State of the Art*, Anthology Series 23, Singapore: SEAMEO Regional Language Centre.

Tognini-Bonelli, E. (1992) 'All I'm saying is', *Literary and Linguistic Computing*, 7, 1, pp. 30–42, Oxford: Oxford University Press.

—— (1995) 'Italian corpus linguistics: practice and theory' *Textus*, 8, 2.

—— (2000) 'Il *corpus* in classe; da una nuova concezione della lingua a una nuova concezione della didattica', in R. Favretti (ed.) *Linguistica e Informatica*, Rome: Bulzoni Editore.

—— (2001) *Corpus Linguistics at Work*, Amsterdam and Philadelphia: John Benjamin.

Tsui, B.M.A. (1986) 'A linguistic description of utterances in conversation', unpublished Ph.D. thesis, School of English, University of Birmingham.

Van Dijk, T. (ed.) (1985) *Handbook of Discourse Analysis: Dimensions of Discourse*, vol. 2, London: Academic Press.

Weaver, W. (1964) *Lady Luck*, London: Heinemann.

Weigand, E. (ed.) (1998) *Contrastive Lexical Semantics: Current Issues in Linguistic Theory*, vol. 17, Amsterdam and Philadelphia: John Benjamins.

Weinrich, H. (2000), 'Von der Leiblichkeit der Sprache' in *Sprache, das Heisst Sprachen*, Tübingen: Gunter Narr.

Widdowson, H.G. (1991) 'The description and prescription of language' in Alatis, *Linguistics and Language Pedagogy*, pp. 11–24.

Willis, J.R. (1981) 'Spoken discourse in the ELT classroom: a system of analysis and a description', unpublished MA thesis, University of Birmingham.

—— and J.D. Willis (1988) *Collins Cobuild English Course*, London: HarperCollins.

Winter, E.O. (1977) 'A clause-relational approach to English texts', *Instructional Science*, 6, 1, Special Issue.

—— (1986) 'Clause relations as information structure: two basic text structures in English' in Coulthard, *Talking About Text*, pp. 88–108.

Yang, H.Z. (1986) 'A new technique for indentifying scientific/technical terms and describing scientific texts', *Journal of Literary and Linguistic Computing*, 1, 2, pp. 93–103.

Yoshimura, K. (ed.) (1990) *Linguistic Fiesta*, Japan: Kurosio Publishers.

Zipf, G. (1935) *The Psychobiology of Language*, Boston, MA: Houghton Mifflin. Reprinted 1965, Boston, MA: MIT Press.

# Index of authors and names

# Index of themes

Numbers refer to chapters in which these themes are discussed at some length.